An Advanced Guide to Multilingualism

An Advanced Guide to Multilingualism

Larissa Aronin

University Press

Edinburgh University Press is one of the leading university presses in the UK. We publish academic books and journals in our selected subject areas across the humanities and social sciences, combining cutting-edge scholarship with high editorial and production values to produce academic works of lasting importance. For more information visit our website: edinburghuniversitypress.com

© Larissa Aronin, 2022

Edinburgh University Press Ltd
The Tun – Holyrood Road
12(2f) Jackson's Entry
Edinburgh EH8 8PJ

Typeset in 10.5/12pt Janson MT
by Cheshire Typesetting Ltd, Cuddington, Cheshire

A CIP record for this book is available from the British Library

ISBN 978 0 7486 3563 4 (hardback)
ISBN 978 0 7486 3564 1 (paperback)
ISBN 978 0 7486 3565 8 (webready PDF)
ISBN 978 1 3995 0114 9 (epub)

The right of Larissa Aronin to be identified as the author of this work has been asserted in accordance with the Copyright, Designs and Patents Act 1988, and the Copyright and Related Rights Regulations 2003 (SI No. 2498).

Contents

List of Figures x
Foreword – Muiris Ó Laoire xi

Introduction: How do we approach multilingualism? 1

Part I: The field of multilingualism

1 What is multilingualism? 11
  1.1 What is multilingualism about? 11
    1.1.1 Definitions of multilingualism 12
    1.1.2 Are bilingualism and multilingualism the same or different? 13
  1.2 Individual multilingualism and societal multilingualism 14
    1.2.1 Individual multilingualism 14
    1.2.2 Societal multilingualism 15
  1.3 Historical multilingualism and current multilingualism 16
  1.4 How many languages and speakers are there in the world? 18
  1.5 The purview of multilingualism 20
  Summary 23
  Further reading, chapter review, reflective questions and exercises 24

2 Multilingualism as an exceptional resource 27
  2.1 Resources of multilingualism 27
  2.2 How unique are human language and the ability for multilingualism? 28
    2.2.1 Pavlov's second and first signal systems 28
    2.2.2 Animal communication: can animals be multilingual? 29
    Is using more than one communicative system humans' exclusive characteristic? 30
  2.3 Human language 30
    2.3.1 Language universals 31
    2.3.2 Language features in different languages 35
    Writing systems and scripts 35
    Numerals 36
    Basic colour terms 36
    Time and space terms 37
    2.3.3 Linguistic relativity/linguistic determinism hypothesis 38

	Summary		39
	Further reading, chapter review, reflective questions and exercises		39

3 Multilingualism as modern reality and field of knowledge — 42
- 3.1 Social awareness in languages — 42
  - 3.1.1 Paradigms and stages — 42
  - 3.1.2 The monolingual stage — 43
  - 3.1.3 The bilingual stage — 44
  - 3.1.4 The multilingual stage — 47
- 3.2 The New Linguistic Dispensation — 49
- Summary — 50
- Further reading, chapter review, reflective questions, exercises — 51

Part II: Languages

4 Languages of the world — 57
- 4.1 Languages and dialects — 57
  - 4.1.1 What is a language? — 57
  - 4.1.2 What is a dialect? — 60
  - 4.1.3 Dialect continuum — 61
- 4.2 Language standardisation — 61
  - 4.2.1 Standardisation and codification — 61
  - 4.2.2 Pluricentric languages — 62
- 4.3 Linguistic distance — 62
- 4.4 Kachru's Circles and the World Englishes — 63
  - 4.4.1 Performance varieties — 66
- 4.5 Language varieties resulting from language contact — 67
  - 4.5.1 Pidgins and creoles — 67
  - 4.5.2 Bilingual mixed languages — 71
- Summary — 71
- Further reading, chapter review, reflective questions and exercises — 72

5 Classifications of languages — 75
- 5.1 Linguistic classifications of languages — 75
  - 5.1.1 Word order typology — 75
  - 5.1.2 Linguistic structural typology — 76
  - 5.1.3 Genetic classification of languages — 78
- 5.2 Sociolinguistic classifications of languages — 79
  - 5.2.1 The galactic model (de Swaan) — 80
  - 5.2.2 Economic-related hierarchies — 80
- 5.3 Distinct categories of languages — 82
  - 5.3.1 Lingua franca — 82
    - *English as a lingua franca (ELF)* — 83
  - 5.3.2 Sign languages — 84
  - 5.3.3 Artificial (constructed) languages — 88
- Summary — 89

		Contents	vii
		Further reading, chapter review, reflective questions and exercises	89

Part III: Multilingualism in society

6	Multilingualism at the societal level: basic concepts	95
	6.1 Language contact	95
	6.1.1 Borrowing	96
	6.1.2 *Sprachbund*	98
	6.2 Speech community	98
	6.3 Diglossia	101
	6.4. Domain	102
	Summary	103
	Further reading, chapter review, reflective questions and exercises	103

7	Societal multilingualism: multilingual countries and regions	106
	7.1 How do countries become multilingual?	106
	7.2 Roles and status of languages in multilingual countries and organisations	107
	7.3 Diversity of multilingualism	110
	7.3.1 Measures of linguistic diversity	110
	7.3.2 How multilingual countries differ from each other	111
	Correlation of individual and societal multilingualism in multilingual countries	111
	Proximate and integrative multilingualism	112
	Challenges and issues	112
	7.3.3 Multilingual regions and countries: Africa and India	113
	Africa	113
	India	116
	Summary	119
	Further reading, chapter review, reflective questions and exercises	119

Part IV: Individual multilingualism

8	Individual multilingualism: psycholinguistic and cognitive dimensions	125
	8.1 Who are the multilinguals?	125
	8.2 Special features and language behaviour of multilinguals	125
	8.2.1 Complexity and emergent qualities	126
	8.2.2 Features of linguistic and learning behaviour	126
	8.2.3 Extent of language skills used by multilinguals	127
	8.2.4 Cross-linguistic interactions	128
	8.2.5 Multilingual brains	130
	8.3 Multilinguals in conditions of health and decline	132
	8.3.1 Multilinguals throughout their lifespan	132
	Early and late multilinguals	132
	Age and additional language acquisition	133

		The impact of multilingualism in situations of healthy ageing and disease	133
		Cognitive reserve	134
	Summary		135
	Further reading, chapter review, reflective questions and exercises		136

9 Individual multilingualism: social dimensions — 138

- 9.1 Multilinguality – the identity of a multilingual — 138
  - 9.1.1 Expansion of the identity concept — 138
    - *Technological impact on multilingual identity* — 139
    - *Multimodal dimensions of multilingual identity* — 140
  - 9.1.2 Multilinguality — 141
- 9.2 Trajectories of becoming multilingual — 142
  - 9.2.1 Simultaneous and successive patterns of acquisition — 142
  - 9.2.2 Hoffmann's typology of trilinguals — 143
  - 9.2.3 Becoming or not becoming multilingual: challenges and choices of multilingual families — 144
- 9.3 Various categories of multilinguals — 145
  - 9.3.1 Polyglots — 145
  - 9.3.2 Other exceptional multilinguals — 148
    - *'Savants'* — 148
    - *Deaf and hard-of-hearing language users* — 149

Summary — 149

Further reading, chapter review, reflective questions and exercises — 150

Part V: How we experience and study multilingualism

10 The ways we experience, treat and use languages — 155

- 10.1 The way we treat languages – language nominations — 155
  - 10.1.1 What are language nominations? — 156
  - 10.1.2 How do language nominations emerge? — 156
  - 10.1.3 How expedient are language nominations? — 157
- 10.2 The way we use multiple languages: language repertoire and Dominant Language Constellations — 159
  - 10.2.1 Language repertoires — 159
  - 10.2.2 Dominant Language Constellations — 160
    - *DLC is a unit* — 160
    - *DLC maps* — 160
    - *DLC is adaptable and dynamic* — 160
    - *Languages of a DLC are not arranged in any built-in hierarchy* — 161
    - *DLC is multimodal* — 163
- 10.3 The way we experience languages — 163
  - 10.3.1 Translanguaging and code-switching — 163
    - *What is translanguaging?* — 164
    - *What is code-switching?* — 165
    - *Code-switching or translanguaging?* — 166

	10.3.2 Intercomprehension/receptive multilingualism	167
	10.3.3 The material culture of multilingualism	169
	Summary	170
	Further reading, chapter review, reflective questions and exercises	171
11	**Methods of studying multilingualism**	**174**
	11.1 Features of multilingualism research	174
	11.1.1 Characteristics of research in multilingualism	174
	11.1.2 Challenges	175
	11.2 Research methodologies and types of research	176
	11.2.1 Philosophies, methodologies and types of research in multilingualism	176
	11.2.2 Quantitative research	179
	Language demography	180
	11.2.3 Qualitative research	182
	Ethnographic research	182
	11.2.4 Holistic and complexity research	183
	Complexity approach	183
	Complex interactions	184
	Sensitivity to initial conditions	185
	Emergence	185
	11.2.5 Triangulation	186
	Summary	187
	Further reading, chapter review, reflective questions and exercises	187
12	**Models of multilingualism**	**190**
	12.1 What are theories and what are models?	190
	12.1.1 Theories	190
	12.1.2 Models	192
	12.2 Models specific to multilingualism	192
	12.2.1 Factor Model by Hufeisen	192
	12.2.2 Dynamic Model by Herdina and Jessner	194
	12.2.3 Biotic Model by Aronin and Ó Laoire	197
	12.2.4 Role–Function Model by Williams and Hammarberg	197
	12.2.5 Multilingual Processing Model by Meißner	198
	12.3 Modelling in multilingualism	199
	12.3.1 DLC modelling	199
	Summary	202
	Further reading, chapter review, reflective questions and exercises	203
Conclusion: Reflecting on multilingualism		206
Bibliography		208
Languages index		227
Subject index		231

List of Figures

3.1	The New Linguistic Dispensation embraces multi-, bi- and monolingual arrangements.	50
4.1	The three Circles of World Englishes (after Kachru 1985: 12).	64
4.2	Graddol's modification of Kachru's Circles (Graddol 1997: 10, © British Council, reproduced with permission).	65
5.1	The world language hierarchy (Graddol 1997: 13, © British Council, reproduced with permission).	81
5.2	A language hierarchy for India (Graddol 1997: 12, © British Council, reproduced with permission).	81
9.1	Multilinguality as an ecosystem (Gabryś-Barker 2005: 35, reproduced with permission).	143
10.1	The Russian-speaking community in Israel: language repertoire and Dominant Language Constellation.	161
10.2	Selected Dominant Language Constellation maps (after Kannangara 2020, reproduced with permission). (a) Nursery and preschool. (b) Secondary and upper school. (c) University education – Bachelor's. (d) Current Dynamic Language Constellation.	162
11.1	Types of quantitative research.	180
11.2	Types of research used in multilingualism studies.	186
12.1	(a and b) Previous views of language acquisition development in time (after Herdina and Jessner 2002, reproduced with permission).	195
12.2	Learner multilingualism: overall development (Herdina and Jessner 2002: 124, reproduced with permission).	196
12.3	Plasticine® DLC models comparing Russian/Ukrainian/English and English/Russian/Hebrew.	200
12.4	(a and b) Creating one's own DLC.	201
12.5	Computer-generated 3D Dominant Language Constellations.	201

Foreword

Multilingualism matters in a world characterised by widespread linguistic and cultural diversity. Indeed, multilingualism is the norm and not the exception (Aronin and Singleton 2008). It is not surprising, therefore, that much has been written about multilingualism, especially since around 1990. Before the new century began, the tendency in research was to separate theories of bilingualism and trilingualism. The boundaries were clear and unobscured. Trilingualism was relatively under-researched compared to the volumes of international research on bilingualism that emerged from the 1970s. It was in 2003, at Munster Technological University in Tralee, Ireland, where I now write this Foreword, that the third international conference on trilingualism was held, and here that the fact that research studies on bilingualism and trilingualism had started to morph into studies of multilingualism began to be heralded. The International Association of Multilingualism was founded at this conference and the *International Journal of Multilingualism* thereafter became the arena for a research focus on multilingualism, as distinct from trilingualism. The research agenda appeared to have shifted from trilingualism to multilingualism and this trend continues. While many authors, like De Houwer and Ortega (2018) and Baker and Wright (2017), for example, acknowledge the existence of trilingualism, the discipline now falls more and more under the umbrella of bilingualism or multilingualism, meaning the acquisition of more than two languages or language varieties. There was a growing realisation that multilingualism was not exceptional but rather 'a normal and unremarkable necessity for the majority in the world' (Edwards 1994: 1).

Since the conference, many research studies have renewed our understanding of multilingualism but there is still a need for further work. More and more theories of language are needed to explain and account for the day-to-day and real-world practices of multilinguals, including borrowing, transfer, mixing and translanguaging. More research is needed, particularly on the challenges posed by multilingual education, and especially in the design of curricula, curricular materials and pedagogical strategies. Nonetheless, since the turn of the millennium, research theories and approaches have become more dynamic and fast-changing. The concept and practice of translanguaging among bilinguals and multilinguals, in particular, is receiving increased attention in research, although its meaning is still developing. There has also been a growing number of studies on the extent to which language policies support or hinder societal and individual, bilingual and multilingual development. Different perspectives of academics and practitioners working in indigenous languages in different sociolinguistic contexts have also emerged, although the medium, for the most part, has been and continues to be English. More theoretically and empirically based insights are required that respond to the increasingly complex demands of multilingual societies in a globalised world.

Further research is also needed in the domain of plurilingualism, which was embraced by the Council of Europe at the end of the last century and now defines its approach to language policy. Plurilingualism focuses on the individual's ability to use two or more languages in different contexts, with varying levels of competence in each language. Not all individuals living in a multilingual region, country or city will use more than one language or language variety. People possess differing language competences. Each language learner's individual linguistic repertoire develops and changes over time as more languages are encountered. What was significant about the development of the concept of plurilingualism was the fact that it challenged the pre-existing idea of keeping languages separate at all times. The theoretical foundations of plurilingualism and its correlation to multilingualism have not been fully addressed; nor has sufficient attention been paid to how plurilingualism and multilingualism are being dealt with in the classroom, particularly in early education settings where languages other than the language of the school are often discouraged.

With the rapid shift in thinking and emerging theoretical insights in the discipline, the need is apparent for a textbook on multilingualism, in which important terms and key concepts are introduced and discussions about theories and different methodological approaches are presented. For research students and seasoned researchers alike, there is a need always to return sensibly to the beginnings and foundational concepts that precede and influence discussions and research procedures.

This textbook by Larissa Aronin offers both the research community and future research students access to and information about past and current foci of international research interest on multilingualism, as well as signposting new trends in and possibilities for research in the area. The twelve assembled chapters, each written by a leading researcher in the area, elucidate some of the most recent research findings and their theoretical underpinnings. All aspects and dimensions of multilingualism are covered and treated comprehensively, including definitions, multilingualism as resource and science, the classification and hierarchy of languages, societal and individual aspects, nominations and constellations, methodology and models. Each chapter is underpinned by a comprehensive and scholarly review of relevant research that, more often than not, reveals fresh perspectives, offers discerning insights and proposes challenging possibilities for future research.

An Advanced Guide to Multilingualism is intended for use and study by graduate students; as such, the content appears to be appropriate for expanding their understanding of a range of concepts inherent in the interdisciplinarity that underpins multilingualism. All the topics that one would expect to be covered in such a textbook are discussed in relation to multilingualism in its complex guises and historical and contemporary contexts. There are important insights in the closing chapters regarding the contextual factors and the constantly evolving dominant discourses that challenge contemporary thinking on multilingualism. The growing body of work that helps us understand and research multilingualism is treated comprehensively, with the help of examples and illustrations. The author has presented a text that offers empirical and conceptual insights focusing on the different dimensions of individual and societal multilingualism.

The book lends itself well to face-to face delivery in the lecture hall and to use in private study. Each of the twelve chapters deals separately with the key concepts that underpin multilingualism and correspond with a module semester of twelve lectures or workshops. Knowledge is built incrementally, moving from definitions to a graded introduction of theoretical discussions. The judicious use, here and there, of questions that form the section headings, particularly in Chapter 1, signposts the content and, interestingly, invites reflective participation. There is clear signposting of content in the chapter introductions, and the summary at the end of each chapter provides a helpful barometer of the learning outcomes achieved. The questions and tasks that follow the summary afford a useful opportunity for students to engage with and review the content and to apply it to their own individual context. These questions are suitable for use both during tutorial group work and during private study. The author's approach is pedagogically sound, moving, as it does, from definitions to historical evolutions, methodological considerations and theoretical models. In each chapter, content is presented incrementally in sections that follow on naturally from each other, culminating in a clear, concise summary, a structure and an approach that are consonant with the way the topic would be taught, with discussion questions to engage students in meaningful discussions and further research.

An Advanced Guide to Multilingualism is a very welcome and timely addition to the growing volume of research studies in multilingualism. It spans an impressive range of theoretical lenses, methods and historical and contemporary insights that expand our understanding of the concepts and theories that underpin the discipline. In particular, the author has presented a textbook that offers empirical and conceptual understandings, focusing on the different dimensions of individual and societal multilingualism.

Importantly, as well as adopting a very global and comprehensive perspective on research studies in bilingualism and multilingualism over the years, it provides a useful and timely 'one-stop shop' for new and practised researchers in the field. It is full of valuable references and enlightening insights that will be an asset to tutorial work as well as to private study. This is undoubtedly a useful scholarly resource.

Professor Muiris Ó Laoire
Munster Technological University
Tralee, Ireland
April 2021

References

Aronin, L. and D. Singleton (2008), 'Multilingualism as a new linguistic dispensation', *International Journal of* Multilingualism, 5(1), pp. 1–16.

Baker, C. and W. Wright (2017), *Foundations of Bilingual Education and Bilingualism*, 6th edn, Clevedon, Bristol: Multilingual Matters.
De Houwer, A. and L. Ortega (2018), *The Cambridge Handbook of Bilingualism*, Cambridge: Cambridge University Press.
Edwards, J. (1994), *Multilingualism*. London: Routledge.

Introduction:
How do we approach multilingualism?

This textbook is dedicated to *multilingualism*, the social and individual language practice that has come to the fore in today's human society, and which is the focus of this textbook. The various aspects of multilingualism relate to spheres as diverse as human physiology, cognition, communities and their traditions and material objects, and, of course, languages. Multilingualism concerns education, engineering and commerce, policy-making, family life and entertainment, to name only some of its dimensions, but it cannot be reduced or equated to discrete disciplines of sociology, psychology, cultural studies or linguistics. Despite such a diversity of facets, everything in the realm of multilingualism invariably boils down to one of its three basic constituents – language, user and environment – or, rather, to their interaction. The result of this unique and complex interplay is manifested in the *practices of multilingualism*, so exciting and so enticing to understand.

The field of multilingualism is not entirely new; numerous books and articles treat it from a variety of angles, some representing it geographically and politically, others focusing on educational and social aspects, or exploring the identity of multilinguals in depth (see, for example, Pattanayak 1990; Todeva and Cenoz 2009; Rindler-Schjerve and Vetter 2012; Phipps 2019; Banda 2020). In addition, there are not that many books to date that provide a general and systematic understanding of the entire field of multilingualism. This textbook is intended to fill this gap and to demonstrate how the multiple dimensions of multilingualism work in concert, constituting the complex reality that we encounter today.

Usually, students of various specialisations such as linguistics, sociology or pedagogy are taught only selected issues inherent in multilingualism, closely linked to the specific interests of each discipline. For example, out of all possible multilingualism content, students of sociology and political science are offered topics related to minority and language rights, identities in post-colonial societies, and indigenous languages. These students are less likely to be exposed to the issues of teaching second and third languages, unlike those studying education and pedagogy. To balance and complete the expertise, this textbook offers a panoramic perspective on multilingualism and provides students in various fields of learning with a basic introduction to both classic and current issues of using and learning multiple languages.

The purview of multilingualism is so wide that it is impossible to deal with all the concepts, theories and findings that have been accumulated to date. Therefore, several prominent topics perceived as urgent, and those intensely discussed in current academic discourse, were selected for treatment in this textbook. Among them are the similarities and differences between bilingualism and multilingualism, models of multilingualism, individual multilingualism and special characteristics of multilinguals, the diversity of multilingual countries and communities, the roles and status of languages in them, translanguaging, Dominant Language Constellations, and methods of studying multilingualism. Many of these areas are interdisciplinary and therefore each chapter of the textbook draws upon a number of disciplines. For instance, Chapter 2 brings in material from linguistics (such as word order typology, linguistic structural typology, genetic classification of languages, borrowing, dialects), sociolinguistics (diglossia, speech community, indigenous and post-colonial languages), philosophy (language universals, holistic and complexity research perspectives), anthropology (the Sapir–Whorf hypothesis, perception of colours and numbers in various human societies) and biology (such as animal communication). Other issues, also interwoven into the fabric of multilingualism – issues that were raised years ago, as well as those enthusiastically debated in the 2010s – are touched upon (code-switching, domain, the material culture of multilingualism, receptive multilingualism, Kachru's circles and World Englishes, sign languages). Others are only mentioned, rather than discussed as a separate topic.

An Advanced Guide to Multilingualism will enable students to develop a deeper understanding of their discipline and engage in independent thinking on the issues and current discussions in multilingualism. They will be able to respond to the challenges of multilingualism and approach the constantly arriving streams of new information on multilingualism in an informed manner.

About this textbook

Purview and scope

This textbook is a general introduction to the subject area of multilingualism for university and college graduate students before they take more specialised courses in their disciplines. It examines current multilingualism: that is, the way various languages are acquired, used, treated and researched today.

While making multilingualism the focal point around which all the discussions in this textbook revolve, we will, of course, speak about bilingualism, which is sometimes equated with multilingualism - not only by non-specialists, but also by some scholars. Bilingualism is the use and acquisition of two languages or dialects. Multilingualism, in very general terms, can be defined as the use and acquisition of three or more languages. Bilingualism and multilingualism are obviously similar and much of the knowledge on multilingualism originated from bilingualism studies. Having said that, and as will be seen from this textbook, we must acknowledge that these two kinds of language practices are seen today not only as similar but also as differing in many significant aspects. It follows that while topics related to bilingualism and Second Language Acquisition (SLA) will necessarily be discussed in this textbook, these are not exhaustively presented here and will be included to the extent that they have relevance to multilingualism.

Taking into consideration the fact that students specialising in various disciplines (such as linguistics, language teaching, sociology or political science) might have different prior knowledge related to multilingualism, the textbook conveniently provides information on the topics without which an understanding of current multilingualism would be impossible. Experience shows that students of multilingualism may need to complete, expand or update their knowledge on some important subjects. To this end, the book contains information on human language, dialects and languages, and language distance, which some but not all students may know from their previous studies. Facts and issues that students of multilingualism frequently ask about in order to form a comprehensive understanding (such as animal communication) are included too.

This is an elementary textbook in the sense that it provides a basic coverage of the fundamentals and central issues of multilingualism for professionals who, by virtue of their professional tasks, are involved in one way or another with multilingual individuals, groups, spaces and communities. The book will be instrumental for those who specialise in education, linguistics, translation, language teaching and language policy. In fact, everyone who faces multilingualism daily as a multilingual speaker and is concerned with the languages used by their children and grandchildren will find here answers to many of their questions, free of common misunderstandings and myths. For these people, this textbook can be used occasionally as a reference book.

Structure of the textbook

The structure is designed with an average twelve-week module semester programme in mind. The content is organised into five parts. Part I introduces the field of multilingualism. The three middle parts of the textbook are ordered in succession, according to the three constituents of multilingualism - languages, environment and users. The last, Part V, deals with the ways we experience and study multilingualism. Here is a more detailed overview.

Part I, 'The field of multilingualism', contains three chapters devoted to a broad general description of the field, the scope of multilingualism as a domain of knowledge, and its key terms and concepts. Chapter 1, 'What is multilingualism?', discusses current multilingualism in broad terms, explains what multilingualism is, and how unique and, at the same time, how common this phenomenon is, and introduces the basic terms used in the field. Chapter 2, 'Multilingualism as an exceptional resource', offers a discussion of multilingualism in light of the resources – linguistic, human, technological and others – that it affords to individuals and to society. Chapter 3, 'Multilingualism as modern reality and field of knowledge', postulates the distinction between bilingualism and multilingualism, traces the three stages of societal awareness of languages and introduces the notion of the New Linguistic Dispensation.

Part II is devoted to 'Languages' and includes two chapters that provide an overview of 'Languages of the world' (Chapter 4) and 'Classifications of languages' (Chapter 5).

Part III is about 'Multilingualism in society'. Its chapters describe social settings that accommodate and adapt to language speakers with their languages and cultures. It examines the interconnected linguistic, geographical and social processes that lead to various language arrangements. Chapter 6 introduces the basic concepts of societal multilingualism, such as diglossia, language contact and language community, and Chapter 7 gives an overview of multilingual countries and regions.

Part IV is dedicated to 'Individual multilingualism' and its two chapters concentrate on how a multilingual person lives with their languages across ages, affordances and settings. Chapter 8 looks into the psycholinguistic and cognitive dimensions of individual multilingualism, and Chapter 9 examines the social dimensions that influence the life of a multilingual.

Finally, Part V is concerned with 'How we experience and study multilingualism.' Its three chapters consider the way we now experience, treat and use languages (Chapter 10), the methods of studying multilingualism (Chapter 11), and the theories and models within it (Chapter 12) which are increasingly diverging from the methodology and theories of bilingualism.

The topics explored in this textbook are briefly summarised in a concluding précis. The volume is complemented by a bibliography and languages and subject indexes. In addition, a glossary is easily available for the use of readers (see below).

How to use this textbook

An Advanced Guide to Multilingualism is suitable for use in various institutional frameworks and modalities of study – face-to-face, distant or mixed. It is intended primarily for use in twelve-week module semester programme, but it is also well suited to a more comprehensive year-long course. Whether you are a teacher or student involved in a university or college course or an independent reader, a *glossary* containing the most important and up-to-date entries is immediately available for you on the complementary EUP website (edinburghuniversitypress.com/multilingualism) for your convenience. It can stimulate and accompany themed discussions and workshops, and may result in international discussions and collaborations on the topic of multilingualism as well.

The logical order of the chapters and the design features of the textbook are organised towards the pedagogical goals of enhancing learning and providing students with the tools for further development of knowledge, as well as for making informed decisions in situations associated with multilingualism. You will see that the content is presented in stages and moves from definitions to historical evolutions and then to methodological considerations and theoretical models. In this way, knowledge is built step-by-step by means of a measured supply of information and a graded introduction of theoretical discussions.

The detailed *contents list* helps with quick orientation and makes the book a user-friendly reference source, suitable for complementing, refreshing or updating your knowledge of multilingualism. You can simply search through the contents list for the topics you wish to read about, or look for a particular term or language in the *subject index* and *languages index*, respectively.

Each chapter consists of the *text* and a *learning/teaching unit*. This formatting is uniform across the book to ensure consistency and convenience in your studies. The subject matter is indicated in the *introductions to the chapters*, thus preparing students before they embark on their reading and thinking activities.

Introduction

The text of each chapter is divided by subheadings into clearly discerned sections. Although, together, they constitute a logical whole, each section is a complete and independent segment of information on a particular topic. Therefore, if necessary, you can use each section as a reference source or teach it separately.

You are invited to *make good use of the questions that form the section headings*, such as 'What is multilingualism about?' in Chapter 1; 'How unique are human language and the ability for multilingualism?' and 'Animal communication: can animals be multilingual?' in Chapter 2; and 'What is translanguaging?' and 'How expedient are language nominations?' in Chapter 10. These can serve as pre-teaching reflective questions for your class, or topics for discussion before reading the chapter.

A concise *summary* at the end of each chapter features the key words and issues discussed there.

Although a full *bibliography* is provided at the end of the book, each chapter also suggests a few pieces under the rubric *further reading*. The items recommended for students' reading both support and supplement the content of the chapter. The carefully selected journal articles and book chapters were preferred over others, and also chosen for their accessibility and moderate length. Among them, you will find chapters and articles that are already considered classics and intensively discussed in the field, along with ones that supply basic information that students specialising in adjacent disciplines might have missed. The reading items may serve as a basis for a dedicated classroom discussion if you are particularly interested in a topic.

Along with the information on its particular topic, each chapter is equipped with a *teaching/learning unit*. This is a block of didactic instruments that contains a *chapter review*, *reflective questions* and *exercises*. The didactic block opens with a *learning table*, specially devised to help in processing and remembering the material. Filling in the table requires the student to recycle the material in a chapter in various ways by defining and describing important terms, concepts and ideas, and prompts comparison, classification and other cognitive operations. To stimulate thorough and personalised processing of the material, a special column in the table is assigned for the student's comments and thoughts. In this way, working on a learning table takes students through the processes of learning towards a better understanding of the material. At this stage, additional internet materials may be employed to expand the purview beyond basic reading, if and when teacher and students find it appropriate. Web resources are plentiful today but they quickly become outdated. Specific web addresses are not provided in this textbook simply because of their volatility; it also seems sensible for students and teachers to conduct their own searches for additional internet resources according to the needs of the moment.

The next rubric contains *reflective questions*. Their order and formulation follow the logic of the chapter and check for understanding of the main issues and terms. You may find some of the answers to these questions, usually the first ones in the list, within the chapter. These are posed in a straightforward way and the answers are easily located when you review the content of the chapter. Others are more open-ended and involve comparing, summarising, going beyond the facts provided in the chapter, and applying the knowledge to a student's individual context. Different types of questions provide a useful opportunity for students with different learning styles to engage with the material in the way they prefer.

The *chapter review* includes interactive and multimodal activities and offers topics for discussion. The tasks, exercises and questions are suitable for use during tutorial group work and hands-on explorative sessions, such as creating handmade plasticine models of one's Dominant Language Constellation (see Chapter 10), as well as for online activities.

The last rubric in the learning block is aimed at developing students' presentation skills, as well as providing necessary practice in academic communication, including delivering presentations, preparing posters and participating in discussions, in addition to question–answer sessions. The rubric is labelled *exercises* and relates to both face-to-face (classroom and conference hall) and previously recorded and real-time internet presentations. The exercises in presentation skills involve various modalities and increase in difficulty from the first chapters of the book onwards, progressing from ones that are easier, both in a technical sense (from a poster to an e-poster, using figures and tables, creating interactive pictures, producing a short video) and organisationally (from preparing a presentation to organising a student conference or an exhibition), to those requiring more skills. The initial presentation tasks are based on the material already provided in the chapter, and then expand to those requiring students to collect additional information on the topic, or to provide information about themselves and the environment. Further along in the course, the tasks change to more complicated ones, requiring thorough examination of a topic and involving the skills of collecting and summarising data and providing arguments to support the presenter's point. Not all the exercises are compulsory; rather, teachers are invited to select their preferred ones in accordance with their personal teaching goals.

This textbook supports distance learning, as well as a hybrid (face-to-face and distance) course design. You can use it in a lecture hall but also online, for teaching via communication platforms such as Zoom or MS Teams. In the case of distance learning, reading of chapters and sources should be completed before or after the online sessions, according to the teacher's plan, so that the online meetings can be dedicated to discussions, watching videos, posing new questions and sharing ideas with classmates. For distance teaching and learning, a glossary is available via the EUP website (edinburghuniversitypress.com/multilingualism).

The content and teaching bloc can serve as a basis and inspiration for *themed workshops* that focus on certain topics in multilingualism. To this end, you, as the organiser, may select various parts or chapters dedicated to particular issues, such as 'languages of the world', 'multilingualism in society', 'individual multilingualism' or a workshop focusing on 'how we experience and study multilingualism'.

Depending on the students, goals and allotted time, the parts of the textbook (I to V) are individually suitable for *short online courses*. These became especially popular in the time of COVID-19 and seem to have stayed with us as a convenient way of learning. For each such mini-course dedicated to a particular topic in multilingualism, you can choose the corresponding parts of the book to accompany and support your teaching.

The student-friendly design and the structure of the textbook guide the reader through its content and make it expedient for personal individual study and enrichment. An individual learner is invited to follow its logic and be particularly responsive to the instructions in a learning/teaching unit. To make the most of your individual study of multilingualism, you can do the following:

- Read the title of the chapter, its introduction and section subheadings. Ponder the topics proposed for this chapter, formulate questions that arise when you read, and then try to answer these questions, based on your previous knowledge of the topic. Consult the EUP online glossary (edinburghuniversitypress.com/multilingualism) when needed. Write down what you think it is important to know in order to answer your questions.
- Read the chapter section by section. Check whether you obtained the information 'promised' by the subheading. If not, or if it is not fully clear, read the section one more time. As you read, jot down the main ideas, important statements and questions or comments that arise, but also point out things that are new to you or that contradict your previous knowledge. Highlight the information that is important for your professional or personal growth.
- Write your own summary of the chapter. Make sure you mentioned all the important themes and described the crucial concepts. Compare your summary with the one in the book.
- Fill in the learning table. Start with the things that you can enter immediately. Return to the chapter if you forgot something. If you encounter difficulties, you can partially fill in the learning table and proceed to the next rubric. You can resume the work on the chapter review later.
- Answer the questions. The definitions and explanations are easily located in the text. Remember that answers to the open-ended questions that require consideration and involve your personal experience cannot be right or wrong. You may wish to discuss your answer with other individual learners, whether through face-to-face communication or online via social media.
- Work on the learning tasks. First carry out those that you can do individually. Think of how and with whom you can discuss the task.
- To develop and enhance your understanding of the material in a chapter further, write an essay on the topics discussed in it. You may use the chapter subheadings as the titles of your essays. When you feel more confident, formulate your own essay titles.
- Expressing your knowledge and understanding in a visual form is also a good way to enhance your grasp of multilingualism. Draw figures and mental maps as you progress through the theories and figure out complex multilingual situations.

I wish readers the very best of success in using and teaching their languages in an informed and conscious way. I hope that this book will stimulate further interest and the reading of other works that are specific to the particular areas of multilingualism that readers choose to pursue.

Acknowledgements

I am grateful to the EUP editorial team, and especially Laura Williamson, for their infinite patience and generous support of this project over many long years. I wish to thank the reviewers, whose valuable comments were constructive and improved the book. I must acknowledge the contribution of Muiris Ó Laoire, well-known scholar, Irish language enthusiast and cherished co-author of many years. My thanks go to Professor Kary Smith of the Norwegian University of Science and Technology, who translated the excerpt from Russenorsk into modern Norwegian.

Part I
The field of multilingualism

1 What is multilingualism?

It is hard to imagine an aspect of modern life that is unaffected by multilingualism. The majority of the world's population is bi- and multilingual; those who are not are still influenced by the mostly multilingual world they live in. This chapter explains what multilingualism is, and how unique yet, at the same time, how common this phenomenon is, as well as how important it is for the global society and for each of us. It also outlines the scope of multilingualism as a domain of knowledge, explains how to refer to the numerical data in the field and introduces some basic terms.

1.1 What is multilingualism about?

Consider these questions. How many languages are there in Laos? Is it normal that grandchildren and grandparents do not understand each other because they speak different languages? Which words and expressions are to be taught to adult German learners of Dutch who already know French? Should funding be allocated for preparing and marking driving licence tests in languages other than English in America? What is an optimal age to start teaching English as a third language to a child living in Barcelona who also speaks Catalan and Spanish? Which kinds of schools – monolingual, bilingual or multilingual – are appropriate in present-day Vienna and which language or languages should be taught in these schools? Why are people concerned by language loss and how long does language revival take? Are there more and less economically beneficial languages? How are languages selected for work and international meetings? Why is everyone not a polyglot, as Cardinal Mezzofanti was (see Chapter 9)?

Alternatively, decide which language, out of several known to a multilingual, should be the language of treatment in the case of *aphasia*[1] in multilinguals, in the situation described by Kiran and Goral (2012):

> You have a new outpatient client who had a stroke a year ago and has aphasia. Mrs. R is 63 years old and multilingual. She was born in Colombia, South America, and spoke Spanish as a child and young adult. She studied and learned to speak French in college and spent a summer in France. She moved to North America when she was 22 and married an American who speaks only English. In which language will you provide

---

1. Aphasia – language disorder characterised by either partial or total loss of the ability to speak, read or write.

treatment? Would you provide treatment in Spanish, the first acquired language, or in English, the language learnt later but the one the client has been speaking with her immediate family? (Kiran and Goral 2012)

These are only some of the questions that arise daily in all parts of the world. All of them relate to multilingualism. All of them are highly relevant not only to specialists in the fields of education, communication, healthcare, social work or economics, but also to people in all walks of life. Multilingualism has a bearing on all of us, as we have to contend with it through all the stages of life while acquiring language, pursuing a career, socialising and getting older, as we live out our lives in the roles of language speakers, family members, citizens and professionals.

To answer these questions, along with considering the global and local multilingual environment, one has to refer to the corresponding fields of practice and knowledge, such as healthcare, organisational and globalisation studies, pedagogy and education, and didactics – the study and development of teaching and teaching methods, depending on the particular issue under examination.

Although one part of the term 'multilingualism' may lead to an assumption equating multilingualism with linguistics, this would not be correct. *Linguistics* is the scientific study of language and its structure. Linguists concern themselves with morphology, syntax, phonetics, semantics and pragmatics. While it is true that linguistics is an important part of multilingualism, multilingualism is not about languages as such; rather it is about *how people use multiple languages*. Multilingualism researchers are interested in how, by whom and in what conditions languages are acquired, spoken and dealt with; how many and which language varieties are used or not used, and why; and what the implications of this are on individuals and society as a whole. Therefore, *language* is only one of the three *constituents of multilingualism*; the other two are *speakers*[2] and the *environment* in which people use their languages. Multilingualism is a vibrant and highly dynamic intersection of these three elements which we encounter daily in learning and working environments, in medicine, business, transport and economics, across geographical areas and in urban and rural multilingual hubs.

1.1.1 Definitions of multilingualism

At this point, it must already be clear that there is no universal, 'one size fits all' definition of multilingualism that is suitable for all occasions and purposes. In this book, *the term multilingualism is used to refer* to *the use and acquisition of three and more languages*, and is distinguished, where appropriate, from *the use and acquisition of two languages*, which is termed *bilingualism*.

In literature, multilingualism is often broadly defined as the use of more than two languages. While this is correct, this definition is rather general and basic for something that is considered to be *a natural state of humankind*. For a more specific understanding of what multilingualism is, definitions characterise it through the lens of the discipline and the purpose at hand.

---

2. It would be more exact to say 'users' rather than 'speakers' because people also sign and write.

What is multilingualism?

Thus, it is quite normal to encounter the following rather divergent definitions.

- Multilingualism is the *presence* of a number of languages in a country or community.
- Multilingualism is the *use* of three or more languages.
- Multilingualism is the *ability* to acquire and speak several languages.

Those dealing with different dimensions of multilingualism usually emphasise the particular facets of it that they are concerned with. In neuroscience, for example, scholars discuss multilingualism in the context of the way the brain is organised among those who speak several languages. Ordinary computer users and IT specialists employ the term 'multilingualism' to imply the opportunity to communicate and receive information via the internet, and to participate in social webs and knowledge societies in cyberspace through the medium of multiple languages and with regard to software development. Ideologies also often play their role in the generation of a definition of multilingualism. In the context of minority languages and associated ethical, ethnic and political issues, the term 'multilingualism' often points to efforts to revitalise dying languages and maintaining endangered and lesser-used ones.

1.1.2 Are bilingualism and multilingualism the same or different?

This question is not only a matter of terminology and definitions. It is amazing how much is linked to the answer. The organisation of education, methods and outcomes of learning and teaching languages, reliability and validity of research and more are all dependent on what we think about how similar or different multilingualism and bilingualism are.

Recognising the actual relationship between bilingualism and multilingualism in their social and individual guises took place gradually. For a long time, multilingualism was considered to be simply the 'addition of one more language', whether to a community or to an individual's repertoire. The similarities were obvious and the differences have been largely overlooked. Often, it was simply taken for granted that bilingualism and multilingualism are 'the same'. Still, multilingualism is not extended bilingualism.

On the face of it, bilingualism and multilingualism look like the same phenomenon. Both can be described as an individual's use of at least one more language beyond the mother tongue, or as the existence of more than one language in a community or a country. Both bilingualism and multilingualism occupy the interface area between language and society, and both require multidisciplinary treatment from physiological, cognitive, emotional, pedagogical and social points of view. The areas of practice of bilingualism and multilingualism overlap. Therefore, when we find the terms bilingualism and multilingualism used interchangeably in literature, especially in neurolinguistic and psycholinguistic studies, it may be justified.

That being said, it has become increasingly clear that similarities between bilingualism and multilingualism do not mean that they are identical. Evidence from multidisciplinary research since around 1990 has revealed *meaningful differences* between the two. The word 'meaningful', applied to differences between bi- and multilingualism, emphasises their crucial implications for all the domains of human life. Data from neurolinguistic, psycholinguistic and sociolinguistic studies, which we cannot ignore, indicate *systemic and significant differences* between bilingualism and multilingualism.

The crucial difference that accounts for all others lies in the level of complexity. While both bilingualism and multilingualism are complex, rather than simply complicated,[3] multilingualism is remarkably more complex than bilingualism. This underlies both quantitative and qualitative divergence between bilingualism and multilingualism, relating to language acquisition and learning, processing of languages in the brain, emergent qualities of trilinguals as compared to users of two languages, and organisation of education and other things that will be discussed in more detail in Chapter 8. *Bilingualism and multilingualism are similar and overlapping in many ways, but at the same time, significantly dissimilar in many important aspects.*

1.2 Individual multilingualism and societal multilingualism

Traditionally, distinctions are made with regard to individual and societal multilingualism.

1.2.1 Individual multilingualism

The mental faculty to acquire and use many languages, the identity of multilinguals, their emotions, feelings and attitudes, and the behaviour associated with the use of languages, as well as multilinguals' life trajectories, fall within the purview of *individual multilingualism*. Sometimes, instead of 'individual multilingualism', the term *plurilingualism* is used, mostly in Francophone scholarship and documents of the European Union. In this book, we follow the tradition of using the term 'individual multilingualism'. Individual *trilingualism, quadrilingualism* (four languages), *pentalingualism* (five languages) and more-lingualisms are all covered by the term 'individual multilingualism'. For an individual, the mother tongue or native language may also be termed L1. The additional languages are traditionally marked as L2, L3, L4, L5 and Ln, with *n* denoting any subsequent language.

Ideally, definitions of multilingualism and of *a multilingual* should serve as a kind of measure for practice, enabling an understanding of whether we are encountering a case of multilingualism or not. This has not proved to be easy. Firstly, it is often hard to distinguish between two languages or between a language and a dialect (see Chapter 4). Is a person who speaks Italian, High German and Swiss German a bilingual or a trilingual? Secondly, can someone who uses one or two languages on a daily basis and a third language very infrequently and only on specific occasions be called a multilingual? Consider a Finn using Finnish and Swedish at home, at work and with friends, who only once in a while may read work-related material in French, especially if his knowledge of French is very basic. Is he a trilingual? There is no

---

3. 'Complicated' means consisting of many parts or elements; 'complex' refers to change in quality due to the interactions of multiple parts and elements of a system.

consensus among researchers on what frequency of language use a person requires to be counted as a language speaker. There is also disagreement regarding the degree of proficiency in a language that is needed for one to be considered a speaker of this language. There is no strict and reliable way to define how many words a person has to know to be considered a speaker of an additional language. Are three words – such as *bonjour, merci* and *au revoir* in French – enough? Or 200 words? Or 2,000 words? Perhaps it is only when an individual can discuss politics, fashion and philosophical issues, write a legal document properly and read Gustave Flaubert or Guy de Maupassant in the original that s/he can be designated as a multilingual? To add to the confusion, there are discussions among linguists and sociolinguists as to whether all aspects of language – reading, writing and oral communication – should be acquired at an equally high level of mastery for someone to be considered a speaker of a language. Questions remain as to whether those who can read a language but not speak it, or those who can communicate only in oral form, are to be considered fully-fledged language speakers. The current consensus seems to accept a person as a multilingual if s/he has some degree of functional capability, and uses several languages on different proficiency levels, each sufficient for carrying out the practical tasks required for work and daily life. Hufeisen and Jessner (2019: 65) note that 'in multilingual contexts, it is common that language skills are developed in various languages for their use in certain domains but that the language proficiency in some of the languages can be limited'.

1.2.2 Societal multilingualism

When the attention is directed to the routine use of three and more languages in a country or by all employees in an organisation, it is the realm of societal *multilingualism*. The term *societal multilingualism* refers to the organised and unorganised language practices involving three and more languages and the handling of these languages by either some or all members of a community, as well as the implications of these practices and their handling for the society and its members. 'Handling' includes activities, policies, attitudes and the assumptions underlying language use in a particular community.

Societal multilingualism as a particular organisation of language use takes place across the globe in countries, communities, physical and internet groups, organisations and educational, political and business establishments – in groups of any size and rank. In day-to-day reality in a multilingual country, it may have an impact on how easily you can communicate, catch the right bus, get a job or obtain medical help. Likewise, choosing one nursery or school over another, receiving a letter from a municipality in only one language or in a version in two or three languages, hearing unfamiliar speech on the street, and having to study additional language are also matters of societal multilingualism.

In addition, the issues that are within the scope of societal multilingualism include how multiple language varieties intersect in society, what the status and social opportunities of people are, and what the language policies consist of. A separate line of interest in society is multilingualism in education, which is connected with the aspirations of learners and their understanding of events in wider society. The study of societal multilingualism touches multiple other issues that are of interest to business people, politicians and public figures.

Despite different subjects under research in individual and social multilingualism (a person or a grouping), the two are tightly interconnected. Societal multilingualism cannot be understood without knowledge of how multilingualism affects individuals, and the opposite is also true. Knowing about earlier forms of multilingualism, both individual and societal, is also important.

1.3 Historical multilingualism and current multilingualism

Multilingualism is obviously not a new phenomenon. It has been present in society since the dawn of humanity and continues to exist at all times. Anthropologist Alan Barnard, the author of *Language in Prehistory*, thinks that 'there were once many more languages in the world than there are today' (Barnard 2016: 133). Our ancestors

> lived in small bands, and they came from many places, and their languages and dialects had diversity too. Multilingualism was the norm, and multilingual peoples were made up of individuals from different linguistic backgrounds, whose groups intermarried and passed on their genes and their linguistic diversity. (Barnard 2016: 133–4)

From the history of the ancient world, and what we know of earlier multilingual territories, countries or empires of previous epochs, the world was always pretty multilingual. In the monarchies and empires ruled by a king/queen, emperor/empress or sultan/sultana, the population belonged to many ethnic groups who spoke their own languages. For example, in Central Europe, the Austro-Hungarian Empire (1867–1918) listed Croatian, Hungarian, Czech, German, Italian, Polish, Romanian, Serbian, Slovak, Slovene and Turkish among the official languages of its citizens (Schjerve-Rindler and Vetter 2007).

Historical documents allow us to glimpse the attitudes and ways of dealing with multilinguals and multiple languages in medieval Europe. Historian Jacques Le Goff cites a captivating testimony showing that some people might have preferred to manage without additional languages:

> Common people were saddened to realize that other people spoke differently. For example, the thirteenth century German peasants did not recognize their prodigal son when he returned home pretending to speak several languages.
>
> 'My dear children,' he said in Low German, 'may God make you always blessed'. His sister ran up to him and hugged him, whereupon he said to her, 'Gracia vester!' The children then ran up and the old parents came up behind, and both of them welcomed him with boundless joy. He said to his father, 'Deus al!' and to his mother, Bohemian-fashion, 'Dobra Ytra!'. The man and his wife looked at each other, and the mistress of the house said, 'Husband, we are mistaken, this is not our child. This is a Bohemian or a Wend.' The father said, 'He's a Frenchman! He is not our son (may God preserve him), and yet he looks like him.' So then Gotelint, the sister, said, 'It's not your child. He spoke to me in Latin, so he must be a clerk.' 'Faith,' said the servant, 'if I judge from what he said, he was born in Saxony or Brabant. He spoke in Low German, so he must be a Saxon.' The father said simply, 'If you are my son, Helmbrecht, I shall be won over

to you if you pronounce one word according to our custom and in the manner of our ancestors, so that I may understand you. You are always saying "Deu sal", and I don't understand one word of that you are saying. Honour your mother and myself – we have always deserved this. Speak one word in German and I will rub down your horse, I myself, not the servant...' (Le Goff 1991: 275)

This evidence from the thirteenth century does not, of course, deny the fact that there were many multilingual individuals throughout history, and that many of them made good use of their multilingual abilities, as we will see in Chapter 9.

Through the centuries, some individuals and groups of people have always had a more pressing need than others to acquire at least partial proficiency in several languages. Among these were people living in border areas between tribes or nations, merchants travelling between countries, scientists who regularly used Latin and Greek, or members of royal families arriving in another state to marry – all were compelled by their life circumstances to master more than two languages. The illustrious story of a German Princess who became the Russian Empress Catherine the Great shows how the persistence of the young monarch in learning Russian that was totally unfamiliar to her, in addition to her native German and French she was brought up with, equipped her to survive and become sovereign of the vast country. Upon ascending the throne, Catherine actively exploited all her languages, each for a particular task: she spoke and thought in German, corresponded with the philosophers Voltaire, Diderot and other French thinkers in French, and ruled and loved in Russian. The reign of this 'enlightened despot', as she was called by her contemporaries, is considered the golden age of Russia. Catherine the Great of Russia is an example of successful individual multilingualism and multiliteracy.

For specific professions, crafts or castes, mastery of a few languages was much appreciated and even respected, but the point is that this need arose quite selectively and only for the skills that supported other priorities that were more important for that society and that time. For example, in ancient Egypt, where thousands of people were united under the power of the Pharaoh spoke many different languages, possessing such skills proved useful. In the main, however, these were writing skills as opposed to the multilingual abilities that were central to the politics, religion, agriculture and economy of that vast empire. In a civilisation that believed in the magical power of written or drawn signs, the caste of scribes played a key role in the centralised and rigid hierarchy, and writing skills were more significant in ancient Egypt than the ability to speak several languages.

In other regions and centuries, the role of multilingualism was conspicuous but somewhat limited. Basically, in previous epochs, however imperative multilingualism was for certain individuals and groups, it was not critical for the entire community or country, and was nowhere near as important for the entire world as it is now. Rather, maintaining many languages was largely supplementary to the development and continuation of previous societies. Previous multilingual social arrangements tended to be more local in nature and often required only a particular additional language, language-related knowledge or a number of specific language skills for sustaining economic, political and religious systems. The multilingual arrangements that, historically, were in place before globalisation are labelled '*historical multilingualism*'. Our current day-to-day existence and social behaviour differ markedly from those of previous generations. Contemporary practices of using multiple languages are called '*current multilingualism*' (Aronin and Singleton 2008; Aronin and Singleton 2012; Singleton et al. 2013b).

Current multilingualism differs from the historical forms of using multiple languages in society on a number of important points: first of all, in its scale, made obvious by its territorial and unprecedented numerical spread. Thousands of languages are currently spoken around the world. The reference source *Ethnologue* list 7,139 languages spoken in the world today (Eberhard et al. 2021) and about 142 language families as of 2020 (Ethnologue 2021). Millions of people speak 'big' languages such as English (estimated as between 1,132 million and 1.5 billion speakers), Mandarin Chinese (about 1,117 million speakers) and Hindi (about 615 million speakers). At the same time, we increasingly hear more about less-spoken languages of the world than ever before. For example, the 2016 Census of Canada[4] lists more than 70 Aboriginal languages in use across Canada; among them is Tlingit, the language spoken in Alaska and on the Pacific Northwest coast of British Columbia by 255 speakers, and Kutenai, with as few as 170 users in British Columbia. Another characteristic of current multilingualism that differentiates it from the historical one is that most countries and regions of the contemporary world are multilingual, whether officially or de facto.

Beyond rising numbers of multilinguals and multilingual countries and organisations, there is a more significant specificity of the current multilingualism. As the increasing breadth and width of its effects couple with the overwhelming pace of technology, new patterns of mobility and super-diversity, current multilingualism has acquired *a distinctive quality*. The emergent multilingualism of today generates particular societal impacts and outcomes. One of them is that, in the modern world, multilingualism *is the norm* for people of all walks of life, whatever their profession and status. And this is because of another important emergent quality – current multilingualism is *systemic*, in that it is embedded in the contemporary functioning of society, both globally and locally. The crucial difference between current and historical multilingualism lies in the degree to which multilingualism is or was integral to the construction of a specific social reality (Aronin and Singleton 2008, 2012). Permeating countries and villages, schools and clubs, laboratories and army units, the multilingualism of today has acquired global importance as *one of the most essential social practices in the world*.

1.4 How many languages and speakers are there in the world?

In order to assess the scope of multilingualism in the world and its geographical regions and polities, data on numbers of speakers and languages are often sought. We want to know how many languages and dialects there are in the world and in various countries; how many people in the world speak Spanish and how many people learnt Tok Pisin as a second language; how many heritage language speakers there are

---

4. <https://www12.statcan.gc.ca/census-recensement/2016/as-sa/98-200-x/2016022/98-200-x2016022-eng.cfm> (last accessed 31 August 2021).

in the USA; and how many endangered indigenous languages survive today. The answers will always be approximate and in need of continuous updating.

For example, the simple question 'How many languages are there in the world?' may yield a range of figures varying from 5,000 to 14,000 (compare this with the numbers given earlier in this chapter: 7,117 and 8,515).The most popular conventional figure cited in various sources including academic papers is around 6,000 languages (see, for example, Graddol 1997).

Such a scatter of numeric data on speakers and languages is an expected phenomenon, known to specialists. There are several reasons for it. Among these is the fact that the term 'language' is elusive, allowing a number of interpretations, and people differ in their ideas about what is to be counted as one language. Current estimations of the total number of languages have risen, compared to earlier assessments, in the light of social and political developments. In recent decades, language varieties such as pidgins, creoles and some dialects which used to be stigmatised are generally no longer seen as corrupt versions of their source languages, but rather as languages in their own right; they are therefore counted as separate languages. A significant number of sign languages, in addition to 'oral' languages, have been taken into consideration in recent times. In addition, the number of languages cited has increased owing to developments in the perception of World Englishes: Indian English, Irish English and African American Vernacular English (AAVE) are now often treated as distinct languages (McArthur 1987; Kachru 1985; Kirkpatrick 2007; Nelson et al. 2020). Yet another factor behind the increase in the total number of languages is the reinvigoration of *languages in decline*, examples being the revival of Hebrew, and the revitalisation of Basque, Catalan, Maori and Welsh (see, for example, Zuckermann 2020).

On the other hand, many languages are in a state of extinction and disappear every day. As the speakers of such languages lose their skills and fluency, they may be gradually replaced by semi-speakers and rememberers (Thomason 2015: 54). There is often no way of knowing whether and when exactly a language is lost due to the death of its speakers or to the shift to another language dominant in a region. Instances when we do know the date and time of a particular language loss are rare. Such is the case with Boa Sr, an Indian Great Andamanese[5] elder and the last speaker of Bo, or Aka-Bo, an ancient language in the Andaman Islands. In the last years of her life, Boa Sr, who also spoke Hindi and another local language, had no one to converse with in the Aka-Bo language because she was the last person to be fluent in it, the rest of the tribe, who numbered fifty-two at the time, no longer remembering it (Abbi 2006). In this case, we know that this language became extinct, as the event was widely reported in the media (for example, Watt 2010) and Boa Sr was, for many years, in contact with linguists. But the dynamics, survival or loss of thousands of other languages mostly goes unregistered. Language populations all over the world swell and shrink for various reasons, reorganising as their speakers move around the globe, learn new languages or lose others.

Obtaining the exact numbers of languages in a geographical region, country or city at any particular time is a challenging task. Demographic and linguistic changes

---

5. Port Blair, Andaman and Nicobar Islands, India.

occur every single day, and we will always lag behind the reality. With that in mind, specialists point out that the language statistics and population counts available today are already good enough to be useful, in terms of what they might tell us about language populations, endangerment of languages and the global situation with regard to language diversity (Paolillo 2006). When we discuss multilingualism, the figures indicating the number of speakers of particular languages and the number of languages are to be taken for what they are – approximate, always in flux, but helpful for general orientation and decision-making.

1.5 The purview of multilingualism

The three elements that constitute multilingualism explain the wide assortment and diversity of fields of knowledge that contribute to it.

The element 'language' is studied by linguistic disciplines – such as comparative linguistics, historical linguistics and computational linguistics. Other disciplines pertaining to the domain of linguistics are discourse studies, stylistics, semiotics, the study of signs and symbols and how they produce and communicate meaning, and the areas of expertise that examine writing systems and scripts.

The 'user/speaker' element is investigated by the knowledge provinces that refer to the study of individuals and groups. The human capacity to acquire more than two languages is endowed by physical abilities and neurological processes in the brains of healthy, challenged and gifted individuals. Therefore, multilingual performance and perception are studied by a host of areas that include physiology, psychology and cognitive studies. Neurolinguistics is the study of how and where our brains store our languages and how these languages are processed in the brain. Psycholinguists, in their turn, examine the relationships between linguistic behaviour and psychological processes.

The disciplines referring to the study of groups of people and their lives are, in the first place, *sociolinguistics* and *sociology of language*, which occupy a notable position in multilingualism. Both disciplines study the relationship between language and society, and their interests often overlap. To distinguish between them in rough terms, it is worth remembering that sociolinguistics has its main focus on language and investigates how societal factors affect language. It scrutinises regional, class and occupational dialects, gender and age differences, language change and variation. For example, the sociolinguistic study by Yaron Matras (2004) describes the dialect of the Romacel community of Parakalamos, in Greece – a language referred to by its speakers as Romacilikanes. *The Palgrave Handbook of Romani Language and Linguistics*, edited by Matras and Tenser (2020), contains sociolinguistic studies on the Romani language, including its dialect divisions, major external influences on the language through contact with other key languages, such as Turkish (Friedman), Hungarian (Bodnárová and Wiedner) and Slavic (Meyer), Romani dialectology (Elšik and Beníšek) and Para-Romani varieties (Bakker).

The main focus of the sociology of language is the 'reverse' of that of sociolinguistics, in that it studies how language affects society and the interplay between social conditions, events and ideologies on the one hand and use of languages on the other. The sociology of language 'focuses upon the entire gamut of topics related to the social organisation of language behavior, including not only language usage per se but also language attitudes and overt behaviors toward language and toward language users' (Fishman 1997: 25). Typically, it investigates larger social and political contexts than sociolinguistics. The province of the sociology of language is language use at a macro level, investigating entire countries or continents, and language contact among social groups, especially phenomena such as language conflict and multilingualism. For example, a volume edited by Isabelle Kreindler ([1985] 2015) on Soviet national languages tackled the languages and language policies in Estonia (Raun), Byelorussia (Wexler) and Ukraine (Solchanyk), Daghestan (Bennigsen and Lemercier-Quelquejay), and also the languages of smaller communities, such as the Mordvinian languages (Kreindler) and the Chuvash language (Krueger) in the time of the USSR.

It is not difficult to notice that these areas of interest also deal with multilingual settings. *Linguistic ethnography* and *linguistic anthropology* that traditionally contribute information and insights on multilingualism, whether concerning endangered languages or the ways that language influences social life, beliefs and social identity in various peoples. Ethnographic approaches (Davis 2013) in various areas of multilingualism have been around for several decades, starting with seminal works on the *ethnography of communication* and *interactional sociolinguistics* (Gumperz 1982b; Hymes 1972, 1974), and moving on to sociocultural studies of first language socialisation, second language development, situated language use and sociopolitical issues that were developed with regard to bilingualism (see, for example, Zentella 1997, 2018; Wiley and Valdés 2000).

Multilingualism discourse has integrated some newer ways of thinking from the perspectives of post-colonial and indigenous communities (Canagarajah 2005; Lo Bianco 2021; Phipps 2019; Skutnabb-Kangas and Philipson 2017; Zuckermann 2020; Zuckermann et al. 2014). These deal with implementing human rights instruments, legal protections at the national and international level for vulnerable and endangered languages, and language reclamation and salvation.

The issue of *post-colonial languages* is complicated by the thorny dilemmas that emerged from the ramifications of a historical colonial period and later developments in a given state. The drive of the post-colonial states and individuals to reclaim their indigenous languages in the contexts of power and education is met with the discourses of economic and practical considerations (Wolff 2017; Anchimbe and Mforteh 2011). Roughly speaking, one debated option is a complete return to the use of indigenous languages in all spheres of life. Another alternative is to continue using a colonial language (such as English, French or German) to enable easy communication in a state. Each particular country deals with such challenges in its own way. Consider the following examples.

Australia is a country with a complex linguistic demography. This immigrant and post-colonial nation can boast of its achievements in addressing indigenous and community language needs. Its scholars and practitioners continue their investigations in the field of language policy to fulfil educational aspirations that are advantageous for all the diverse inhabitants of Australia. In addition to English, the country's national and de facto official language, the language education policy has to embrace the remaining Aboriginal Australian languages of today, indigenous speech forms such as koines or *lingua francas*, mixed languages, and pidgins and creoles, as well as immigrant languages other than English that are known as 'community languages' (Lo Bianco and Slaughter 2017).

Banda's study (2020) provides an effective analysis of current language policies and sociolinguistic reality, including historical and ideological considerations and practical language use in the multilingual African state of Zambia. In a country with seventy-two spoken indigenous languages and where English is used as the primary language of education, numerous language clusters (called Dominant Language Constellations; see Chapter 10) operate across individual, household, community, regional and national boundaries as a consequence of intense language and interethnic contact.

Lo Bianco (2020) examines the state of indigenous and post-colonial languages in Vietnam through the trigraphia (use of three scripts) in Chinese, French and Vietnamese. This cluster of scripts demonstrates the competition of languages to function as the main national means of communication. The author concludes that

> In most post-colonial settings pragmatic management of public life has involved compromises involving continued use of current and former colonial states' languages and their demands to be granted continuing status in education and political/administrative and economic life, struggles around finding an 'honourable' or 'dignified' place for national language and at local levels, languages of tribal groups, hill populations or minority urban immigrant clusters. (Lo Bianco 2020: 52)

Language policy and planning is the area of research and the practices that deal with 'ideas, laws, regulations, rules and practices intended to achieve the planned language change in the societies, group or system' (Kaplan and Baldauf 1997).

A wide range of disciplines contributing to multilingualism often intersect in variously defined fields of interest, and the boundaries between them are blurred. Such are the interdisciplinary fields of *second language acquisition* (SLA), *third language acquisition* (TLA), *multiple language acquisition* (MLA) and *foreign language acquisition* (FLA). Multilingualism also includes the field of *applied linguistics*, which, in its turn, is a wide and interdisciplinary area of study and practices. Applied linguists aim at finding solutions to diverse real-life issues of education, communication, psychology, SLA and TLA.

The above does not yet exhaust the list of domains related, contiguous to and sharing with multilingualism. Some domains of knowledge, at first sight unrelated to multilingualism, have nevertheless shone their light on multilingualism investigation by virtue of the attentiveness and deep, scholarly thinking of their researchers. An illustrative example is Sir William Flinders Petri (1853–1942), a British Egyptologist, who was the first to start paying attention during his digs not only to the precious artefacts but to all the finds, which allow us to have information about languages, as Bernard Comrie and his colleagues noted in their *Atlas of Languages* (2003: 174). Now *material culture* is a province of multilingualism which describes, counts and interprets multilingual artefacts with inscriptions in a variety of languages as they define, modify and alter individual and communal life. In order to know more about the manifold dimensions of multilingualism, we draw on an ever-expanding array of disciplines that are seemingly distant to it, such as geography, philosophy, computer technologies and data science.

In recent years, multilingualism has been enriched by the cross-disciplinary fields of neurophilosophy and neuroarchaeology as they established *the close connection between brain, body, culture and the physical world.* Their theories underlie the interest of multilingualism in three intertwined elements – language, speaker and environment (see more on this in Chapter 9).

Thus, on the one hand, multilingualism relies heavily on disciplines much older than itself, such as linguistics, anthropology, psychology and philosophy. On the other hand, it promptly incorporates new ideas from the frontlines of science.

With such an array of fields of knowledge involved in multilingualism practices and studies, no wonder that the scope of *subjects* of study is also exceptionally huge. In multilingualism, researchers investigate speakers and sentences, slips of the tongue and feelings, choices and fleeting memories, along with educational establishments. In dialectal studies within the area of the sociology of language, for instance, communities of people are under research, with the focus being on the pronunciation of sounds as realised by various groups. Applied linguistics and language acquisition studies may investigate cross-linguistic interactions in oral and written language production and the responses of different age groups of students to methods of teaching additional languages. Investigations of entire communities, schools and families have helped us understand language users in terms of their linguistic and ethnic background, life trajectories, language attitudes and motivation.

Summary

Multilingualism is the acquisition and use of three and more languages. It is neither an extended bilingualism nor a sum of several bilingualisms. Multilingualism is a unique phenomenon of human existence and a field of practical and research interest that embraces a spectacular array of various elements: languages and abilities, language practices, and geographical and social contexts.

The various definitions of multilingualism are produced with the particular subfield of multilingualism in mind and depend on differing scientific backgrounds and ideologies.

Individual multilingualism refers to a private sphere and the domain of personal abilities, acquisition and use of languages. Societal multilingualism transpires through the manifestation of the organised and unorganised language practices involving three and more languages, and the handling of these languages in countries, communities and organisations. The implications of these practices and the way they are handled for a society and its members also lie within the purview of societal multilingualism. The ad hoc numerical data on speakers and languages are always dynamic and have to be perceived as given for general orientation.

Multilingualism did not always have the role, characteristics and forms it has now.

The differences between historical and current multilingualism lie in the degree of multilingualism spread and its intensity, but most significantly in the criticality of multilingualism for sustaining and advancing human society in general. Being aware of the specific features of current multilingualism allows it to be dealt with in an informed way. The overarching interest in multilingualism inquiry is the acquisition and use of multiple languages by individuals and in societies.

The study of multilingualism draws on a wide and ever-expanding range of scientific areas from the linguistic disciplines and cognitive and social studies, to seemingly distant ones such as geography, philosophy and data science. Multilingualism is an exceptionally broad, diverse and fascinating field of knowledge with multiple sources of information, subjects of study, methodologies and insights from the continuum of connected and distant disciplines.

Further reading

Anderson, Stephen (2004), *How Many Languages Are There in the World?*, Washington: Linguistic Society of America.

Kemp, Charlotte (2009), 'Defining multilingualism', in Larissa Aronin and Britta Hufeisen (eds), *The Exploration of Multilingualism: Development of Research on L3, Multilingualism and Multiple Language Acquisition*, Amsterdam: John Benjamins, pp. 11–26.

Chapter review

Fill in the table by (1) using material from the chapter, and (2) giving your own examples/illustrations.

Concept/keyword	Definition or explanation	Example from the chapter	Your own example	Your considerations and comments
Multilingualism	Give a definition			
Constituents of multilingualism				
Bilingualism	Give a definition			
Individual multilingualism				
Societal multilingualism				
Multilingual				
Bilingual				
Linguistics				
Sociolinguistics				
Sociology of language				

Contd

Concept/keyword	Definition or explanation	Example from the chapter	Your own example	Your considerations and comments
Historical multilingualism	Describe			
Current multilingualism	Describe			
Third language Acquisition (TLA)				
Multiple language acquisition (MLA)				

Reflective questions

1. Why is multilingualism so important today? Why study multilingualism?
2. What are the similarities between bilingualism and multilingualism?
3. List and describe the meaningful differences between bilingualism and multilingualism.
4. What are the implications if the differences between bilingualism and multilingualism are not recognised? Provide a minimum of three examples.
5. Based on the material in this chapter, provide your own definition of multilingualism relating to only one of its aspects, or try to define multilingualism as a phenomenon in its entirety.
6. Describe the scope of societal multilingualism. What are the issues it deals with?
7. How are individual and societal multilingualism interconnected?
8. What is the difference between current and historical multilingualism? Why is it important to distinguish between the two?
9. What are the sources of numerical data on languages and people using these languages? What can be learned from these data?
10. What are the areas of knowledge that contribute to multilingualism?

Exercises

Exercise 1.1

Select three individuals who are multilingual. Ask each of them whether they would consider themselves multilingual and why. Compare their definitions with each other and with the definitions and descriptions of multilingualism supplied in this chapter.

Exercise 1.2

Bring to your classroom photos and/or pictures that demonstrate your life in a multilingual environment.

Exercise 1.3

Prepare a five-minute presentation for your class using PowerPoint or Prezi, summarising this chapter.

Exercise 1.4

Prepare a five-minute presentation using PowerPoint or Prezi, illustrating *one* of the topics presented in this chapter: What is multilingualism? What is societal multilingualism? What are the sources of numerical data on languages and people?

2 Multilingualism as an exceptional resource

In order to understand the extraordinary might and potency of multilingualism, we have to appreciate the resources that the gift of human language delivers for humankind. Animals also have various communication systems, but human language and the human capacity for language are unique. This chapter brings together the themes that demonstrate multilingualism as exceptional, unique as a kind of resource. It draws on linguistics, biology, SLA, applied linguistics and globalisation studies. The chapter begins by emphasising human language species specificity by referring to Pavlov's theory and comparing human language with animal communication systems. Then, distinguishing between the abstract but very real concept of human language and concrete named languages, the chapter goes on to describe the functions that language performs for individuals in human society and language universals. Despite the universal functions and properties, particular named languages vary in morphosyntactic structure, scripts, expression of numerals, colours, morphology and time and space terms. These will be discussed in the rest of this chapter, along with the Sapir–Whorf hypothesis of linguistic relativity. Logically, the final topic of this chapter is linguistic diversity and the existing measures of it.

2.1 Resources of multilingualism

The dictionary meaning of the word 'resource' is a stock or supply of any natural or human wealth that can be drawn on by a person or organisation in order to function effectively. Contemporary humans have at their disposal language-related assets of various kinds, including broadly understood materials, people and tools that allow them to maintain their social and physical lives. Human language in the generic sense and concrete named language varieties, such as Dutch, Hakka or Haitian Creole, cumulatively constitute the linguistic resources of multilingualism. Language users are normally endowed with the mental faculty that allows them to learn languages, produce and understand utterances, write poetry and documents, switch from language to language and express their anger or joy. This would not be possible without appropriate physiological capacities, including the vocal apparatus, and the organs that together construct the neural architecture required for acquiring and producing language. These are multilingualism resources too.

With globalisation, resources of multilingualism have grown in terms of accessibility and distribution. Mobility and technology advancement have provided the whole of human society and each individual with additional affordances to use multiple languages through numerous modalities and channels.

It is also useful to know how various social groupings, families and individuals manage these resources, whether using them fully or partially, increasing them, or neglecting and losing them carelessly. Much of the information indicating multilingualism resources and their actual use can also be found in other chapters of the book: for example, on languages and language varieties in Part II, on the patterns in which language resources are experienced and organised in today's multilingual world in Part V, or the transmission of multiple languages in trilingual families in Chapter 8. This chapter specifically focuses on multilingual resources, not only providing arguments but also describing some points at greater length to illuminate the nature and profoundness of the human gift of language and multilingualism.

2.2 How unique are human language and the ability for multilingualism?

2.2.1 Pavlov's second and first signal systems

The aim of identifying the essential features of human intelligence and language was behind the works of Russian physiologist Ivan Petrovich Pavlov (1849–1936). He developed the concepts of the first and the second signal systems and formulated his theory in 1930. Pavlov attempted to draw a line between human language and the ability of animals to communicate (1935). He called the direct impressions of the world of reality 'the first signal system'. These include sensations, representations and thinking in terms of situations and images, arising from outside world stimuli. The first signal system comprises the impressions of reality that come directly to our visual and auditory tactile receptors.

The first signal system is at work in all animals that react to physical reality. Let us imagine that a dog sees the word 'food' written in red ink on white paper. It is hard to expect the response of the dog to the event of the paper with an inscription on it to be identical to that same dog's response to the actual food placed in front of it. Commonly, dogs do not internalise the information concerning the two distinct events, the written word and the food object, at an abstract level.

The second signal system operates with abstractions of reality in the form of speech and symbolic, socially conditioned language. According to Pavlov, this system applies to humans only, and according to some recent research, to dolphins, whales and apes. Human beings are able to form an image, a representation unconnected with circumstances of 'here and now'. When we read the word 'lemon' and visualise it as yellow and sour, we salivate – this, according to Pavlov, is the second signal system at work. The first and the second signal systems interact in human beings. There is a reflex both in people and in other mammals, to salivate over some taste stimuli – the first signal system. People can connect the image of the real fruit – its yellowness, smell, sour taste – with the written sign, the abstraction, and react to it – this is the second signal system.

2.2.2 Animal communication: can animals be multilingual?

Animals are known to have their own communication systems, not languages in the full sense of the term. Animal communication systems range from rather simple to truly sophisticated ones. Horses rub their noses together to show affection; octopi change colour to reveal anger and readiness to mate; eels release electrical pulses in different patterns and rates in order to communicate their location and territory; and fireflies flash light in order to reveal their location, sex and other information to nearby fireflies.

The wide variety of means by which animals communicate includes sounds, gestures, moves and chemicals responsible for colour change, as well as smells, vibrations, tactile displays and light. Male spiders, for example, make their attempts to approach a female with the help of an elaborate sequence of gestures. For adult bowl-and-doily spiders, constant signalling with vibrations and pheromones located on their cuticles are their primary communication signals. They both attract a female and show rivalry between the males for her favours. Fiddler crabs, too, use acoustics and gesture for attracting a female and delivering information to a rival male. The crabs wave their claws in a specific pattern in order to attract females in the daytime. At night, from just inside his shelter, a male crab uses two different sounds to deliver information to the female, and also to rival males.

Birds, especially, are widely known for their vocal abilities. They can imitate accents and voices, and sing. An exceptional African Grey parrot, Alex, whose language abilities surprised linguists (and zoologists), had an intelligence on a par with that of dolphins and great apes. According to the animal psychologist Dr Irene Pepperberg, who trained Alex for about thirty years till his death in 2007, Alex used words creatively, and was seen answering various types of questions. But birds' ability to produce sounds similar to those used in human language, and even Alex's outstanding accomplishments, do not amount to possessing a system as complicated, flexible and multipurpose as human language.

Scientists found out that animal communication is often seasonal, mostly accompanying life cycle changes, such as courtship behaviour, which take place at specific times of the year. Further restriction of the communication systems of mammals, birds, insects and fish, from a human point of view, is that when animals communicate on specific occasions their communication signs evoke specific behaviours. While humans may chat with their friends over the phone or at a picnic for pure fun, animal communicating behaviours are connected to food, reproduction, territorial claims and warnings, nesting and flocking recognition and greetings. Honey bees perform their dances to tell others the location of rich stores of honey, where and how far it is; wolves compete for food using facial expressions, staring into the eyes of the competitor and baring their teeth. They mark their territory by urinating on its boundary. In other words, the functions of animal communication are somewhat limited.

The mainstream literature on the topic of human and animal communication states that it would be more exact, at least in the current state of knowledge, to describe non-human systems of communication as 'animal communication' rather than 'animal language'. It is assumed that the interaction between animals by such communication is fundamentally different in its underlying principles from human language, rather than that human language is superior to that of animals.

Is using more than one communicative system humans' exclusive characteristic?

Jean Aitchison (2008: 24) begins the discussion of whether language is restricted to humans with a short poem by Robert Desmos:

> An ant who can speak
> French, Javanese and Greek
> Doesn't exist.
> Why ever not?

Indeed, while pet owners report addressing their cats, dogs, snakes and alligators in two or three languages, there are no consistent data about animals actually using several codes for their communication. Probably a good example of an animal that was reported to use two languages is the case of the 'Speaking Elephant', Batyr. The famous elephant, who sparked a wave of attention in 1979 in the former USSR, lived in the Karaganda Zoo in the Republic of Kazakhstan in 1969–93. Reportedly, he said the words by manipulating his trunk. Having put his trunk in his mouth, and pressing the tip of his trunk with the bottom of his jaw and manipulating his tongue, the elephant allegedly used about twenty words, both in Kazakh and in Russian. These included 'Батыр' – Batyr (the athlete in Turkic); 'Батыр хороший' – good Batyr (the trunk in the mouth); 'Дурак' – the fool; 'Ой-ё-ёй' – oh-yo (it is very sonorous – the trunk in the mouth); 'Бá-бa' (short for 'babushka' – the grandmother); and the short children's sound 'ba' (the trunk in the mouth).

This controversial case very possibly was largely exaggerated by the media. Many reports contained considerable fabrication and wild conjecture; even if we believe that he used words from the Kazakh and Russian languages, Batyr was not bilingual, of course. It is very difficult to claim that he used the two codes as human language users would, or even distinguished between the languages.

Even if we admit that some of the most eloquent and resourceful animals, insects and birds use two codes for their communication, this cannot be compared with the common bilingualism and multilingualism that are more the norm than the exception for the human race. It is not our aim here to prove the superiority of human language over the animal communication systems. Rather, this comparison precedes and informs the discussion of the unique features, richness and possibilities of human language, marvellously multiplied in multilingualism.

2.3 Human language

The first and foremost resource of multilingualism is *human language*. This abstract but very tangible phenomenon, which enables the life and development of human beings, is universal for all humans. People normally master their mother tongue by a very early age, regardless of whether they receive special language-related attention in their family. Even those children who grow up in an environment where adults are not particularly intent on developing a child's language skills nonetheless, in due course (except in circumstances of some type of brain malfunction), become able to communicate thoughts and feelings and manage personal and social relationships.

Having said that, no one speaks the 'human language'; in real life, human language is reified in a large number of concrete language varieties, such as French, Amharic or Lagunen-Deutsch.[1] *Named languages* are arbitrary systems of written and auditory signs governed by grammatical rules that enable humans to communicate, express themselves and manipulate objects in their environment. Thousands of named languages throughout the world allow human communities to maintain their culture and pass it on to new generations.

Human language performs several essential *functions* as humans use their language capacity to perform numerous tasks. We use language to deliver and receive innumerable bits of information, express nuances of feeling and emotions, tell and understand jokes, express compassion and love, carry out work, buy and sell, conduct global business, create literature and culture and pass it along to our children and grandchildren, elaborate ideas and discuss complicated matters. It is with the help of language that people dream and fantasise, lie effectively, perform virtual communication, and sometimes take on another identity. In fact, the number of functions of human language appears to be never-ending.

The *primary functions of language* are communication, thinking and cognition. Language has instrumental utility and carries out a symbolic function. In fact, language, along with the capacity for reasoning, is considered a particularly human endowment that has brought humans to a stage of development distinct from other species. All named languages are characterised by language universals, distinctive characteristics of all human languages that are described in the next section.

2.3.1 Language universals

Language universals demonstrate the uniqueness of the human language faculty and relate to many named languages concomitantly. They were singled out by linguists and philosophers long ago. In globalised multilingual conditions, the features universal to many languages modify: some become less pronounced, while others acquire new shades and significance. In 1960, Charles F. Hockett provided a list of the characteristics of human language, which, he suggested, distinguish human language from animal communication. Some of the items known as language universals are discussed below.

1. *Vocal-auditory channel.* The fact that language is mostly performed by the vocal organs and perceived via the auditory channel may be accidental in humans' development, but it is fairly convenient since an individual can engage in many other activities, leaving hands and legs free for other tasks. Another advantage of using acoustic signals is that they are independent of light conditions and can be transmitted in the darkness; they can also flow over obstacles and do not require much energy for their production. The use of the vocal–auditory channel ensures the quality, which is called *complete feedback*: that is, the ability of a speaker to hear everything of what is said. The way of producing acoustic sounds and transmitting

---

1. Lagunen-Deutsch – a dialect of German spoken in Chile.

them through the air is species-specific for humans. We are capable of producing a wide range of sounds: British linguist Peter Ladefoged (2005) estimated that there are about 200 different vowels in the world's languages and more than 600 different consonants. Each language has its own inventory of sounds taken from the existing pool. Some sounds occur more frequently than others and are common for many languages. Others, such as the click sounds of Xhosa, a language spoken in Africa, are very rarely used except by native speakers.

The vocal–auditory way of communication turned out not to be easily available even to our closest relatives, the great apes, which have 99 per cent of their basic genes in common with humans. A series of attempts made in the United States in the 1930s to teach gorillas, chimpanzees and orangutans to speak human language was unsuccessful. Chimpanzee Gua was taught for nine months by the Kellogg family alongside their own son, Donald, but was not able to pronounce a single word (Kellog and Kellog 1933). A female chimpanzee named Viki was reared in the home of scientists Catherine and Keith Hayes, as their own child. She could not master spoken language beyond poorly articulated versions of 'mama', 'papa' and 'cup' (Hayes 1951). The lesson was well learned, and the next generation of 'talking apes' was taught American Sign Language. The legendary chimpanzee Washoe, for example, signalled but did not speak. The most generally accepted reason nowadays, which was not so obvious initially, is that the vocal apparatus of the ape is not equipped for emitting human-like sounds.

The vocal–auditory channel is not the only way that people communicate. Deaf people, for example, communicate in various sign languages where gestures and lip-reading are used (see Chapter 5 on sign languages). Technology provides numerous opportunities for communication for those who, for any reason, do not wish to or cannot communicate using their voice. Deaf and hard-of-hearing children and adults and people with autism spectrum disorders increasingly use supplemental means to replace speech and writing. Augmentative and alternative communication (AAC) encompasses the use of gestures, photographs, pictures, drawings and also various multimedia and communication devices (see, for example, Dada et al. 2017) to help people cope with their learning and daily routines. A feature of current multilingualism is that, today, people often use a cluster of languages and communication means, instead of a single one, and their Dominant Language Constellations (see Chapter 10) consist not only of natural languages but also of sign languages and alternative means of communication.

2. Long ago, people noticed that the nature of the sounds produced by people is fleeting: sounds disappear very soon after they are produced. *Rapid fading* of oral language sounds is also characteristic of human language. It is due to this characteristic of human language that we do not know how ancient languages sounded: examples include Assyrian, the language of diplomacy and culture spoken from the third millennium BCE[2] to the early first millennium in the Middle East, or Urartian, once spoken in Armenia. We can only guess how Latin originally sounded. Sometimes, however, due to technological progress, we may have a taste of the sounds that may have been heard on Earth 300,000–500,000 years ago.

---

2. BCE – before the current era (BC – before Christ – in other notations).

Preserving fleeting words was one of the reasons for people to invent *writing*, an astonishing language feature that is believed to have existed for about 7,900 years. Since then, humans have created a range of *writing systems*: systems of symbols visually representing language. Their major types are logographies, syllabaries and alphabets (see the next section for further detail).

In more recent times, new channels of saving and passing linguistic information, such as the internet and modern technological devices, have been added to handwriting and print. Languages using these new ways of language transmission are flexible enough to accommodate themselves to the new forms of transmission – texting, sending images and videos via messaging programs – and thus become *multimodal*.

3. Characteristics of *cultural transmission* are found in all human languages, regardless of the extent of effort involved, and whether the language is handed down to other generations consciously or unconsciously. One traditional expression regarding cultural transmission is that, in a particular setting, a child acquires the language of the community they hear around them: 'We do not expect a child born into a family and community speaking only Chinese to start speaking in Spanish.' Today, however, we do expect that, in multilingual families and settings, since bilingual and multilingual early language acquisition allows for multilingual cultural transmission.

Let us proceed to a discussion of the fundamental characteristics of human language.

4. The quality of *arbitrariness* refers to the fact that there is generally no rational or 'natural' connection between a linguistic form (sound or sign) and its meaning. You cannot determine the meaning of the words [huā] in Chinese, *fleur f* in French, цветок in Russian and *die Blume* in German to be a plant that is cultivated or appreciated for its blossoms – that is, *flower* – from how they sound or how they are written. With the exception of a few words that do indeed seem to have a link between the meaning they are intended to convey and the sound signal or written form they use to convey it, such as *giggle, murmur, moo, oink, phew, wham* and *crackle* in English, human words are arbitrary.

5. The quality of *displacement* describes the ability of humans to refer to things that are not in the immediate vicinity, either spatially or temporally. Human languages can be used to communicate ideas about things that are currently not present (cf. first and second signal systems above). Although animals, especially domesticated ones, are known to be sometimes extremely sensitive in communicating with their owners, you do not normally expect an answer from a parrot on what they think of the outfit your girlfriend might have worn last Friday. Humans, on the other hand, can discuss events removed from them in time and space. With the help of language, we can express our future plans, dreams and actions that can take place only if a certain condition is fulfilled.

6. *Discreteness*. Language is composed of discrete units that are linguistically and meaningfully specific and that are used in combination to create meaning. Each sound of a language is meaningfully discrete. Different sounds in **d**og and **f**og, for example, effectively differentiate between the creature and water vapour in cloud-like masses that possibly limits visibility. The meaning of 'log', a usually bulky piece or length of a cut fallen tree, is understood if we substitute only one phoneme for another, 'l'.

Like other universal qualities, discreteness is manifested differently in different languages. In some languages, some sounds are discrete, while others are not. For example, in English the difference between the sounds 't' and 'd' is meaningful, while the same sounds in Russian can be perceived as the same without having a difference in meaning if they are not in a stressed position at the end of a word, as in the word 'город', for example.

7. The feature that allows any of the human languages to produce an infinite variety of words, phrases and utterances for any particular specific need and circumstance, to create novel utterances continuously and actively, and to produce them is variously called *productivity, spontaneous usage, creativity* or *openness*. An important aspect of human language productivity is that human speech is *stimulus-free*. While animals, as we saw in the previous section, use their communication signals in specific situations and for specific purposes (for example, an ant releases a chemical in order to signal an alarm situation, and on receiving the signal the nearby ants travel towards the scent to help their nest mate; a kangaroo stomps its back legs to communicate danger to nearby kangaroos), humans have the ability to say anything they like in any context.

Other traits of human language that were named to capture the essential nature of human language and separate it from animal communication are *turn-taking, prevarication* and *reflexiveness*.

9. *Taking turns* is the typical manner in which orderly conversation takes place: that is, one interlocutor waits until the other has finished their utterance, and only then produces their utterance. How is this universal connected to multilingualism? In social life, it translates into specific timing in conversational response and differing perceptions of speakers of different languages of their timing as 'delayed', 'on time' or 'simultaneous'. Scholars (Stivers et al. 2009) analysed turn-taking behaviour in speakers of ten languages that fundamentally varied in terms of grammar and syntax, including Dutch, Korean, English, a Mexican indigenous language called Tzeltal, Ākhoe Haiǀom, a Khoe language of the Khoisan family spoken in Northern Namibia, Japanese and Yélî-Dnye, used by a small population in Papua New Guinea. They found that speakers from five continents, ranging from hunter–gatherer groups to urban metropolis dwellers, displayed universal turn-taking behaviour across languages and cultures. Stivers and her colleagues (2009) reported that the objective time measures of turn transition speed (in milliseconds) registered meant that the offset of the next turn in each language departed by no more than a quarter-second from the overall mean in the average gap between turns, within a range of 250 milliseconds from the cross-language mean. The actual difference between the ten-language norm and the average turn transition in Danish is confined to the time it takes to utter a single syllable, which should not imply fundamentally different types of turn-taking systems in different languages. As speakers of different languages aim to minimise the time gap before producing a following turn at talking, and at the same time to avoid overlaps in their conversations, they, according to the researchers, are hypersensitive to perturbations in the timing of responses, measured in 100 milliseconds or less. This sensitivity to subtle variation may be responsible for the subjective impression by outsiders of 'huge silences' in Danish and Lao (202 and 203 milliseconds respectively, in the case of Nordic languages).

An exceptional resource 35

10. *Reflexiveness* or *metalinguistics* is the human ability to discuss language itself and how we use it. The value of this trait is especially marked in people learning and using their second and subsequent languages.

11. The ability to read intentions, *prevarication*, which, according to scientists, emerges early in the first year of life, allows young children over the age of eight to discern utterances expressing praise, sarcasm and blame. As mentioned earlier, human language enables its speakers to lie, pretend, fantasise, dream and gossip. In his book *Grooming, Gossip and the Evolution of Language* ([1996] 2004), Robin Dunbar argues that gossiping[3] is vital to a society and strengthens some kinds of relationships within it. This ability, as we can judge from SLA, TLA and applied linguistics scholarship, is manifested in each of an individual's languages to various degrees and may not appear in the first stages of learning a foreign language.

2.3.2 Language features in different languages

Linguists and philosophers long ago noticed often dissimilar approaches to expressing reality in world languages. Diversity in conveying meanings, numbers, colours, time and some other aspects of human existence are investigated not only in linguistics, but also by ethnographers, sociologists and psycholinguists. The implications of the differences in languages' structure, vocabularies and pragmatics have been debated for decades. Differences do not mean that any linguistic forms of expression are 'better' than others; all of the features are valuable linguistic resources and add to the variety of life forms.

Below are some dimensions in which differences between languages are more readily noticed.

Writing systems and scripts

For thousands of years, people have devised a large range of means to express information in writing. Various *scripts*, sets of written characters, were created in different parts of the world for different needs. The earliest ones were ideographic, where ideas and concepts are sometimes represented by pictures; the best known of these are Egyptian hieroglyphs. Writing systems can be roughly divided into logographies, alphabets and syllabaries. While logographic writing systems are based on a letter, symbol or sign used to represent an entire word, without relation to sounds, syllabaries and alphabets are phonographic writing systems in which a symbol represents a sound or sounds.

Logographies, such as the Sumerian cuneiforms of Uruk used in the mid to late fourth millennium BCE, and modern Chinese (Hanzi), Japanese (Kanji), Korean (Hanja) and Vietnamese, are writing systems that use symbols that stand for words or morphemes.[4] They may count thousands of symbols.

---

3. In Robin Dunbar's study the word 'gossip' is used in its wider sense, meaning conversations on social topics (Dunbar [1996] 2004).
4. Morpheme – the smallest meaningful unit of a language that cannot be further divided (for example, 'kind' and 'ly', forming 'kindly').

Alphabets are sets of letter symbols, each standing for a single spoken sound and/or a phoneme, either consonant or vowel.

Latin, Cyrillic, Roman and Greek alphabets (writing systems) have long histories of origin and modification through the centuries. A number of languages can have their own alphabets based on one writing system.

Arabic and Hebrew scripts, as well as Pahlavi, a written form of various Middle Iranian languages, are abjads: sets of graphemes[5] that represent consonants; vowels are indicated or not by diacritics.

An *abugida* is a writing system based on consonants, but in which a vowel following a consonant modifies it through diacritics, such as Devanāgarī and other South Asian scripts.

Syllabaries are phonographic systems in which each character represents a syllable: a unit of speech composed either of a combination of consonant and vowel sounds or of a vowel sound (na, ni, nu, no). Writing systems that use syllabaries wholly or in part are Cherokee, Japanese and the ancient Cretan scripts (Rogers 2005; Daniels and Bright 1996; Coulmas 1999).

Among less obvious things that people noticed, for example, is that languages present a rich palette of stress patterns. Some European languages, such as English, French and Portuguese, have a phrase stress rhythm, while others, such as Spanish and Italian, have syllable stress patterns. The African Bantu languages, such as Swahili, also follow a syllable stress rhythm, which in practice makes speech a bit slower than in phrase-stress languages.

Numerals

Numerals, words denoting numbers, are constructed differently in different languages. In Chinese, Japanese and Korean, for example, numerals are more systematically transparent than numerals in English and other European languages.

To add to the diversity, Korean, unlike many other languages, has two systems of numerals – Native Korean and Sino-Korean. These are used simultaneously: for example, in telling the time (as in 12.30 p.m.), the hours are said in Native Korean, and the minutes in the Sino-Korean system.

Basic colour terms

The influential 1969 study by Brent Berlin and Paul Kay showed that the speakers of about 100 different languages that were used in their experiment classify the same physical stimuli – a chip with colours – in different ways because their languages provide them with different numbers of colour words. In particular, Berlin and Kay found that languages may have the following patterns of colour terms:

1. two colour words: black (covers most of the dark hues) and white (embraces most light hues)
2. three colour terms: black, white and red

---

5. Grapheme – the smallest meaningful contrastive unit in a writing system, a written symbol, letter or group of letters that represents a sound in a word. For example, the letter 'o' in the word '**dog**' is a grapheme, as is 'ch' in the word '**chef**'.

3. four colour terms: black, white, red and either green or yellow
4. five colour terms: black, white, red and both green and yellow
5. six colour terms: black, white, red, green, and yellow plus blue
6. seven colour terms: the above six colour terms plus brown
7. more than seven terms: the above seven plus colour terms for purple, pink, orange, grey or a combination of these.

The first two patterns are thought to be found only rarely nowadays. Examples of four-colour languages are Ibo and Urhobo, languages of Nigeria; among five-colour-term languages are the Mayan languages of Mexico and Guatemala; seven-term languages can be found in India among the dialects of Malayalam and in Africa – the Bari and the Siwi languages.

Other examples include Urdu, which has terms for black, white, red, green, yellow, blue, brown and purple; Cantonese, which, according to Berlin and Kay (1991: 35), has the first six basic terms but lacks brown, purple and orange; Tagalog and Vietnamese, having the colours of the first few patterns and lacking the term for orange; Catalan, which has no terms for pink and orange, but has first several basic colour terms. The eight-, nine-, ten- and eleven-term languages are widely found today. Japanese, Zuni, Hebrew and English are eleven-term languages; Hungarian and Russian have twelve basic terms – Hungarian has the standard eleven with a distinction between *vörös* 'dark red' and *piros* 'light red', while Russian has the standard eleven with a distinction between синий (siniy) 'dark blue' and голубой (goluboy) 'light blue'.

The study stimulated a wave of further investigations and discussions on the topic from linguistic, ethnological, anthropological and philosophical angles. In 1976 the authors of the 1969 study and their colleagues carried out the *1976 World Color Survey*, with the extended scope of samples from 110 unwritten languages from around the world, in order to investigate the main findings of Berlin and Kay. A curious scholar can visit *The WCS Data Archives* (Cook et al. 2012). Analyses and interpretations of the data followed (Kay et al. 1997, 2009; Regier et al. 2010; Kay and Cook 2015).

Time and space terms
The time and space terms of world languages were also found to be not always similar. Especially thought-provoking was the study by Benjamin Lee Whorf (1956a, 1956b). After studying the tribe of Hopi Indians and their language, Whorf (1956a: 57) came to the conclusion that Hopi 'is seen to contain no words, grammatical forms, construction or expressions that refer directly to what we call "time," or to past, present and future'. Whorf explained that, in the same way as it is possible to have other geometries in addition to the Euclidian, it is possible to have a perfect description of the universe that is different to the common descriptions of time in standard average European language. The Hopis' way, according to Whorf, does not express our familiar contrasts of time and space.

Like the colour studies, the investigation by Whorf on time and space expressions, which implied that language shapes thinking, stirred a wave of further explorations, discussions and disputes (such as Pinker 2007; Brown and Lenneberg 1954).

Ekkehart Malotki, who explored the Hopi too, argued that the tribe does have temporal concepts and gave multiple examples; unlike what Whorf called standard average European languages (SAE), however, Hopi employs the device of spatial–temporal metaphor in order to convey concepts of space and time (1983). The position of the sun indicates their perception of time, and this is expressed by special linguistic means. A 'spatial expression *haq 'iwta* by drawing on the base *haq* – "far" is said to locate the sun "way along" its diurnal path' (Malotki 1983: 281) and may be interpreted as 'afternoonish', as used in utterances like 'The sun was already far (into the day) when we came to you here.' When the speaker wishes to refer to the midday point *taawanasave*, the terminology changes to expressions reflecting the downward trend of the sun's journey (Malotki 1983: 281).

2.3.3 Linguistic relativity/linguistic determinism hypothesis

Despite the controversy, the research of Whorf, which drew on the views of the Yale linguist and anthropologist Edward Sapir, proved to be influential and is often referred to as the *Sapir–Whorf hypothesis*, although the two never formulated their views together. In various interpretations it can be understood as stating that the structure of a language determines or greatly influences how people think and behave, and that their understanding of the world depends on the structure of the language they habitually use. To keep more faithfully to the original statements of each of the two scholars, the two illustrious quotes are provided below.

Edward Sapir wrote:

> Human beings do not live in the objective world alone, nor alone in the world of social activity as ordinarily understood, but are very much at the mercy of the particular language which has become the medium of expression for their society. It is quite an illusion to imagine that one adjusts to reality essentially without the use of language and that language is merely an incidental means of solving particular problems of communication or reflection. The fact of the matter is that the 'real world' is to a large extent unconsciously built up on the language habits of the group. (1929: 209)

In turn, Benjamin Lee Whorf expressed his vision as follows:

> We dissect nature along lines laid down by our native languages. The categories and types that we isolate from the world of phenomena we do not find there because they stare every observer in the face; on the contrary, the world is presented in a kaleidoscopic flux of impressions which has to be organized by our minds and this means largely by the linguistic systems in our minds. (1956b: 213)

With time, Sapir's and Whorf's enquiries into the possible influence of language on human thought and cultures developed into a large pool of ideas and research on what is now called the *hypothesis of linguistic relativity/linguistic determinism*.

The formulations of the hypothesis are generally interpreted as 'weak' and 'strong' versions. The strong one, 'linguistic determinism', says that language determines thought. It holds that linguistic categories limit and determine cognitive categories and, therefore, that a world view is imposed on speakers by a particular language. In such a formulation this view is currently considered by many scholars to be quite extreme. The weak version, or 'linguistic relativism', says that linguistic categories and usage do not determine but rather influence thought and perception of the world. To which extent this influence is exerted and through which mechanisms – for example, through the categorisation of words – are still to be determined.

Summary

The gift of human language, inseparably intertwined with the physiological, cognitive and neurological capacities of language users, produces the remarkable and unique resource of multilingualism. While human language was always considered a unique human feature separating the human race from the rest of nature, the human ability to acquire and use a multiplicity of languages has not been stressed enough as an aspect of the specialness of humankind.

Animals are known to be able to use various types of communication, but using more than one language is humans' exclusive characteristic. The interaction of the first and second signal systems, according to Pavlov, and the species-specific physiological and neuroarchitecture lie behind this facility. Today, the resources of human multilingual endowment are multiplied and restructured to numerous modalities and channels. Language universals are reified in named languages in a variety of ways and their current expression in concrete languages and cultures bears new meanings under global multilingualism. Multiple linguistic features, such as structure, vocabulary, stress, writing systems and scripts, represent a realm of exciting diversity and stimulate insights for sociologists, ethnographers and philosophers into the essentials of human life. The Sapir–Whorf hypothesis and its two basic components, linguistic determinism and linguistic relativism, pose questions regarding whether human thought is shaped by language, and if so, to what extent. Recognising various types of resources that multilingualism affords society, in general and to particular individuals, it is possible to make informed decisions about the management and optimal use of these riches. How people have been dealing with and organising their common resources is discussed in the next chapter.

Further reading

Aitchison, Jean ([2008] 2011), *The Articulate Mammal: An Introduction to Psycholinguistics*, 5th edn, New York: Routledge: Chapter 2, 'Animals that try to talk. Is language restricted to humans?', pp. 24–48.

Coulmas, Florian (1999), *The Blackwell Encyclopedia of Writing Systems*, Oxford: Blackwell.

Trask, R. L. (1998), *Key Concepts in Language and Linguistics*, London and New York: Routledge.

Chapter review

Fill in the table by (1) using material from the chapter, and (2) giving your own examples/illustrations.

Concept/keyword	Definition or explanation	Example from the chapter	Your own example	Your considerations and comments
Human language				
Named language				
Functions of human language				
Animal communication				
Design features of human language/language universals	Enumerate and explain			
First signal system				
Second signal system				
Augmentative and alternative communication (AAC)				
Writing system				
Basic colour terms				
Linguistic relativity				
Linguistic determinism				

Reflective questions

1. Why, in your opinion, did David Cooper (1973: 3) call human language an 'extraordinary institution'?
2. What is the difference between the terms 'human language' and 'named languages'? How do the concepts denoted by these terms relate to each other?
3. Name as many functions of human language as you can.
4. What are the means of communication used by animals, insects, birds and fish?
5. What are the functions of animal communication? What are the limitations of animal communication systems? How can the linguistic achievements of apes be interpreted and can they amount to human speech?
6. Compare alphabets, abjads and syllabaries, and say how these different writing systems (a) contribute to societal multilingualism, and (b) can affect individual multilingualism.

7. What might the implications of studies on basic colours in various languages be? Provide at least three implications in relation to social life, education and economics.

Exercises

Exercise 2.1

Select five language universals and explicate how they are manifested when you use each of your languages.

Exercise 2.2

Discuss the resources of multilingualism that you have employed in the course of your life. Draw a plan for more appropriate management of the resources of multilingualism in your workplace.

Exercise 2.3

Choose or formulate your own interpretation of the linguistic determinism/linguistic relativity hypothesis. Provide arguments for and against it.

Exercise 2.4

Prepare a poster describing the writing system(s) of local/indigenous languages in your region.

Exercise 2.5

Organise a class conference with four or five short presentations that focus on arguments and illustrations related to the presenter's interpretation of linguistic determinism/linguistic relativity. Allocate time for answering questions from the audience and discussion.

3 Multilingualism as modern reality and field of knowledge

The previous chapter was dedicated to demonstrating the riches of multilingualism in terms of what it may offer to human society. This chapter is devoted to how people are aware of and deal with their languages in social time and space. It accounts for the current multilingual reality and the ways in which contemporary people organise their common linguistic resources. To this end, the chapter traces the three stages of societal awareness of languages and prevalent ideas, research and policies relating to languages and their users as they correspond to these stages. The multilingual stage is associated with the New Linguistic Dispensation, the modern sociolinguistic order brought about by globalisation.

3.1 Social awareness in languages

3.1.1 Paradigms and stages

Despite the use of multiple languages from the dawn of humankind, the phenomenon of multilingualism seems to have attracted social and academic attention only recently. It has become especially noticeable since the turn of the millennium, to the extent that 'multilingualism' has become a buzzword. The good news is that it is now being extensively pursued by scholars in various areas. Gradually, issues and phenomena that previously went unnoticed or were not deemed worthy of attention have come into the spotlight. The history of multilingualism as a field of research is not yet written, but we can already trace its main developments, name its classic works and make use of an extensive pool of findings.

The particular combination of focal interests in societal discourse and science in each particular period is not accidental. Its selection is governed by contemporaneous scientific development and religious, cultural and political beliefs that together produce societal mindsets. The focus established by a particular blend of social and scientific attitudes leads to some real things being seen as extremely important, and other things being considered as irrelevant to societal and scholarly attention.

It is possible to distinguish roughly three stages in societal and scientific awareness with respect to language and languages. These stages differ in *paradigms*, the perspectives from which the sociolinguistic reality is seen and managed accordingly. *The monolingual paradigm* has one language as a point of departure; *the bilingual paradigm* recognises two languages as active and influential; and *the multilingual approach* (paradigm) deals with many language varieties that intersect and interact in all dimensions of contemporary human existence.

The approximate periods of time when monolingual, bilingual or multilingual assumptions and arrangements (paradigms) dominated society are called *monolingual, bilingual* and *multilingual stages*. The stages are not exactly chronological and are not neatly defined in time and place, rather, they can be indicated very approximately. This approximate division does not mean that the so-called monolingual stage in a given context is characterised by the use of a single language only, nor the bilingual stage by the use of just two languages. Rather, the stages of societal and scientific awareness with respect to language and languages are characterised by the particular monolingual, bilingual or multilingual ambience and the prevailing corresponding ideological paradigm.

This overview of the stages of human interest in language and languages invites readers to consider how people have been aware of and utilised the resources of multilingualism for the last two centuries. Matching the paradigms accepted by wider society to stages demonstrates how people value, control and regulate the language resources available to them, whether these are spoken or sign languages, dialects or other forms of communication.

3.1.2 The monolingual stage

Paradoxical as it may sound, we find the beginnings of multilingualism in the monolingual thinking that pervaded the general views on social arrangements and human nature in the second half of the nineteenth and early twentieth centuries. The outstanding linguists and philosophers of the time provided the under-structure of knowledge that researchers of multilingualism still use. They left us their considerations on languages and language typologies, their philosophy of language, and detailed information (including grammars and dictionaries) about various languages of the Americas, Asia, Australia, Europe and Africa. Without this background knowledge of language as a human attribute, as well as the detailed data on separate languages, multilingualism would not have such a comprehensive linguistic and ethnographic basis. In the twentieth century, language has become a prominent focus of philosophical studies. The philosophy of language was, in fact, concerned with philosophical questions rather than with linguistic ones. Logicians posed 'general questions about language as such' (Lacey 2001: 172) rather than about specific languages. At the same time, theoretical and philosophical linguists, such as Ferdinand de Saussure (1916), Edward Sapir (for example, 1921, 1947), Benjamin Lee Whorf (for example, 1956a) and Noam Chomsky (1957), were interested in exploring language in and of itself and were also concerned with language use and acquisition.

In the nineteenth century, throughout the twentieth and thereafter, interest in language was limited by an assumption that looked quite natural: that individuals and groups speak *a* language or *the* language. In other words, *one* language was the point of departure in thinking and reasoning, planning and measuring everything connected with languages. The abundance of languages was acknowledged in linguistic studies but it was considered normal that a person should speak one language rather than a number of them.

Since the world has moved away from the so-called 'monolingual paradigm', not everyone remembers a time when the predominant assumption was that using only one language was a natural state of things, at least across Europe and North America. Even bilingualism, to say nothing of multilingualism, was thought to have a detrimental effect on both the language and the cognitive development of a person. As a consequence, society tended to treat bilinguals as those outside the norm, at times as deficient because the knowledge and competencies of those who acquire and use more than one language have been measured against the high level of proficiency of an educated monolingual. The following quotation shows the argumentation for that view:

> If it were possible for a child to live in two languages at once equally well, so much the worse. His intellectual and spiritual growth would not thereby be doubled, but halved. Unity of mind and character would have great difficulty in asserting itself in such circumstances. (Laurie 1890: 15, quoted in Baker 2011: 139)

The conscious or unconscious presumption is that using one language is *the norm* and that ways of thinking, theories, practices and attitudes derived from it characterise the *monolingual perspective*. That view, which is now labelled the *monolingual paradigm*, originated and persists in various forms, even now. It was only later that experience of and research into the 'bilingual stage' led to an understanding that bilingualism is not an exceptional condition, but rather the norm, and that being bilingual has both beneficial and less favourable implications.

3.1.3 The bilingual stage

As linguists and philosophers continued researching human language and uncovering the particularities of separate languages, there came a point when the facts of bilingualism could not be ignored. They appeared visibly in reference to communal and educational realities in societal and academic discourse. Society was becoming aware of the fact that many people and communities actually employ two languages on a regular basis in a range of specific social situations. Once bilingualism became a salient issue in areas such as education, politics, economics and the cognitive sciences, researchers began to raise burning questions in relation to the social, psychological, ethical, educational and many other impacts of bilingualism. Several major topics emerged.

Early bilingual development was one of the subjects that aroused great interest at the beginning of the twentieth century. A child can become bilingual in one of two ways. Either both languages are acquired from infancy *simultaneously*, which is, then, *a bilingual first language acquisition* (BFLA), or the second language is added when the first is already established to some extent, and this is *successive* or *sequential* bilingualism.

Simultaneous bilingual development was famously described by linguistically minded fathers Jules Ronjat (1913) and Werner Leopold (1939). Both studies were based on diary records of their children's early language development. Ronjat (1913) described the simultaneous acquisition of French and German by his son, Louis, until he was about five. On the advice of their friend, the French linguist Maurice Grammont, the parents used the strategy of *'une personne, une langue'* – *'one parent, one language'* (OPOL). Ronjat himself and his relatives spoke only French to his son, and his wife and her relatives only German. According to Ronjat, the strategy proved successful in bringing Louis to a mastery and appropriate separation of the two languages. Importantly, Ronjat also came to the conclusion that his son's intellectual development was not impeded in any way by acquiring two languages simultaneously.

Leopold, who undertook a ten-year study (1939–49) that was thoroughly documented in four volumes, gave an account of the simultaneous acquisition of English and German by his daughter, Hildegard. In this case, the parents had also adopted the *'one parent, one language'* approach. The father spoke German to the daughter, and the mother spoke English to her. Hildegard was also successful in becoming bilingual, but she passed through a stage when she used words from both languages in the same utterance. This, along with other details noted in Leopold's meticulous documentation, was interpreted as evidence of confusion of two languages and initiated further research into both the merits and the dangers of a bilingual beginning to life (see 'The case of Hildegard', in Baker and Prys Jones 1998: 39, or in Grosjean 1982). More case studies on bilingual development followed.

Other topics on individual and social aspects of bilingualism started being seriously investigated in the twentieth century. In the 1950s and 1960s, a broader perspective on bilingualism, importantly including sociolinguistic aspects, was provided by studies conducted by Uriel Weinreich, Einar Haugen, Charles Ferguson, Joshua Fishman and John Gumperz. Their research is now classic and remains a foundation not only of bilingualism, but also of multilingualism studies. As a result of their and other scholars' research, we now have a picture of bilingualism in populations and groups that are geographically, socially and experientially diverse, using various combinations of languages. A description of some of the milestones in bilingualism research that are essential for multilingualism studies follows below. Other studies important for bilingualism and multilingualism will be discussed in the following chapters where appropriate.

Uriel Weinreich's *Languages in Contact* (1953) is an insightful classic work that deals with the psycholinguistic, grammatical and sociolinguistic aspects of circumstances in which languages and populations meet. These issues, especially *interference* and his oft-cited classification of bilinguals, are still most relevant as a point of departure on which more recent understandings have been built.

For his part, also in 1953, Einar Haugen published a highly influential study of Norwegian–English bilinguals in the United States under the title *The Norwegian Language in America: A Study in Bilingual Behavior*. This book made a major contribution to bilingualism studies through its wide-ranging and very useful account of cross-language borrowing phenomena. Another of Haugen's great contributions was made later, in 1972: his origination of the *ecological approach to language*. Haugen suggested that we should attempt 'to see language in relation to its human environment' (Haugen 1987: 27), and the term *ecology of language*, the concept and the approach, have been widely embraced since then. Importantly, they have found special application in later times in situations where more than one language is involved, and in language teaching contexts (Hornberger 2009).

Despite the pioneering and, to a great extent, descriptive studies of bilinguals, the prevailing attitude towards the influence of learning one more language in addition to the native one was initially very negative. Most researchers and non-specialists were convinced that bilingualism was detrimental to children's development. Adding one more language was thought to be harmful, both psychologically and socially. However, new, ground-breaking studies gradually eroded these traditional negative views on bilingualism and bilinguals. A 1962 study by Elizabeth Peal and Wallace Lambert at McGill University in Montreal had the greatest impact and became a benchmark reference in a very gradual understanding that mastery of a second language is an asset rather than hindrance for an individual (Peal and Lambert 1962). This now much-cited research was conducted on 110 bilinguals and monolinguals, ten-year-old Montreal children, all from middle-class backgrounds. Peal and Lambert (1962: 20) found that 'bilinguals performed significantly higher (than monolinguals) on 15 of 18 variables measuring IQ'.

Other studies followed and more evidence was found to suggest that bilinguals not only are as good as monolinguals, but in some situations surpassed their monolingual counterparts. The findings of Hamers and Blanc, for their part (2000: 89), note that bilinguals had advantages regarding a whole range of other abilities. A series of studies by Ellen Bialystok demonstrated that bilingual children process language differently from monolingual children (see, for example, 1991: 139) and provided precise data about the benefits of bilingualism for specific cognitive processes.

The studies of bilingualism put forward the issues that continue to be debated – interference and positive transfer, the age factor, code-switching, interlanguage and multicompetence. To date, these questions remain under scrutiny and we will refer to them in subsequent chapters of this book. Bilingualism and SLA are well developed and currently developing domains of knowledge and here we refer the reader to only some of the classic luminary books on the subject: Suzanne Romaine, *Bilingualism* ([1989] 1995); Tove Skutnabb-Kangas, *Bilingualism or Not* (1981); Hugo Baetens-Beardsmore, *Bilingualism: Basic Principles* ([1982] 1986); and more recently, *Encyclopedia of Bilingualism and Bilingual Education* (1998), edited by Colin Baker and Sylvia Prys Jones.

The key insights from the bilingual period were the realisation that the 'bilingual is not the sum of two multilinguals' (Grosjean 1989, 1992), and that an L2 learner is not a failing, under-achieving imitator of a native speaker but a language user in his/her own right (Cook 1992, 1993; Grosjean 2010). Grosjean insisted that the bilingual speaker should be seen as someone 'with a unique and specific linguistic configuration'(1985: 470). In his perspective, being bilingual does not necessarily mean knowing two or more languages equally well, as would be expected from someone using his or her L1/native language. Depending on a person's experience, needs and interests, each of his or her two languages may be similar or differ in the degree of proficiency, in communicative purposes and in terms of domains of use.

A similar view has been expressed in the domain of SLA by Vivian Cook, who established the concept of 'multicompetence'. This represents the overall system of a mind that allows multicompetent speakers to share lexical, syntactical, emotional and other skills, competencies and experiences across their languages and enables transfer, codeswitching and translanguaging. The development of proficiency in one language is enhanced by proficiency in another language. Cook's scrutiny of the notion of *native speaker* has turned bilingual individuals into *multicompetent language users* who differ from monolinguals in terms of the nature of their linguistic knowledge, metalinguistic awareness and cognitive processes (Cook 1992; Cook and Li Wei 2016). Cook's (2016) conception of multicompetence, defined as 'knowledge of two or more languages in the same mind', naturally and fittingly extends to multilingual speakers.

These truly revolutionary views, implying that bilingualism is not an exceptional condition but rather the norm, are clearly rich in implications: for example, in education, where the difference between the acquisition of the first language and learning of the second language is widely accepted. When users of two or more languages are no longer seen as the sum of two or more monolinguals, their proficiency in languages other than their mother tongue is not strictly measured against that of native speakers. Realistic aims for the bilingual learners in accordance with their linguistic and communicative needs are set in curricula, and different methods of teaching are used compared to those aimed at learners of L1.

Following the research of the 'bilingual' stage and consequent modifications in educational and social attitudes and practice, the consensus in accepting bilingualism as a norm meant crossing an important threshold.

3.1.4 The multilingual stage

The second threshold has been crossed with the advent of the current 'multilingual stage' of societal awareness of languages, which is a consequence of globalisation processes. The research data accumulated by this stage provided reasons to ask questions such as: do bilinguals differ from multilinguals in terms of cognition and communication? Should the same methods be used when teaching additional languages to a bilingual learner and to a multilingual learner? Do the language acquisition processes of a multilingual repeat the acquisition processes of a bilingual? Does processing three and more languages in the brain occur in the same way as processing of two languages? The issue of similarity and divergence between bilinguals and tri-multilinguals came to the fore.

Today, multilingualism is necessary to the functioning of major components of the social structure. It is increasingly deep and broad in its effects and overtly manifested in many areas of life encompassing technology, finance, politics and culture.

The sheer number of languages, multilingual individuals and communities, and the unprecedented territorial spread of multilingualism and its greater density in the current multilingual stage, imply a reconfiguring of language practices. We neither speak in the same way as people used to in the not-so-distant past, nor use the languages, whether at work or at home, in the same way that our grandparents did. Instead of a single language being habitually used in the places where it has been a tradition, clusters of tightly connected languages, Dominant Language Constellations, are used by individuals and in organisations and communities to perform the essential functions of communication, cognition and identity. The scientific conceptions and popular beliefs regarding the ways of social interaction have changed.

Because it is so visible and challenging, multilingualism in its various forms is supported and promoted by international institutions. Some examples include the European multilingualism formula 2+1, which suggests mother tongue, regional language plus one international language as the optimal configuration for the benefit of Europeans. In 2005, the portfolio of one of the commissioners of the European Union explicitly included multilingualism, and a foundation text on multilingualism was put in place by the Commission of the European Communities (a new framework strategy for multilingualism). A more recent affirmation of multilingualism as a desired norm was declared in the 'Salzburg Statement for a Multilingual World', issued by Salzburg Global Seminar (2017, released 21 February 2018).

The constant public turmoil around the issues related to languages and multilingualism is, to a large extent, conditioned by two powerful global trends that work concomitantly and yet in opposite directions. While each of these trends carries in itself strong positive growths, their clash may be said to lie behind and motivate political disputes, public protests and other controversies in social and educational spheres. The trends are defined as:

1. the unparalleled spread of the use of English as an international language; and
2. a remarkable diversification of languages in use (Fishman 1998; Maurais 2003).

The novelty of the situation described by these trends, as opposed to historical multilingualism, was expressed by Joshua Fishman with the phrase 'never before'. 'Never before in human history', writes Fishman, 'has one language been spoken (let alone semi-spoken) so widely and by so many' and 'Never before in history have there been as many standardized languages as there are today: roughly 1,200' (Fishman 1998: n.p.). The spread of English at the end of the twentieth century and the beginning of the twenty-first is indeed unprecedented. The visibility of other languages and efforts in favour of international, majority, minority and lesser-used languages – in short, Languages Other Than English (LOTE) – are unparalleled, too.

We can add that never before has the meeting of the two trends been so active and influential. This inescapable co-dependency comprises the whole continuum of consequences from conclusively positive to allegedly extremely negative.

More often than not, the two trends are seen contradicting each other. The spread of English and the diversification of languages are accompanied by a troubling decline in the vigour of many languages, to the point where many are simply dying out, and this causes fervent controversy, especially in the face of the chronic and sometimes violent conflict that is associated with states' refusal or inability to accommodate linguistic minority rights (Canagarajah 2005; Lo Bianco 2020; Skutnabb-Kangas and Philipson 2017).

No less formidable is the practical challenge of accommodating the implications of the two trends. Particularly sensitive in this respect is the area of education. Educators and parents are compelled to discuss the choice of languages to be learned and taught, some to be included on school or university curricula as a discipline or as a means of instruction. Decisions regarding each particular choice are especially far-reaching in bilingual and multilingual environments where minority and heritage languages and English compete for precious teaching time. Each requires careful and informed judgements and the flexibility to find the balance. In fact, there is no 'either/or' dilemma. Rather than 'English *versus* other languages', the workings of global trends are better described as 'languages *with* English'.

In terms of research, the multilingual stage separates multilingualism from bilingualism more straightforwardly than before and employs specifically multilingual methods that more often reveal the nature of multilingualism. The issues of importance examined in the multilingual stage include:

- tri- and multilingual early development
- multilingual identity, multicompetence
- multilingual education and the education of multilinguals, including education via minority languages; translanguaging
- the cluster of issues related to minority languages in a variety of specific circumstances, such as language rights and language maintenance and revitalisation.

The newly emerged focal issues are:

- multilingual urban and rural hubs and other super-diverse environments where various dynamic and multimodal practices of social interaction are employed
- material culture of multilingualism and visualisations
- Dominant Language Constellations
- technology applications and involvement in multilingual communication and language teaching/learning.

The current multilingual stage of societal awareness in language and languages corresponds with the modern-day linguistic–social condition – *New Linguistic Dispensation*.

3.2 The New Linguistic Dispensation

The word 'dispensation', with its multiple dictionary definitions applied to the current sociolinguistic global situation, transparently captures the essence of linguistic arrangement in society. It refers, firstly, to allocation, supply, allotment and distribution of languages across the world and in very local niches. It also denotes, secondly, management, administration and regulation of linguistic riches, as well as, thirdly, permission, indulgence and privilege to use them in certain communities.

By calling current multilingualism 'a new linguistic dispensation' (see also Chapter 9 for current patterns of language practices), we acknowledge and emphasise the fact that today's multilingual practices are the *patterned regularities manifested on a world scale*. These regularities are evident in nations, firms, interest groups, class or status groups, armies, churches, communities and so on.

The overall order of things regarding languages that was in action in the past has been transformed in contemporary society and shaped into what is termed the New Linguistic Dispensation (Aronin and Singleton 2008, 2012). This is a modern-day linguistic–social condition that affects civilisation as a whole and is manifested in specific patterns and dispositions of human activities dependent on or related to language use.

The reality of a new linguistic dispensation is unfolding through the contact between three kinds of arrangements – mono-, bi- and multi-, with multilingualism having the prominent role (see Figure 3.1).

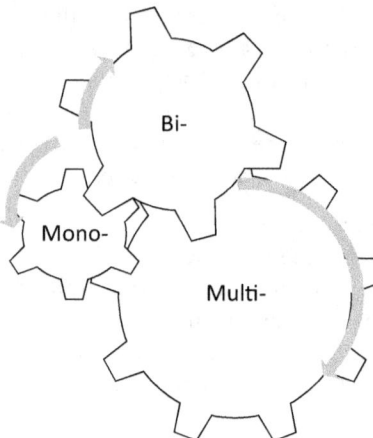

Figure 3.1 The New Linguistic Dispensation embraces multi-, bi- and monolingual arrangements.

Monolingual or bilingual approaches are sometimes justified for teaching or for dealing with particular individuals and communities, even in the multilingual context.

Multilingual language practices are the vehicle of the New Linguistic Dispensation, and play a central role in it as, at present, virtually every facet of human life depends on multilingual social arrangements and multilingual individuals, whether directly or indirectly.

Summary

This chapter presented the theoretical perspective on multilingualism that reflects current sociolinguistic reality. Distinguishing between bilingualism and multilingualism, as well as being aware of their common ground, is of the utmost importance because many necessary things depend on how we define these crucial concepts.

People variously distribute their language resources according to the spirit of the times, developments in science, ideology, attitudes and customary practical arrangements. The three stages of social awareness of language and languages broadly reflect the evolution of language research. These three stages – monolingual, bilingual and multilingual – signal social paradigms inherent in each roughly outlined period. The paradigms governing each stage of societal awareness reproduce predominant perceptions and practices, and reflect social ideas and predispositions with regard to both scientific and everyday interest in language.

The stages are not intended to demonstrate an ascension from bad to good, from wrong to right, or from primitive to sophisticated, but rather may demonstrate how, gradually and depending on the level of development, scientific and wider communities in the world started discerning and appreciating the use of more languages.

Today, when dealing with any practical issue in multilingualism, be it in connection with minority languages in a community or the choice of school languages, it is important to realise how the interplay of the two global trends – the unparalleled spread of the use of English as an international language and a remarkable diversification of languages in use – is involved.

The New Linguistic Dispensation, as the term aptly points out, is the contemporary patterned settings and activities by which individuals and societies allocate, permit, regulate and manage their languages. Monolingual, bilingual and multilingual linguistic arrangements exist concurrently. They are engaged in intricate interactions and are dominated by the global role of multilingualism.

Further reading

Aronin, Larissa and David Singleton (2008), 'Multilingualism as a new linguistic dispensation', *International Journal of Multilingualism*, 5(1), pp. 1–16.

Chapter review

Fill in the table by (1) using material from the chapter, and (2) giving your own examples.

Concept/keyword	Definition or explanation Short outlines	Example from the chapter	Your own example	Your comments and considerations
Bilingualism				
Multilingualism				
Monolingual paradigm Monolingual stage				
'une personne, une langue' – 'one parent, one language' (OPOL)				
Bilingual paradigm Bilingual stage				
Simultaneous early language acquisition				
Successive or sequential bilingualism				
Multilingual paradigm Multilingual stage				
The Two Trends				

Contd

Concept/keyword	Definition or explanation Short outlines	Example from the chapter	Your own example	Your comments and considerations
LOTE (Languages Other Than English)				
New Linguistic Dispensation				

Reflective questions

1. What is meant by a language-related paradigm in multilingualism? How do paradigms evolve?
2. What are the most important distinctions between the three stages of social awareness of languages?
3. What are the two thresholds in the development of knowledge about multilingualism in human society?
4. From the beginning of the bilingual stage, the 'one parent, one language' (OPOL) strategy was reported as the most successful of all parental strategies for simultaneous early language acquisition. Could OPOL be used in trilingual families? In which way? How successful do you expect this strategy to be if modified for use under current multilingual conditions?
5. What are the two sociolinguistic trends in the current sociolinguistic arrangements of the world? How do they shape the multilingual reality? Give three examples of challenges in decision-taking that, to your mind, emerged from the interplay between the two trends.
6. What is the message of Fishman (1998) when he uses the word 'unprecedented' while referring to each of the trends?
7. Characterise the New Linguistic Dispensation in your own words. How are monolingual, bilingual and multilingual arrangements accommodated within it?

Exercises

Exercise 3.1

Draw a table or a figure that represents monolingual, bilingual and multilingual stages of awareness of languages in comparison. To this end, choose not less than two criteria of comparison.

Exercise 3.2

Prepare a poster with your own table or figure that would best represent monolingualism, bilingualism and multilingualism in the contemporary world. Discuss your poster with your classmates and teacher, correct and edit if necessary, and design an e-poster.

Exercise 3.3

Design a poster with a table or figure that would most clearly show the three stages of social awareness of languages.

Exercise 3.4

Design a poster with a table, figure or collage that would demonstrate the distinctions between monolingual, bilingual and multilingual paradigms.

Exercise 3.5

Prepare a ten-minute presentation describing the advantages of a parental strategy for simultaneous early language acquisition of your choice. Be ready to answer the questions and provide arguments to support your opinion.

Part II
Languages

4 Languages of the world

Different disciplines look at languages from different angles and multilingualism studies bring these together in order to work out a comprehensive view on multiple languages of the world. This chapter deals with some frequent and general questions pertaining to the most essential human resource – language. How can we distinguish one language from the other? How can we tell a language from its dialect? Is it possible to measure differences between languages and language varieties? What are pidgins, creoles and World Englishes? These are the issues explored in this chapter.

4.1 Languages and dialects

4.1.1 What is a language?

If asked, everyone would say that English, Japanese, Spanish (Castilian) and Swedish are languages. Usually, we can easily distinguish one *named language* from another, even without mastering all of them. But language varieties exist that have a very similar structure and vocabulary. How can we know whether there are two different languages or just one? And are they languages or dialects?

This is a complicated matter. Languages and dialects are studied in linguistics, dialectology, sociolinguistics and sociology of language. The perspectives of these areas of knowledge on language are somewhat different. Due to this, and also to the well-known elusiveness of the notion of 'language', approaches to what can be defined as a language, and on what premises, differ as well. Linguistics and sociolinguistics alike acknowledge that it is impossible to decide what a language is solely on the basis of linguistic criteria. Nor does there exist any unambiguous linguistic measure or series of features that could allow a distinction to be made between two close languages. Likewise, designating a language variety as either a language proper or a dialect cannot be performed on the basis of the linguistic features of a language, since there is no intrinsic value in the morphology or phonology of any linguistic variety. One of several English dialects, South-East Mercian, which dates back centuries, has become Standard English, 'the bearer of nationhood, to carry the flag, or standard, of the emerging nation' (Halliday 2020: 334), and is therefore a language, not a dialect. The idea of languages and dialect division being more of a social phenomenon, rather than a purely linguistic one, is well summarised in a famous saying dreamed up by a young man who had attended a lecture by the linguist Max Weinreich in the early 1940s: 'a language is a dialect with an army and a navy'. This emphasises the social nature of the designations 'language' and 'dialect'.

Whether a language variety is awarded the status of language or a dialect is, to a great extent, defined by historical and political factors. The criterion of *mutual intelligibility* is traditionally used to decide whether we are dealing with one language or with two different languages. If speakers of the two language varieties do not understand each other, such as speakers of French and Chinese, then we may assume we are dealing with different languages. But in the case of Swedish, Danish and Norwegian, three different languages which can be mutually understood by their speakers, we immediately see that the criterion of mutual intelligibility is not always reliable for the purpose of distinguishing between languages. The linguistic structure and the vocabulary of Serbian and Croatian, as well as Hindi and Urdu, are also very similar, but each of the languages in these pairs is now a separate language, emphasising the ethnicity and statehood of its speakers.

Consider another example: the case of the Moldovan–Romanian language (see, for example, Alpatov 2000: 185). The Language Act of 1989 nominated Romanian as the state language of Moldova. Then a struggle took place between radical nationalists oriented to Romania and more moderately inclined parties who preferred the term *Moldavian* language. In 1994, the President managed to include an Article in the new Moldavian constitution using the name *Moldovan language*. In 1995, a student demonstration ensued, in which one of the main demands was a return to the previous Romanian language designation. About a year later, the Speaker of the parliament suggested a compromise, 'Moldovan (Romanian) language', which was also rejected. To make the point that these are two different languages, a Moldovan–Romanian dictionary, *Dicționar Moldovenesc–Românesc*, compiled by Vasile Stati, was published by the Moldovan side in 2003. It is comparable to an English–American dictionary.

We can see from the above examples that, linguistically, at least at the moment of their separation, the languages were nearly the same and diverged mainly due to ethnic and political considerations. Given the social and historical changes that happen with similar languages, *intelligibility* not only involves a straightforward understanding of words, but goes hand in hand with the *appropriate interpretation*, as accepted in the 'understood' language variety, which happens when an interlocutor is familiar with the sociocultural reality of its users (Smith and Nelson 2020).

With time, the diverged languages naturally acquire different lexes and each evolves in its own way; often, the script is changed in order to differentiate it from its counterpart. (For example, Romanian is written in the Romance script and Moldavian in Cyrillic; Hindi, one of the official languages of India, uses the Devanāgarī alphabet, while Urdu, the official language of Pakistan, is written in the Arabic script, although both are derived from the Hindustani language.)

Another difficulty is that languages that are identical from a linguist's point of view are sometimes perceived as self-evidently different by the different communities who speak them and are familiar with them. The speakers of a language and those outside their particular community apply different names to the same language, as in the case described in Mesthrie et al. (2009: 10) in connection with the fuzzy boundaries between languages in Papua New Guinea.

The language spoken in Bolo village is also from a linguist's point of view identical to Aria, but Aria speakers from other villages say it is not Aria. They say Bolo speakers really speak Mouk. However, the people of Salkei village, who speak Mouk, say that Bolo people speak Aria. As for the Bolo speakers themselves, they claim to be Anêm speakers (Romaine 1994: citing Thurston 1987). If this were not complicated enough, the Anêm people of another village do not think that the Bolo speak acceptable Anêm any more. (Mesthrie et al. 2009: 10)

Thus, separating one language from the other is far from clear and easy; it is based not only on linguistic differences in structure and lexis, but also to a great extent on societal criteria that may be historical, religious, economic and political.

For this reason, the term *language variety* is used in literature to refer to languages, dialects and mixed forms of language use, such as pidgins, as a more general umbrella term. One more term that is often used in relation to languages, dialects and other language varieties is *vernacular*. Vernacular is the local or native speech of common, everyday communication that is transmitted from parent to child.

From a linguistics perspective, all languages are dialects, and not a single dialect has any superiority over the other in terms of its linguistic features. Nor does there exist any universally accepted criteria for distinguishing languages from dialects. For instance, Filipino, the official national language in the Philippines, is based on Tagalog. The country also lists such languages as Cebuano, Ilokano, Hiligaynon, Bikol, Waray-Waray, Pangasinan, Kinaray-a, Maranao and others. Some linguists are convinced that Tagalog is the only language and the others are dialects. Others firmly believe that the latter are languages in their own right.

The following criteria are generally used to distinguish between a language and a dialect:

1. Mutual intelligibility: if intelligible, these are dialects; if unintelligible, different languages (although we have discussed the lack of certainty regarding this criterion above)
2. Size: that is, number of users. A larger number of users is normally connected with languages and a smaller number of users with dialects. This criterion does not fully work in a situation where language varieties with fewer speakers are labelled as languages, and others with far more speakers are referred to as dialects. For instance, Bashkir, a state and titular language of an ethnic group in an autonomous region in Russia, is spoken by 1,450,000 people, and Tabasaran, spoken by about 98,000 people in Dagestan, are considered languages, while Cantonese, spoken by millions of people, is often referred to as a dialect of Chinese.
3. Prestige: in popular thinking, dialects are sometimes seen as less prestigious and as being used by less educated and provincial people, as opposed to central, standard varieties, often called language.
4. Languages are also linked to a state and a territory, while dialects are thought to be spoken by ethnic groups of the regional areas or those without their own land.
5. Languages are associated with a richness of expressive means and a long history of literary traditions more often than dialects.

In this sense, languages serve as a means of identifying and ordering social groups. Dutch, for instance, used to be described by some not as a language, but as a dialectal form of German. Afrikaans, in its turn, was sometimes considered to be a variant of Dutch. The link between Afrikaans and Dutch is now perceived differently, in light of political developments in South Africa, and Afrikaans has since been recognised as a separate language.

4.1.2 What is a dialect?

Most languages are known to have dialects. For example, German has several major dialects in addition to Standard German, or Hochdeutsch: Friesisch (Frisian), Niederdeutsch (Low German/Plattdeutsch), Mitteldeutsch (Middle German), Fränkisch (Frankish), Alemannisch (Alemannic) and Bairisch-Österreichisch (Bavarian–Austrian). In their turn, these are subdivided into smaller varieties, or 'sub-dialects'.

Peter Trudgill, an authority on dialects, defines them as sub-varieties of languages (1999: 121). In their turn, Baker and Hengeveld (2012: 381) state that 'Dialects are, in general terms, the forms of language use that occur in a certain area or community.'

Just as with languages, linguistically, no dialect (or language variety) is 'better' than another and the difference in status originates from non-linguistic factors. Many dialects are identified by their individual or local 'flavour'; the well-known dialects have a savour and tang to them (for example, Cockney is a very distinctive dialect with its own accent).

There exists a wide variation in dialects at every linguistic level: phonological, morphological, syntactic, lexical, semantic and pragmatic. Pronunciation is the most noticeable aspect of a language variety; therefore an *accent* is usually detected immediately by the conversers. Technically, accent is the description of aspects of pronunciation and therefore, every language user has an accent.

Variation in forms of speech is determined by geographical and social factors. Dialects are geographical or social sub-varieties of a language that is characteristic of a certain area or of a certain social group that show systematic differences or regular variations. Most dialects have a particular geographical distribution; these are called *regional dialects*. Examples are the dialects of German referred to above and also Appalachian in the USA, and Liverpool English and Newcastle English or Tyneside English, the latter also nicknamed 'Geordie', in Britain.

Dialects that are used by particular social groupings are referred to as *sociolects*. The use of different forms of language by different social classes is associated with the socioeconomic status, level of education, profession, age, ethnicity or gender of the speakers. Some varieties become more prestigious than others. An individual speech pattern, characterising the linguistic behaviour of individuals, such as specific sounds, vocabulary and idioms, habitually used grammar, and a style unique to this individual is called an *idiolect*.

Dialects of one language are normally mutually comprehensible. A speaker of Yorkshire dialect, Cheshire dialect and Cockney English can understand each other as well as those, of course, who speak Standard British English. But a different case is also possible. Germans in Berlin speak German in a different way from Germans living in Bavaria, and Swiss German, Schwyzerdütsch, is not easy to understand for Germans from Bonn or Frankfurt.

4.1.3 Dialect continuum

While some languages have a number of clearly distinctive dialects, others are barely distinguishable from one another. In the latter case, we can speak of a *dialect continuum*. A dialect continuum is a chain of mutually intelligible dialects unfolding as one moves across some countries and regions. Gumperz (1971b: 7) speaks of a chain of mutually intelligible varieties in India stretching from Sind in the north-west to Assam in the north-east, explaining that it would thus be possible to traverse the subcontinent from the north-west to the north-east without discerning any radical differences in speech characteristics from one village to the next.

Dialect continua exist throughout the rural dialects of Portugal, Spain, France and Italy; they can also be found in Germany and in Scandinavia. There is always intelligibility among neighbouring dialects of the North Germanic language area of Denmark, Sweden and Norway. The dialects of neighbouring villages across the continuum are always mutually intelligible.

Speakers are often capable of switching between local dialect and the standard language, depending on context and interlocutors. As Ralph Fasold (1987: 43) points out, a local dialect can be used at home or among local friends, while the standard language is automatically selected by speakers when they are communicating with speakers of other dialects or for public or professional functions. And this is also a sign of multilingualism.

4.2 Language standardisation

4.2.1 Standardisation and codification

Some, but not all, languages have a standard dialect when countries accept one of the regional or social dialects as a model, or 'correct', form of a language. Wardhaugh (2010: 33) defines *language standardisation* as 'The process by which a language has been codified in some way. That process usually involves the development of such things as grammars, spelling books, and dictionaries, and possibly a literature.' In other words, standardisation is the arrangement and ordering of languages for systematic description in grammars, spelling books, dictionaries and reference books.

This process of *codification* takes place in some or all the aspects of a language, such as spelling, vocabulary and pronunciation, and involves a major conscious effort on the part linguists and enthusiasts of language. The 'formal' codification of language, which normally has a stable written form, usually continues in the use of the standard form in media, education, commerce, the courts and administration. Standardisation gives a legal or officially authorised status to a dialect. A standardised language is usually a more prestigious variety, associated with the more educated echelons of society.

There are special institutions specifically charged with the task of codifying language and setting standards for its pronunciation, orthography and usage. They are usually state-affiliated and have the authority to judge and keep an eye on correct usage of this codified language variety. One of the most respected institutions of this kind, the principles of which were copied by some other countries, is the French Academy (l'Académie française),[1] the official authority in matters of language, established in 1635 by Cardinal Richelieu. The Academy publishes an official dictionary of the French language, *Dictionnaire de l'Académie française*.

In Israel, the Academy of the Hebrew Language was established in 1953 by a Knesset law to direct the development of Hebrew as a living language. Since Modern Hebrew is a revitalised language, the mission of the academy is twofold: to carry on historical research into the language, and on this basis, to establish the norms of modern usage by creating or approving new words from Hebrew roots, setting rules for grammar, spelling, transcription and punctuation, and coining professional terminology.

The Swedish Language Council, Svenska Språkbyrån, embraces several corporations and organisations such as the Swedish Academy, Swedish Radio and the Swedish Broadcasting Corporation which promote and cultivate the well-established and well-standardised Swedish language.

Increasingly, more language varieties are being codified across the globe. We know, for example, of Standard Singapore English following the government's promotion of the 'Speak Good English Movement', and of Standard Nigerian English (Ekpe 2007).

4.2.2 Pluricentric languages

A number of languages are codified and standardised in more than one country. These are called *pluricentric languages*. *Pluricentric languages* are languages with several interacting centres, each providing a national variety, with at least some of its own (codified) norms (Clyne 1992a,b). Chinese, Korean, English, French, German, Swedish, Dutch and Spanish are considered to be pluricentric. English has centres and the standard versions in the United Kingdom and the United States of America, as well as in Australia, Canada and South Africa. The German language has one centre in Germany and another in Austria, as well as a third in Switzerland. As for French, apart from France, it has centres in Canada, Switzerland and Belgium.

4.3 Linguistic distance

It is always important to know just how different or how similar the languages that we speak or learn are. *Linguistic distance* (sometimes *language distance*) is the degree of contrast between language varieties, the measure of which is important for multilingualism. While there is no definite and fully valid way of determining linguistic distance, some interesting ways have been suggested. The degree of contrast is evaluated by comparing the grammar and vocabulary of the two languages. It is possible to compare the percentage of similar words. The weak points of this method

---

1. http://www.academie-francaise.fr/ (last accessed 20 August 2021).

are that it is hard to quantify grammar distance, and in comparing vocabulary items subjective judgement plays a significant role.

Barry Chiswick and Paul Miller (2004) based their measurement on the difficulty that Americans have in learning other languages. They have shown that when other determinants of English language proficiency are the same, the greater the measure of linguistic distance, the poorer is the respondent's English language proficiency. The authors believe that this methodology can also be applied to linguistic distance measurements for other languages.

To avoid subjectivity, Filippo Petroni and Mauruzui Serva (2008) likened the vocabulary of a language to the DNA of organisms (vocabulary for a language is the same as DNA for organisms). They used the method of computing the distances from the percentage of shared *cognates*.

4.4 Kachru's Circles and the World Englishes

In the middle of the twentieth century, it became especially noticeable that the number of people using English was growing from day to day. By the mid-1980s, the growing spread of English in diverse sociocultural contexts across the globe, often in settings distant from the precincts of its historical development, received ample research attention. The growing numbers of language users in all parts of the world, the appearance of localised varieties of English, and the implications of these changes for society, identity of speakers, education and entire communities were to be documented, clarified and understood.

In his seminal early works, Braj Kachru (1985) presented the spread of English in a simple and inspiring way. He classified all the speakers of English and the varieties of English they use into three Concentric Circles of English.

> The term 'cognate' means 'blood relative' in Latin (cognatus). Cognates are words with similar meanings and forms in two or more languages, believed to emerge as a result of genetic ties between the language varieties and their common origin. For instance, the English word night is a cognate of 'nicht' in Scots, 'Nacht' in German and 'nuit' in French, and also of 'ночь', 'noch', in Russian, and 'noc' in Czech, Slovak and Polish. The speakers of many Indo-European languages would understand the English words 'culture' and 'mother', and would figure out the meaning of the Spanish words 'gigante', 'manuscrito' and 'secreto'.
>
> Cognates and similarities in the structure of typologically related languages are helpful for linguistic transfer and for intercomprehension (see Chapter 9), and their understanding and use while learning or teaching an additional language can save effort and time for learners and teachers.

The *Inner Circle* refers to the varieties of English used in the countries where English is historically the primary language and is a native language for most. These countries are the USA, UK, Ireland, Canada, Australia and New Zealand. The language varieties developed there through centuries are considered the most prestigious and influential (Kachru 2020: 454), even today. They are marked as 'norm-providing' in Kachru's scheme.

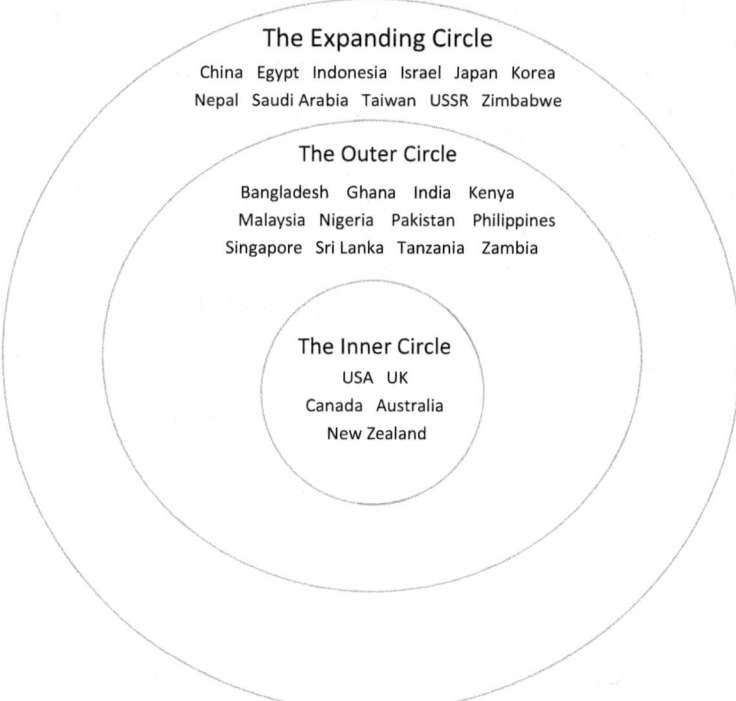

Figure 4.1 The three Circles of World Englishes (after Kachru 1985: 12).

The *Outer Circle* includes the varieties of English that evolved in post-colonial territories such as India, Malawi, Nigeria, Kenya, the Philippines and Singapore. They are the outcome of the first wave of expansion of English in non-native settings. Under those historical conditions, English in these countries was institutionalised, and was in formal use in media and the main state institutions, being an important second language. Kachru called the Outer Circle varieties 'norm-developing'.

The *Expanding Circle* embraces the varieties that are connected neither with the history of the use of English in these settings, nor with colonial expansion. Such varieties emerged in the countries where English is not engrained in their inner life but rather used alongside a country's other important national and official languages for particular purposes. These are, for example, Germany, Brazil, China, Russia, Japan and Korea. The Expanding Circle varieties are 'new' compared to the long-established ones of the Inner Circle, and evolved for different reasons from those relating to the varieties of the two other concentric circles. The transplantation of English happens due to the appearance of new functions of this language, coupled with increased opportunities in language contact and use. Technology allows swift connection and greater mobility of individuals, as well as shared participation in business, education and entertainment. In the countries allocated to the Extended Circle, English is normally a 'foreign' language, but is also used increasingly for international, academic and business purposes; for some, it is a second language. Originally, the Expanding Circle varieties were denoted by Kachru as 'norm-

Languages of the world

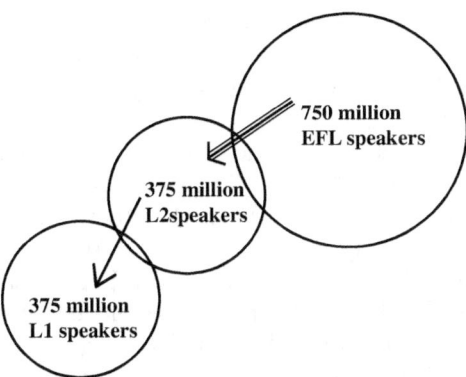

Figure 4.2 Graddol's modification of Kachru's Circles (Graddol 1997: 10, © British Council, reproduced with permission).

dependent'. Today, as we will see below, many Expanding Circle English varieties developed or are developing their own linguistic and usage norms.

The number of non-native users of English exceeds its native speakers by a ratio of 3:1, in some estimations 4:1. In other words, there at least are three times more speakers of World Englishes and those who speak it for intercultural communication than native speakers (Crystal 2003: 69; also see Jenkins 2003: 3–4 and Kirkpatrick 2007). Graddol's modification[2] of Kachru's Circles illustrates the numerical prevalence of speakers in the Outer and Expanding Circles.

The works of Braj Kachru (1985) and his colleagues (Kachru and Smith 1985; Kirkpatrick 2007, 2010a; Bolton and Kachru 2006; Kachru et al. 2006, Nelson et al. 2020) marked a shift of perspective on the global proliferation of English from one centred on *native varieties of English* to one that emphasises the *pluricentricity* of this language. Distinct and numerous regional and local varieties of English that emerged in various geographical and political contexts all over the globe justify the appearance of the term *World Englishes* – in the plural, rather than World English in the singular.

World Englishes (WE) are dynamic and constantly reshaping, acquiring new norms of usage and linguistic features. They are not homogenous either and may have further variations within a 'bigger' variety. For instance, Aboriginal Australian English (AAusE), although it overlaps with Australian English (AusE) in many respects, differs from it in linguistic structure and norms of use (Kiesling 2020).

Current sociolinguistic reality challenges the traditional views that only the English speakers in the Inner Circle countries are the gatekeepers and norm-providers. Language changes, both linguistic and pragmatic, are brought about by the linguistic creativity of users of English who live in their particular environments and adapt the language to local cultures and traditions. The issue of the ownership of English is debated. Do native speakers of English 'possess' English? Who has the

---

2. This form of depiction was disputed by some scholars because it shows the norms coming down from the native varieties, as given, and does not include the creativity of the speakers of the non-native varieties.

right to change or modify it, establish norms in pronunciation, vocabulary and structure, and decide the appropriate use? Who may write poems and produce works of literature in English? Who owns the English language? From the point of view of the World Englishes paradigm, 'The language now belongs to those who use it as their first language, and to those who use it as an additional language, whether in its standard form or in its localized forms' (Kachru and Smith 1985: 210).

Tom McArthur elaborated Kachru's model further and came up with a popular picture intelligibly illustrating the multiplicity of World Englishes. Each of the World Englishes, whether that found in traditional English-speaking countries such as UK or Canada, or that found in different regions of Europe, Africa or Asia, is considered a variety in its own right. This entails changes in teaching, education and the respective application of these pluricentric understandings to social practices. Which variety of English is, then, to be taught in various parts of the world? Who can teach English, native speakers, or non-native teachers who may speak a variety from the Outer or Expanding Circle?

4.4.1 Performance varieties

English and some other languages such as German, French, Russian and Spanish also have what Kachru called *performance varieties* (1985: 13). The most developed range of these varieties belongs to English. In relation to this language, Kirkpatrick defined performance varieties as a 'range of Englishes whose *roles and features are determined by their function*' (Kirkpatrick 2010a: 2, italics added). Such, he goes on to explain, are the Englishes of business, computer-mediated Englishes, the Englishes of pop-culture and the Englishes of academia. English as a Native Language (ENL), English as a Foreign Language (EFL) and English as a Second Language (ESL) are widely used in English language teaching. The performance varieties, along with their usefulness and the teaching of them, are often contested. Bolton (2020: 750) maintains that 'the earlier threefold distinction between ENL, ESL, and EFL was ideologically loaded and intellectually flawed' because this categorisation foregrounds a distinction between 'native' and 'non-native' speakers; as Hilgendorf (2020: 217) also argues, this reflects a situation that was relevant towards the end of the 1980s. The performance variety called English as a Lingua Franca (ELF) became notable in research and also formed the subject of debates in the late 1990s (Jenkins 2009, 2018; Seidlhofer 2001; Cook 2013); it is now considered a complementary paradigm to World Englishes. ESL, EFL, ELF, WE and also EAP – English for academic purposes – have emerged as disciplinary fields with teaching resources, educational programmes and courses, methodologies and objectives. As with many other language varieties, there are no clear-cut distinctions between them; what we have to remember when we are involved in teaching, learning or researching them is their specific and differing functions for users. Consequently, different methods and courseware for teaching and learning, as well as differing outcomes, must be thought through.

4.5 Language varieties resulting from language contact

In language contact situations, new languages originate between two or more existing languages. Such varieties are clearly distinct linguistically from either of their source languages and are not members of any language family (see the next chapter about language families, in the section 'genetic classification of languages'). Several kinds of mixed languages can appear, depending on the communicative needs of the contact groups, their previous knowledge of other languages, and the length and intensity of contact between the two: *pidgins*, *creoles* and *bilingual mixed languages*. For a long time, approximately until the 1950s, contact-induced language varieties were not regarded as 'real' languages and were therefore neglected by academics.

4.5.1 Pidgins and creoles

Mufwene (2020: 299–30) provides the following definition:

> Strictly speaking, creoles and pidgins are new language varieties which developed out of contacts between colonial nonstandard varieties of a European language and several non-European languages around the Atlantic and in the Indian and Pacific Oceans during the sixteenth through nineteenth centuries.

A *pidgin* is a simplified form of speech that is usually a mixture of two or more languages. Pidgins emerged in groups of people, typically of different social standing with no common language, and with no real need or possibility of learning each other's language, in restricted contexts such as trade, mining, agriculture, on plantations and especially in conditions of forced labour. In these conditions, people speaking different languages had sporadic and limited contact and needed only a basic form of communication.

Typically, pidgins have rudimentary grammar and vocabulary; most pidgins entirely lack inflectional morphology, as well as any complex derivational morphology. The grammar and phonology are usually as simple as possible, and pidgins also lack categories such as tense, aspect, person and number.

Development of many pidgins in the sixteenth century up to the early nineteenth century, between Europeans and the indigenous peoples of Asia, Africa and the Americas, is associated with European conquests and colonisation of vast territories throughout the world. Pidgins appeared to provide a means of communication between masters and slaves, and between slaves among themselves, in order to bridge various ethnic and linguistic backgrounds such as Wolof, Malinke, Fulani, Akan, Yoruba, Ibo, Hausa and Mandinka. Such slave groups worked mostly on the plantations of the New World and fortified posts along the West African coast, and pidgins such as Belizean and Negerhollands sprang up and then faded in these regions (Mesthrie et al. 2009).

Many pidgins appeared in trade contexts and in other parts of the world. An example of a trade language is Russenorsk, the pidgin language created and used extensively in northern Norway in the eighteenth and nineteenth centuries. For about 150 years, the barter trade between Russians and Norwegians in the north was restricted to a few months in summer, and Russenorsk arose to facilitate communication between Russian traders and Norwegian fishermen in the Arctic.

Its last use is thought to be at the beginning of the twentieth century. As in other pidgins, the grammar of Russenorsk is rudimentary, and its vocabulary consists of fewer than 400 attested words, mostly referring to Arctic fishing and trade, such as 'fish', 'weather', 'water', 'buy' and 'grain'.

A rare example of communication in Russenorsk was, according to Kortland (2000), recorded by A. W. S. Brun, cited and translated by Peterson (1980: 253f.), and reproduced by Broch and Jahr (1984: 130f.). It is also published, along with an English translation, and discussed at length by Kortlandt (2000), and reproduced in Russian script with a translation into Russian in the 'Saint-Petersburg University' Journal by Alexandr Russinov.

Below is the version compiled with the addition of a Norwegian translation done by Kari Smith. The first line is in Russenorsk, the second line is in Russian, the third line is in English and the fourth line is in Norwegian.

1. Kjøpn in seika, treskar, tiksa on balduska?
   Покупаешь сайду, треску, пикшу и палтус?
   Are you buying pollack, cod, haddock and halibut?
   KJØPER DU POLLACK, TORSK, HYSE OG KVEITE?

2. Dar, dar – mojar kopomr altsamman, davair po skipn komn.
   Да, да — я куплю все, поднимайся на борт.
   Yes, yes - I'll buy all of it, come on board.
   JA. JA. JEG VIL KJØPE ALT, KOM OMBORD.

3. Spasibar! Harn in mokkar, harn in groppar?
   Спасибо! У тебя есть мука, у тебя есть зерно?
   Thank you! Do you have flour, do you have grain?
   TAKK. HAR DU MEL? HAR DU KORN?

4. – Dar, dar! Davair po skipn komn, bratr, po tjeir drikin.
   Да, да! Поднимайся на борт, брат, выпей чая.
   Yes, Yes! Come on board, brother, drink some tea.
   JA. JA. KOM OMBORD, TA DEG EN KOPP TE.

5. Blagdarur pokornar! Kokr tvojar betalomn forn seika?
   Покорно благодарю! Как платишь за сайду?
   I humbly thank you! What are you paying for pollack?
   TAKKER YDMYKT. HVA BETALER DU FOR POLLACK?

6. – Petr pudofr seika 1 pudr mokir.
   Пять пудов сайды за один пуд муки.
   Five poods of pollack for one pood of flour.
   FEM TØNNER POLLACK FOR EN TØNNE MEL.

7. Korn in tykjen en den lagan? In mon gjern den billiarn!
   Какого черта такой расчет? Давай дешевле!
   How the hell is that figured out? You have to make it cheaper!
   HVORDAN I HELVETE KOM DU TIL DET? DU MÅ GJØRE DET BILLIGERE!

8. Kakr sprek? Mojer nietr forston.
   Что сказал? Я не понимаю.
   What did you say? I don't understand.
   HVA SIER DU? JEG FORSTÅR DEG IKKE.

9. Dorgor, dorglor Rusmainn – prosjair!
   Дорого, дорого, русский – прощай!
   Expensive, expensive, Russian – goodbye!
   DYRT, DYRT, DU RUSSER. FARVEL.

10. – Nietsjevor! Sjetirir – galln!
    Окей! Четыре — и половина!
    Okay! Four and a half!
    OKEY, FIRE OG EN HALV.

11. – Davair firn – nietsjevor verrigodn.
    Давай четыре, окей, хорошо.
    Make it four, okay, good.
    LA DET BLI FIRE, OKEY. BRA.

12. Njetr, bratr! Kudar mojar selomn desjevlir? Grot djurn mokkar po Rusleienn deinn orn.
    Нет, брат! Где я продам дешевле? Четыре очень дорого в России в этом году.
    No, brother! Where can I sell it cheaper? Flour is very expensive in Russia this year.
    NEI BROR, GODE VENN. HVOR KAN JEG SELVE DET BILLIGERE? MEL ER DYRT I RUSSLAND DETTE ÅRET.

13. Tvojar nietr sainferdin sprek.
    Ты говоришь неправду.
    You are not telling the truth.
    DU FORTELLER IKKE SANNHETEN.

14. Jes, grot sainferdin, mojar nietr lugomn, djurn mokkar.
    Да, это правда, я не лгу, четыре дорого.
    Yes, it is very true, I'm not lying, flour is expensive.
    JA, DET ER HELT TIKTIG, JEG LYGER IKKE. MEL ER DYRT.

15. Kakr tvojar kopomr – davair firn pudr; kakr tvojar nietr kopomr – son prosjair!
    Если хочешь купить – четыре пуда; если не хочешь покупать – тогда прощай!
    If you want to buy – four poods; if you don't want to buy – then goodbye!
    HVIS DU VIL KJØPE, SÅ FIRE TØNNER. VIL DU IKKE KJØPE, SÅ FRAVEL.

16. Non, nietsjevor bratr, davair kladir po dekn.
    Хорошо, брат, клади рыбу на палубу.
    Well, okay brother; put the fish on the desk.
    OKEY BROR, SET FISKEN PÅ DEKKET.

Russenorsk is unlike other pidgins in that the users, Russian traders and Norwegian fishermen, had equal social status, and perhaps this explains why it drew equally from both Russian and Norwegian.

Pidgins may emerge in some other contexts of limited contact between the groups of speakers with little knowledge of each other's languages, such as domestic settings. For instance, Indian Butler English (the head of the domestic staff of a European household in India used to be called the 'butler') appeared about 200 years ago in the time of the British Raj in the Indian subcontinent and is alive to this day, though not confined to butlers, according to Priya Hosali (2005). Another example is a new Arabic-based Pidgin: Pidgin Madam (Bizri 2009). Pidgin Madam is the contemporary language that evolved in many countries in the Middle East from contact with Sri Lankan female domestic workers and their mainly female Arab employers: hence the name. The Sri Lankan maids mainly speak Sinhala – a northern Indo-Aryan language. Pidgin Madam is a contact language where only two linguistic communities are involved and only two languages; it shows an extensive usage of Arabic imperatives as verbal stems, the Sri Lankan maid using the imperative for her affirmative present and past tenses. That is, instead of saying 'I am going to sleep' or 'I want to sleep', she would say 'I, do go to sleep' (Bizri 2009: 138). Many pidgins evolve and disappear to give way to new ones.

If the pidgin is used for long enough, it acquires more words and develops more sophisticated grammar, and can become a *creole*. Like pidgins, creoles evolve or appear abruptly when two or more contact groups do not have a common language, or do not have mastery of any contact language sufficient for minimal meaningful communication. But unlike pidgins, creoles have richer language and more complex structures. Creoles have native speakers – the children born to parents speaking a pidgin as a second language, who learn this pidgin as their first language. Typically, creoles developed in settlement colonies along the Atlantic and Indian Ocean coasts in sugarcane plantations or rice fields where mostly non-European slaves worked. Creoles differ widely from one another; they are not genetically related between themselves because they do not descend from the same parent language, although they belong to one Indo-European language family (Mufwene 2020: 299). Many creoles are based on English, such as Hawaiian Creole English, Gullah (spoken by the African-American population in some coastal regions of America), Jamaican Creole English and Guyanese Creole. Others evolved from contact with Portuguese (such as Cape Verdean Criolou), French (Haitian, Mauritian and Seychellois Creoles) or with more than one language, such as Saramaccan in Surinam, influenced firstly by Portuguese and later by Dutch.

The best-known example of a pidgin with a success story is that of Tok Pisin, also called New Guinea Pidgin. Tok Pisin is considered a language in its own right, even though it originated as a pidgin. It has undergone creolisation (the process where native speakers appear, evolving new identities based on adaptation to a mixed environment, often the creation of new cultures) and there are L1 Tok Pisin speakers. Like all languages, it has evolved over time, now possessing a complex grammar. Not only is it now one of the official languages of Papua New Guinea, but, supported by media, dictionaries and grammar books, it is the most widely used language in that country, spoken by between 3 and 4 million people as a second language (Smith and Siegel 2013) and approximately 122,000 people as a first language, according to some sources (Tok Pisin n.d.).

4.5.2 Bilingual mixed languages

Bilingual mixed languages are combinations of just two languages, and the linguistic material of the resulting blend can easily be traced to the parent languages. Bilingual mixed languages appear in circumstances when at least one of the speaker groups is fluent in both languages.

Bilingual mixed languages typically consist of a grammar derived from one of the languages, and a lexis derived for the most part from the other; in some languages, finer parts of linguistic structure from both sources are intermixed. This is the case with Anglo-Romani, where the grammar is fully English and the lexis includes many basic vocabulary items from the original Romani language, the Indic ethnic-heritage language of north-west India. Media Lengua is a blend of Spanish lexical items and Quechua grammar and phonology; it is spoken in several small towns or village communities in the central Ecuador highlands (Winford 2003).

Bilingual mixed languages differ from pidgins in that their vocabulary and structure are not simplified. They often retain the inflectional complexities of their parent languages. Bilingual mixed languages can emerge relatively rapidly, often within a single generation, as an answer to the aspirations of new social groups or communities that want a language of their own to reinforce their separate ethnic identity. An example is Michif, a mixture of French and Cree, where the nouns and adjectives are mostly French and the verbs are entirely Cree. Michif is an expression of the separate identity of the Metis, who view themselves as a new people of mixed ancestry (Bakker 1997: 13).

Alternatively, slower creation takes place as a result of prolonged contact of two groups in one location, as in the case of Kormakiti Arabic, an Arabic–Greek mixture spoken in Cyprus, which is the result of cultural pressure.

Summary

Thousands of languages that exist in the world are fascinatingly diverse with regard to their linguistic features, origins, development trajectories and role in the societies where they are spoken. Categorisation of language varieties presents certain challenges. There is often no neat criterion that would definitely categorise a language variety as a language or as a dialect. In order to differentiate between two languages and between languages and dialects, one has to consider not only linguistic, but also largely social factors. Each of the named languages, dialects and language varieties of any kind is considered equally capable, at least potentially, of expressing the entire range of information, intentions, emotions and whatever else is expected from a human language.

An increasing number of language varieties undergo the processes of codification and standardisation. In addition to unification of language features and methods of use, standardisation normally grants language varieties status, legitimation and more opportunities for developing the language or dialect in a country.

Linguistic distance between languages is an important facet for multilingual societies and individuals. It impacts acquisition of additional languages, and plays a role in planning for language policy in education; similarities between languages enhance receptive multilingualism.

Pidgins, creoles and mixed languages come into being through particular kinds of language contact and social circumstances.

The spread and recognition of multiple regional and local varieties have led to the appearance of World Englishes – English language varieties in their own right. The shift in focus from the primacy of native varieties to the more recent varieties that sprang up around the globe raised the issue of ownership of English. The ownership is now shared by millions of native and non-native speakers across the world.

Further reading

Comrie, Bernard, Stephen Matthews and Maria Polinsky (2003), *The Atlas of Languages: The Origin and Development of Languages*, New York: Facts on File Library of Language and Literature Series, a Quarto book.

Mesthrie, Rajend, Joan Swann, Andrea Deumert and William L. Leap (2009), *Introducing Sociolinguistics*, Philadelphia: John Benjamins (on pidgins and creoles see pp. 271–81.)

Chapter review

Fill in the table by (1) using material from the chapter, and (2) giving your own examples, considerations and comments.

Concept/keyword	Definition or explanation	Example from the chapter	Your own example	Your considerations and comments
Language				
Dialect				
Regional variety				
Sociolect				
Ethnolect				
Idiolect				
Linguistic variety				
Vernacular				
Dialect continuum				
Language standardisation				

Contd

Concept/keyword	Definition or explanation	Example from the chapter	Your own example	Your considerations and comments
Pluricentric languages				
World Englishes				
Language ownership				
Performance varieties				
Pidgins				
Creoles				
Bilingual mixed languages				

Reflective questions

1. How can we define (if at all) whether we speak a language or a dialect?
2. List four criteria used to distinguish between language and dialect.
3. What is the difference between a dialect and an accent? Between a sociolect and an idiolect?
4. Give an example of a dialect continuum.
5. Explain what standardisation of languages and dialects involves and what it means for people speaking a standardised language or dialect.
6. How is language distance appraised?
7. How are Kachru's Circles associated with World Englishes?
8. What are the implications of the issue of 'language ownership'?
9. What do different performance varieties of languages have in common?

Exercises

Exercise 4.1

Explain and discuss the words of Wardhaugh (2010: 39): 'English is a language, but so are Dogrib, Haitian Creole, Ukrainian, Latin, Tok Pisin, and Chinese. Each satisfies a different sub-set of criteria from our list. Although there are important differences among them, we would be loath to deny that any one of them is a language. *They are all equals as languages, but that does not necessarily mean that all languages are equal!*

Exercise 4.2

Perform a mini-interview with multilingual speakers you know and identify their assumptions about the distance between the languages. Write down the information you receive and/or report it to the class. See whether psycholinguistic distance affects their language acquisition.

Exercise 4.3

Collect material on the dialects of your country's main language(s). Are they all mutually intelligible? Ask the speakers (among your family and acquaintances) to score the prestige of these dialects, to estimate the unifying symbolic power of a dialect. Was it easy to distinguish one dialect from the other? If not, explain the difficulties. Prepare a fifteen-minute presentation.

Exercise 4.4

Prepare a ten-minute presentation about one of the pluricentric languages to give in class. Choose a language that is used in your country (if any) and discuss the qualities of the pluricentric variety that makes your country one of the 'centres' for this language.

5 Classifications of languages

Given the great number and diversity of world languages, varieties and forms, there have always been attempts to organise this abundance into clear categories. A spectrum of classifications and typologies has emerged. At different times the criteria on which scholars attempted to group languages depended on the needs and interests of society. Languages are also distinguished according to their particular function for speakers (*lingua franca*), the channels through which they are expressed (such as auditory or signed) and their origins (natural or constructed languages). This chapter describes the most salient classifications and categories of languages.

5.1 Linguistic classifications of languages

Linguistic typologies categorise languages on linguistic grounds: that is, according to their linguistic properties. They can be holistic, embracing the entire language system, or partial, referring to only one specific feature of languages. Linguistic typologies are examined and applied by the subfields of linguistics – comparative linguistics and linguistic typology. Multilingualism scholars and practitioners draw on these typologies in order to understand cross-linguistic interactions during acquisition and use of various languages and to explain the outcomes of such interactions in daily communication, in education and at work.

5.1.1 Word order typology

Word order is the preferred order in a particular language, or the only allowed sequence of the main sentence elements: subject (S), object (O) and verb (V). The six possible orders are: SOV, SVO, VSO, VOS, OVS and OSV. *Word order typology* classifies languages according to the word order practised in a language. The word order sequences of languages are unevenly spread around the globe.

Some languages allow for variations in their syntactic structure, in the order of sentence elements, and we say such languages have *a free word order*. Latin, Navaho and Russian are among the languages with a free word order. See below the possible variations of word order in Russian:

> Панда ела бамбук
> The panda ate bamboo
> subject – verb – object (SVO)

Ела бамбук панда
Ate bamboo the panda
verb – object – subject (VOS)

Бамбук ела панда
Bamboo ate the panda
object – verb – subject (OVS)

Ела панда бамбук
Ate the panda bamboo
verb – subject – object (VSO)

Панда бамбук ела
Panda bamboo ate
subject – object – verb (SOV)

Most, but not all, languages prefer to put the subject first.

The SVO order (the panda ate bamboo) is observed by users of various languages, including Chinese, Vietnamese, Hausa, Italian and English. The Japanese, Korean, Burmese, Georgian, Cherokee, Tibetan, Armenian and previously mentioned Hopi language also prescribe a word order starting with the subject, but then followed by object and verb – SOV (the panda bamboo ate).

The languages that prescribe starting a sentence with a verb are less numerous. Among *VSO* (ate the panda bamboo) languages are Irish Gaelic, Welsh, Hawaiian and Squamish, and *VOS* (ate bamboo the panda) languages include Malagasy and Tzotsil. Very rarely do we meet word order starting with an object. The language Hixkaryana and a few other languages spoken in Amazonia are usually given as examples of *OVS* (bamboo ate the panda), and the languages of the indigenous people of the Amazon River Basin of South America, such as Yamamadi and Apurinã, are examples of *OSV* (bamboo the panda ate) languages.

5.1.2 Linguistic structural typology

The typological classification of languages according to their structural features, as originated by the brothers Friedrich and August Schlegel and proposed by Wilhelm von Humboldt (1767–1835) in the nineteenth century, is the one most discussed and used by linguists. According to the criterion of relationships between the elements in a sentence, all languages are divided into four groups:

- *analytic* (or *isolating*)
- *agglutinative*
- *inflecting* (or *flective*)
- *incorporating*.

In *isolating languages*, like Chinese, the words mostly consist of the basic roots and have no morphological endings. Words in isolating languages show little variation in their forms. The meaning is determined by the order of the words. Let us compare two sentences with the same words: 'The dog bit the man' and 'The man bit the dog'. Who bit whom, the subject–object relationship, is understood from the order of words.

Classifications of languages

Chinese is a good example of such a language:

Tā qù zhōngguó xué zhōngguó huá.
He/she go China learn China painting
He/she went to China to learn Chinese painting.

An example from the Vietnamese language

khi tôi dên nhà ban tôi, chúng tôi bát dâu làm bài.
When I come house friend I [Plural] I begin do lesson
When I came to my friend's house, we began to do lessons. (Comrie 1989: 43)

The languages assigned to the isolating group are especially common in Southeast Asia but also exist in other parts of the world. Other examples are Lao, Burmese, Yoruba and also English.

The words of *agglutinative languages* consist of a number of invariant endings and affixes glued to a root one after another; each individual component of a word (root, suffix or prefix) has a separate grammatical role. In Swahili this gives:

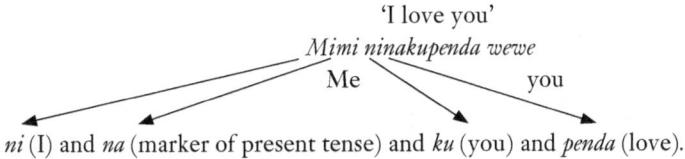

ni (I) and na (marker of present tense) and ku (you) and penda (love).

Turkish, Finnish, Hungarian, Estonian and Basque are agglutinative languages. The primary means of building new words in agglutinative languages is by adding prefixes or suffixes. In the Chukchi language (Northeastern Siberia) 'I have a fierce headache' is rendered as *Təmeyŋəlevtpəytərkən*. This word-sentence can be analysed as t-ə-meyŋ-ə-levt-pəyt-ə-rkən – I- greatly-head- am aching (Bogoras 1922: 833).

English is also capable of agglutinating many word components. The classic example of an agglutinated word in English is 'antidisestablishmentarianism' (anti-dis-establish-ment-ari-an-ism).

Inflecting languages, such as Russian, Latin, Sanskrit, Cherokee, Arabic, Hebrew, Slovenian, Lithuanian and Armenian, normally build up a root plus a component that represents several different grammatical categories. These languages allow roots themselves to be modified to express different grammatical relationships; for example, the Latin word lavo (I wash) consists of the root *lav-* and the suffix *o*. The suffix indicates the first person, singular number, present tense, indicative mood and active voice. The inflection, the *o* ending of the word *amo*, tells us that the meaning is 'I love' – first person singular, present tense, active voice, indicative mood.

In Spanish the *-ó* in *habló* ('to speak') simultaneously codes indicative mood, third person, singular number, past tense and perfective aspect. If any one of these meaning components changes, the form of the verbal suffix must change (Payne 1997: 28).

One more group of languages that is distinguished is *incorporating* languages. They are so called because they often link both subject and predicate into a single word, and this process is known as incorporation. In incorporating languages the difference between a word and a sentence is rather obscure, and a single word stands for a whole sentence. Many Australian languages and Native American languages are incorporating. In Tiwi, an Australian Aboriginal language, the sentence word *ngirruunthingapukani* means 'I kept on eating': *ngi* – (I) and *rru* (past tense marker) and *unthing* (for some time) and *apu* (eat) and *kani* (repeatedly). Another example is the Eskimo sentence-word *angya-ghlla-ng-yug-tug*. 'He would like a big boat.'

No language fits exactly and neatly into one or another of these categories – purely isolating, inflecting, agglutinating or incorporating. It is more often the case that languages possess qualities belonging to several categories. The original typological system of the Schlegel brothers and Wilhelm von Humboldt was criticised, clarified, modified and expanded by the twentieth-century linguists, and usually general classifications are made on the grounds of predominant characteristics. Still, some languages have proved difficult to classify even approximately. The living languages Japanese, Korean and Basque, and the dead languages Etruscan and Sumerian, are considered 'language isolates'. The language of the Ainu – a people living in Hokkaido, Japan, with a cultural and racial background different to that of the ethnic Japanese – did not fit any of the four typological groups.

5.1.3 Genetic classification of languages

Another holistic linguistic classification is *genetic classification* (also referred to as 'genealogical' and 'historical'). This one also came to us from the nineteenth century; it is one of the best-known linguistic classifications and is widely used in linguistics and in multilingualism studies, especially with reference to cross-linguistic interactions. The idea behind genetic classification is that there was a single common ancestor, an original 'proto' language which gave rise to all the languages of the world. This view was established in the nineteenth century by European philologists who suggested that the hypothetical Proto-Indo-European language is the source of modern languages in the Indian subcontinent (*Indo*) and in Europe (*European*).

There is also a hypothesis that there was not one (*monogenesis*: mono – one, single + genesis – origin), but several proto-languages (*polygenesis*: poly – many, several + genesis – origin), such as Proto-Germanic, Proto-Uralic and Proto-Dravidian. Old Norse (more exactly, its dialects) is the proto-language of Norwegian, Swedish, Danish, Faroese and Icelandic. *Monogenesis* implies that all languages in the world are related to each other, in an ancient family of languages, and *polygenesis* that the languages are related to several original 'parents'.

Whether there was one 'great-grandparent' or several great ancestors for human languages, the metaphor proved to work well and scientists set out to trace distinctions between languages from a historical perspective. Scholars were keen to discern meaningful resemblances in languages and to trace the branches of family trees. Through detecting common features in the phonology, lexicology, morphology and syntax of certain languages, they have managed to show the lineage of many modern languages.

There are no proven genetic relationships between languages and no proven existence of a protolanguage or protolanguages. The expressions 'language family' and 'language family tree' are metaphoric, rather than literal, and allow us to imagine and better understand the connection or distance between languages.

A *language family* is a group of related languages with a common origin. Thus, the Astronesian language family consists of the descendants of the proto-Austronesian language: Malay, Formosan Hawaiian and Maori. The Caucasian language family includes the autochthonous languages of the Caucasus (a region at the border of Europe and Asia between the Black Sea and the Caspian Sea, bisected by the Caucasus Mountains): Georgian, Chechen, Circassian, Lezgian, Ingush and Avar.

Below is a list of the ten major language families by language count, as provided by the 22nd edition of *Ethnologue* (2019):

1. Niger–Congo (1,542 languages) (21.7%)
2. Austronesian (1,257 languages) (17.7%)
3. Trans–New Guinea (482 languages) (6.8%)
4. Sino-Tibetan (455 languages) (6.4%)
5. Indo-European (448 languages) (6.3%)
6. Australian [dubious] (381 languages) (5.4%)
7. Afro-Asiatic (377 languages) (5.3%)
8. Nilo-Saharan [dubious] (206 languages) (2.9%)
9. Oto-Manguean (178 languages) (2.5%)
10. Austroasiatic (167 languages) (2.3%)

The 145 language families in the world differ widely in the number of languages and speakers they contain (*Ethnologue* 2019). The largest language families, based on speaker count, are Indo-European (with about 2.91 billion speakers across Europe and Asia) and Sino-Tibetan (for example, Mandarin Chinese), which together encompass over 4.6 billion speakers. Language families are subdivided into branches, and sometimes big branches are also referred to as language families. In this way, the Germanic, Slavic and Romance language families, each including a number of languages, are branches of a larger, more inclusive Indo-European language family.

5.2 Sociolinguistic classifications of languages

> 'Languages are not equal in political or social status, particularly in multilingual contexts.' (Graddol 1997: 12)

Unlike linguistic classifications, in which criteria for organising and categorising languages are linguistic, sociolinguistic classifications of languages consider the social standing of languages and their speakers.

The focus and interest of sociolinguistic classifications involve the influence of languages on various aspects of social life. All the sociolinguistic classifications that have evolved in recent times acknowledge that languages and groups of languages are unequal in their social circumstances, status and position. Such classifications are explicitly hierarchical. Typically, the languages assigned a higher level in such typologies have numerous speakers around the world, and are widely used in literature and in formal and public domains. In the lower levels of the hierarchies, we see languages that are somewhat more limited in their geographical spread and having fewer speakers. These languages on the lower 'floors' of hierarchies are less associated with literary usage and are often oral rather than written. Also, as a rule, they attract fewer L2 learners. The languages higher up the scale are fewer by far than those lower in the hierarchies.

5.2.1 The galactic model (de Swaan)

The galactic model proposed by de Swaan (2001) best reflects the contemporary vision of the language situation. This model is a hierarchy of languages for the entire world, ordered into four layers, according to their role and status globally and locally.

According to de Swaan, the basic layer of the hierarchy embraces the thousands of *peripheral* languages which are used by less than 10 per cent of humankind but comprise 98 per cent of all the world languages. These are, for example, the Wolof language spoken in Tanzania and Senegal in Africa, Chakesang, Deori, Khezha and Lahauli in India, and Occitan and Corsican in France. De Swaan likens these peripheral languages to moons circling a planet (de Swaan 2001: 4).

The next layer of de Swaan's hierarchy is the 'planetary position', to which about 100 *central* languages are assigned. These are usually the 'national' or official languages of states or provinces, used in politics, the law courts, education, textbooks and print and broadcasting media. Examples are Bengali, Italian and Dutch.

On the level of *supercentral* languages, only twelve languages are recognised: Arabic, Chinese, English, French, German, Hindi, Japanese, Malay, Portuguese, Russian, Spanish and Swahili. These are compared to 'suns' in the galactic model and, with the exception of Swahili, they each have more than 100 million speakers. At the top of the hierarchy de Swaan puts a single language, English, which he labels *hypercentral*. The supercentral languages are represented as connected to the central languages, and the latter, in their turn, are surrounded by the peripheral languages. Each layer of the hierarchy is seen as linked to the higher and lower levels via multilingual speakers.

5.2.2 Economic-related hierarchies

One factor that clearly plays an important role in ordering languages is economic reality. David Graddol placed economic matters centre stage when he set himself the task of understanding the role of English and of other languages that are used alongside it (1997: 12). Although, in his books dedicated to investigation of the present and future of the English language (Graddol 1997, 2006), he has not claimed to provide an explicit classification or hierarchy of languages, his discussion of the economic dimension of languages allows us to understand why some languages prevail over others. He comes to the conclusion that languages are hierarchically ordered in accordance with their level of economic power. Ammon (1995) suggests a rather straightforward way of estimating the economic strength of a language by simply ranking the economies of the countries where native speakers of given languages live. Graddol presents graphic schemas showing language hierarchies of the late 1980s at the levels of country (India), politico-economic zone (the European Union) and the world (see Figures 5.1 and 5.2).

Classifications of languages

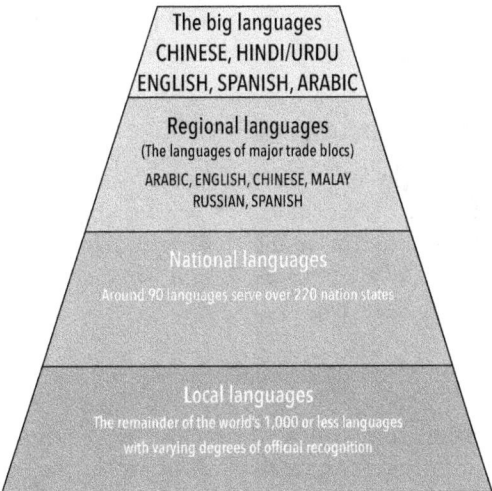

Figure 5.1 The world language hierarchy (Graddol 1997: 13, © British Council, reproduced with permission).

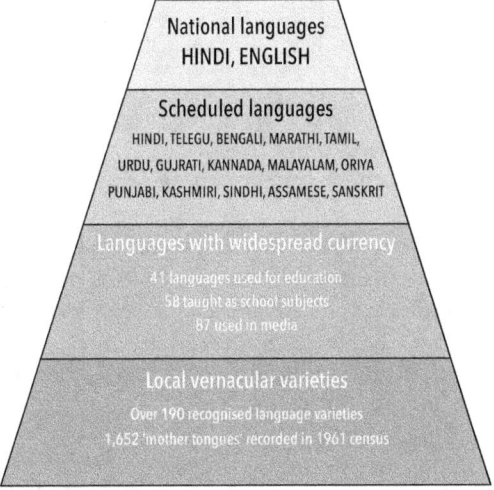

Figure 5.2 A language hierarchy for India (Graddol 1997: 12, © British Council, reproduced with permission).

'The taper of the pyramid reflects the fact that fewer language varieties occupy this position: greatest linguistic diversity is found at the base amongst vernacular languages' Graddol (1997: 12).

Another approach is to take into account all the countries in which a language is spoken and assign to it the appropriate *pro rata* proportion of gross domestic product of each country in question. On this basis, the model calculates for each language the 'gross language product' (GLP) – 'the total value of transactions conducted in a given language' (Ostler 2003: 7).

5.3 Distinct categories of languages

There are separate categories of languages that feature remarkably in multilingualism discourse. In the rest of this chapter, we will discuss the categories singled out as important on the criteria of their particular function – *lingua francas*, the channel through which they are expressed, sign languages and origin – constructed languages.

5.3.1 Lingua franca

Languages that are labelled as a *lingua franca* are singled out from other languages due to the task they perform in situations when other languages are not so helpful for communication. In many areas of the world where people speak mutually unintelligible tongues, they choose one language variety by common agreement in which they communicate for purposes of commerce, religion, administration and so on. Such an auxiliary language used by the speakers of divergent languages is defined as the *lingua franca* (plural: *lingua francas*), according to its function in human society.

The function of a *lingua franca* is to serve as a common means of communication for speakers of different languages over a relatively large geographical area in international trade, tourism and daily interactions. The *lingua franca* may be native to only some of its speakers; others learn it for the purpose of having a medium of communication with speakers of other languages.

The original *Lingua Franca*, now extinct, was used by numerous language communities in medieval times in and around the Mediterranean ports as a trade language to communicate with others whose language they did not speak. It was a mixed language variety of mainly Romance origin, called the 'language of the Franks', thus '*Lingua Franca*', because the Arabs in the medieval period used to refer to Europeans in general as 'Franks' (see Chapter 4 on mixed languages). From that time onwards, other languages were used in a similar way: that is, adopted as a medium for assisting common activities of groups of people with diverging languages. These languages are now referred to as *lingua francas*.

Any language variety can be a *lingua franca* – whether a fully established language which speakers of other language varieties learn, a sign language, a dialect, a pidgin or a creole. The intrinsic qualities of a language are not the factors that promote a language to be a *lingua franca* (Wright 2006). At the same time, some artificial languages were constructed exactly with the intention of using them as *lingua francas*.

In different historical periods, different languages were called to the fore to serve as

> **Languages that used to be or still are *lingua francas***
>
> Arabic,
> Malay,
> Hausa
> Mandarin
> Swahili,
> Sanskrit,
> French,
> Russian,
> English

lingua francas. Certain *lingua francas* arise naturally while others are promoted by government policies.

French is known as the *lingua franca* of diplomacy. For about a millennium, Latin and Greek were the *lingua francas* of Christianity in the West and East, respectively. Among Jews, Yiddish has long served as a *lingua franca*. More frequently, *lingua francas* serve as 'trade languages'. East Africa is populated by hundreds of tribes, each speaking its own language, but most Africans of this area learn at least some Swahili as a second language, and this is used and understood in nearly every marketplace. Swahili as an East African *lingua franca* is spoken by approximately 120 million people, mainly in Tanzania, Kenya and Congo. A similar situation exists in West Africa, where Hausa is the *lingua franca*. Hindi and Urdu are the *lingua francas* of India and Pakistan, respectively. The linguistic situation of this area of the world is so complex that there are often regional *lingua francas* such as Ngambay, an important *lingua franca* of southwestern Chad, or Sadri, the *lingua franca* of the linguistically diverse Chota Nagpur plateau in India.

English as a lingua franca (ELF)

Today, an exceptional and ardently discussed *lingua franca* is English. Seidlhofer describes the English as a Lingua Franca (ELF) phenomenon as 'any use of English among speakers of different first languages for whom English is the communicative medium of choice and often the only option' (2011: 7). ELF users are mostly non-native speakers of English, such as Japanese tourists going to Spain, not to the UK, or French doctors practising medicine through English in Guyana, not in London (Cook 2013: 37). The English of ELF users usually does not adhere to native speaker norms of English; still, it is accepted in its own right and not evaluated against the proficiency of a native speaker. Rather, ELF users adapt the language to suit their own purposes (Jenkins et al. 2011, Jenkins 2018).

ELF scholars in Europe and Asia have worked to identify systematic and regular language features such as lexical and grammatical forms and pronunciation that might be considered characteristics of ELF in each particular context, as well as the existence of specific accommodation strategies intended to enhance mutual intelligibility. Several compilations of ELF corpus, also available online, have been accumulated:

- VOICE – the Vienna–Oxford International Corpus of English, a project run by the University of Vienna in 2005–13 (https://www.univie.ac.at/voice/)
- ELFA – the Corpus of English as a Lingua Franca in Academic Settings (https://www2.helsinki.fi/en/researchgroups/english-as-a-lingua-franca-in-academic-settings/research/elfa-corpus), compiled by researchers at universities in Finland
- ACE – the Asian Corpus of English, which comprises some one million words of naturally occurring English when used as a *lingua franca* between Asian multilinguals (https://corpus.eduhk.hk/ace/, Kirkpatrick 2010b, Kirkpatrick and Sussex 2012).

Since the turn of the millennium ELF has been researched and disputed among both applied linguists and English language teaching professionals in reference to language teaching (see, for example, Kirkpatrick 2011, 2014; Jenkins et al. 2011; Seidlhofer and Widdowson 2009). But the practical goal of teaching ELF instead of English as a foreign language (EFL) or English as an academic language (EAP - English for academic purposes) is not unanimously accepted in academia. Cook (2013), for that matter, questions whether ELF has a national status or its own native speakers (as opposed to the English language), and doubts that L2 users of ELF constitute a single social community, or that they, as a single group, speak a single English-related *lingua franca*. He, along with Canagarajah (2007), rather thinks that ELF is a form of social action, a set of procedures and strategies for communicating with other people (2013: 32).

In recent years, in addition to ELF in business, the workplace and tourism and English for diplomatic purposes, English is especially in demand in higher education. The conspicuous increase in *English as a medium of instruction* (EMI) for staff and students for whom English is not a first language has raised concerns regarding 'the "E" of EMI' (see, for example, Kirkpatrick 2014, Jenkins 2018). The considerations and debates of educationalists in universities and colleges focus on the question of which language – whether native speaker English consistent with American and/ or British norms or ELF – is and should be the model for teachers and students and should constitute the medium of instruction.

Another important point made recently within the discourse of language policy and higher education and English as a *lingua franca* and a medium of instruction is the realisation of the primary role of other languages in these settings. Jenkins redefines ELF as 'Multilingual communication in which English is available as a contact language of choice, but is not necessarily chosen', and suggests that ELF should be renamed EMF - *English as a multilingua franca* (2015: 73, 2018). In this view, multilinguals in *lingua franca* communication are effective users who are able to adjust their languages appropriately to the needs of a particular situation.

5.3.2 Sign languages

As opposed to spoken languages, which are transmitted through the oral–aural modality, *sign languages* (or signed languages) are a big group of languages that are expressed and perceived through the visual–manual modality. Instead of ears and sound, sign languages are 'spoken' through eyes, hand and body gestures, facial expressions and additional tools such as fingerspelling and lip-reading. Sign languages are characterised by simultaneity, iconicity (similarity or analogy between the form of a sign, linguistic or otherwise, and its meaning) and use of space.

These are the languages used for communication by the Deaf or hard-of-hearing. When capitalised, the term 'Deaf' describes the people who identify with Deaf culture and community, and defines them as a member of a linguistic community, while 'deaf' with a lower-case 'd' is an inclusive term for people with hearing loss, which defines them by their level of hearing. Sign languages are also used by hearing people, teachers, family, friends and those living in communities with deaf people.

There are approximately 200–300 sign languages used throughout the world today. The figures, understandably, are likely to be inaccurate, as some languages disappear and others evolve. The 2020 edition of *Ethnologue* lists 144 sign languages

Classifications of languages

that are used exclusively within deaf communities, while another source, *Glottalog*, gives the number as 193 (Power et al. 2020).

Some languages are actively used by large numbers of hearing and deaf signers, such as British Sign Language (BSL), which is employed by around 145,000 people in the UK (2011); American Sign Language (ASL), which is used in the United States and many parts of Canada; Russian Sign Language (РЖЯ), a language with an official status in Russia and also probably used in some other former Soviet countries, such as Moldova, Ukraine, Belorussia and Georgia; Dutch Sign Language (NGT – Nederlandse Gebarentaal), spoken in the Netherlands, Aruba, Curaçao and Surinam; and Chinese Sign Language (CSL), which holds the status of official sign language of the People's Republic of China. Others are local, such as Tebul Sign Language of the village of Uluban in Mali.

It is important to distinguish between signed languages and *manual signed codes*. A code is not a language; it is a representation of a natural language, such as, for example Morse code. *Manual* signed codes are artificial systems which are designed to present a natural language visually. Codes have no structure of their own; they reflect the structure of the language they represent. Codes have no native speakers, as a language would have. Manually Coded English (MCE) is one example of such codes. SSE, Sign Supported English, is a form of MCE that follows the spoken and written English language and its structure. The Deaf normally use both codes and signed languages.

There were times when sign languages were not considered fully-fledged languages, and some misconceptions about them sometimes still persist, such as that all the signers use one sign language or that sign languages are simply embodied copies of the spoken languages in a country.

In reality, sign languages are real natural languages which possess linguistic complexity and an expressive range as wide as those of spoken languages. Sign languages have grammatical and morphological systems and vocabulary, with the help of which they can convey abstract concepts just as all human languages do.

Many features of spoken languages and sociolinguistic phenomena in which spoken languages are involved are paralleled in sign languages. Sign language users, like speakers of auditory languages, have accents that, similarly to spoken language accents, point to a speaker's age, ethnicity, where they are from and what community or subculture they belong to, and also whether or not they are hearing or deaf. It is possible to identify different regional variations in sign language according to the lexical items typically used in an area and even according to the speed of speech (Schembri and Lucas 2015). Esther Inglis-Arkell (2014) illustrates ASL accents in quarterly literary magazine *The Paris Review* in the following way: 'New Yorkers are notorious fast-talkers, while Ohioans are calm and relaxed. New Yorkers also curse more.'

Like all human languages, sign languages are subject to change for various reasons. The most common cause of change is language contact, either with other sign languages or with spoken ones. The forms of language contact may vary from borrowing to shifting to the more dominant language and to disappearance of a language. Socially, sign languages are seen as minority languages surrounded by the spoken languages of the majority. In some communities, indigenous sign languages are being gradually replaced by another sign language that can be more dominant in a given country or by a sign language used in the schooling system. Yoel, who studied Canadian Maritime Sign Language (MSL) in the context of the Nova Scotia Deaf community, describes how a once-thriving signed language was interrupted by language contact, and a language shift from MSL to ASL ensued (Yoel 2009).

Sign languages develop independently from one another and from spoken languages in deaf communities around the world. Contrary to popular misunderstanding, sign languages are independent from the spoken languages of the area surrounding them (that is, majority languages). When communities of deaf people in localities that are often isolated by geographical distances and political borders generate a language which is distinct from the surrounding spoken languages, normally they are mutually unintelligible. Australian Sign Languages cannot be understood by users of Chinese Sign Language, nor can Swedish Sign Language be understood by users of Russian Sign Language.

How do sign languages evolve? We may soundly assume that sign languages have existed throughout human history, although the records at our disposal relate only to the last few centuries. Scholars suggest two common ways in which sign languages emerged in communities with a sufficient number of people to form a sign language community.

One type of sign language is that used in stable signing communities across nation-states or in large urban centres. Examples of such languages, in addition to the above-mentioned BSL, ASL and NGT, are French Sign Language (LSF – Langue des Signes Française), Japanese Sign Language (NS – Nihon Shuwa) and Hong Kong Sign Language (HKSL). Compared to spoken languages, these languages are considered new because the first records relating to them appear, according to different accounts, in the seventeenth to nineteenth centuries. Typically, they evolved within and around special educational institutions, such as residential schools for the deaf which were established at that time. Deaf schools became centres in which deaf children were taught a particular sign language variety and could also meet many other signers to interact and communicate with. It is due to schools and educational policy that sign languages were stabilised and, as historical records show, transmitted not only among the local deaf but also further to other countries and continents.

This type of language development and expansion prompted a classification of sign languages based on educational history and resultant similarities. Linguists track the dispersal of sign languages from several major deaf school centres. One such centre was in France, with its schools for the Deaf and French Sign Language, associated with Laurent Clerc (1785–1869), a deaf LSF signer prominent for his contribution to the spread of deaf education. People from other countries travelled to deaf schools in France with the aim of learning the school's method of teaching the deaf and, upon returning, spread the system in their home countries. Two Dominican sisters and two deaf little girls, students of St Mary's School for Deaf Girls in a Dublin suburb, visited Caen for a period of six months and implemented the FSL system, adapting it to an Irish context (Leeson and Saeed 2012). Thomas Hopkins Gallaudet (1787–1851) not only travelled from America to France but also persuaded Laurent Clerc to relocate to Hartford, Connecticut. In 1817, the first American School for the Deaf was established. That is why French Sign Language, Irish Sign Language and American Sign Language have similarities and are considered related languages. As a result of the institutional links and consequent similarity of this group of sign languages, scholars have proposed a French Sign Language family.

The metaphor of 'family', denoting a group of languages, has proved attractive with regard not only to spoken languages but also to sign languages. In order to find the relation between sign languages, a few comparative studies using the lexico-statistical method have been conducted. Comparisons between the lexicons of pairs of languages have revealed a high percentage of overlap in those of German Sign Language, Austrian Sign Language and Hungarian Sign Language, which is explained by the fact that Germany, Austria and Hungary were all once part of the Habsburg Empire, and teachers of the deaf in these countries were trained in Germany and influenced teaching across the area. In this way, the German Sign Language family, which is also believed to include Polish Sign Language and Israeli Sign Language, emerged. The sign language 'families' consist of languages which are employed in geographically distinct signing communities and are clustered together through links formed by their historical educational origins.

Most recently, a team of researchers (Power et al. 2020) investigated the evolutionary history of sign languages on a larger scale with the help of a computational phylogenetic analysis[1] of 40 contemporary and 36 historical sign language manual alphabets. Using state-of-the-art methods for tracing the relationships and changes in the dispersal of sign language across time and space, these scholars could support and detail the European lineages previously proposed by historical comparative methods, such as the three groups of Austrian, British and French origin. The study also revealed connections more complicated than formerly imagined between the common bases (schools and books) from which the manual alphabets are derived and those of their descendants.

Returning to the ways that sign languages evolve, let us consider the second origin of sign languages, when they evolve naturally in smaller communities with high incidence of deafness. Dissimilar to the larger deaf communities described above, signers in such communities, where the sign languages are variously called indigenous, rural or village sign languages, typically live in close proximity and are related by blood or marriage. In such settings the language is transmitted naturally from older to younger signers as the children are exposed to sign languages from their early years through the signing parents, family members and neighbours (Fenlon and Wilkinson 2015). A classic example of such a community is Martha's Vineyard, described by Groce in 1985. The population, who lived on an island in south-eastern Massachusetts in the United States from the seventeenth century to the mid-twentieth century, was characterised by an extremely high rate of people (about 1 out of 155) who were born deaf due to a hereditary condition. The hearing

---

1. Phylogenetics – the study of evolution, diversity and the way that different organisms and species are related to each other; see <https://www.vocabulary.com/dictionary/phylogeny> (last accessed 20 August 2021). It aims at finding evolutionary ties or histories between organisms among the subjects of interest by analysing changes occurring in different organisms during evolution, finding relationships between an ancestral sequence and its descendants, and estimating time of divergence between a group of subjects that share a common ancestor.

people on this island were bilingual in English and in the island's sign language. What makes this no-longer-existent sociolinguistic setting unique is that both hearing and deaf islanders acquired Martha's Vineyard Sign Language (MVSL) from their childhood and spoke it across their everyday life: for example, for fishing and attending church. The islanders did not see deafness as a handicap, never referring to themselves or to their neighbours with hearing loss as a special group or as 'the deaf', rather considering it 'normal'. The researcher's notes contain the following interview dialogue (Groce 1985: 4):

> [...] in an interview with a woman in her nineties, I asked,
> 'Do you know anything similar about Isaiah and David?'
> 'Oh, yes' she replied, 'they both were good fishermen, very good indeed.'
> 'Weren't they both deaf?' I prodded.
> 'Yes, come to think of it, I guess they both were,' she replied. 'I'd forgotten about that.'

Other such village/indigenous communities typically characterised as having a higher incidence of deafness and their own sign languages are reported to exist or have existed in various parts of the world: the Chican Sign Language, in a village of Chican Mexico, where deafness goes back at least three generations (Delgado 2012), Yolngu Sign Language (YSL) in Australia, Konchri Sain (KS) in Jamaica (Adone et al. 2012) and Inuit Sign Language in the Arctic (Schuit 2012).

From the circumstances in which most signers live in today's world, it is clear that most of them are multilingual by default. The language input such children receive is highly varied and their repertoire may include sign languages, manual sign codes such as MCE or SSE, and literacy in spoken languages as well (see also Chapter 9 on signers as multilinguals).

With the development of medicine and technology, the number of pupils in deaf schools has diminished. Fewer deaf children are being born in countries where the vaccination against rubella that may cause deafness is administered (Fenlon and Wilkinson 2015). As cochlear implants have become increasingly and routinely implanted in deaf children at an early age (Boyes Braem and Rathmann 2010), more parents choose to send their children to mainstream schools rather than to specialised schools for the Deaf. These developments might diminish the number and role of deaf schools as centres of deaf education and sign languages, and disrupt one of the traditional methods of intergenerational transmission of sign languages. Assessment of these developments as positive or negative depends on one's philosophy.

5.3.3 Artificial (constructed) languages

There are also languages which are different from 'naturally evolved' languages. They have been consciously designed by an individual or a group of people and are called *artificial* or *constructed* languages. The urge for invented or controlled languages, which Kachru calls 'linguistic esoterica' (1992: 2), dates from ancient times.

The reasons for creating such languages vary according to the period of their creation. First of all, there has always been a desire to ease communication between people of different ethnic groups and nationalities. The idea of having a convenient and easy-to-use language for all humans was popular at the end of the nineteenth and beginning of the twentieth centuries, the aim being to provide an international language that would connect people of different nations or countries. Auxiliary languages such as Ido, Interlingua, Novial and Volapük were produced. The most successful of these languages is Esperanto invented by L. L. Zamenhof.

Esperanto was created with the aim of making it as accessible as possible, and therefore its grammar is easy and its lexis is based on vocabulary from several European languages. It has probably a million speakers, and there are even some native speakers. Esperanto did not succeed in fulfilling its primary goal – to serve as the global *lingua franca* – but it is still rather widely used by its enthusiasts, the Esperanto community, and Esperantists' congresses are held.

On the whole, despite their reasonable and noble aim, artificial languages have not yet become the new and better means of human communication that their enthusiasts envisaged. Although many such languages have not been appreciated or have been forgotten throughout human history, the fact that languages continue to be designed and perfected is remarkable. Imaginary communities in films or TV series have their own languages, designed by linguists and obeying the rules of linguistic structure. Some of such languages are: Klingon, for *Star Trek* by Marc Okrand, and more recently the language spoken by the fictional Na'vi people on Pandora, in James Cameron's 2009 film *Avatar*.

Summary

In this chapter we have touched upon some current typologies and distinctive types of languages that are employed in the multilingual world to different degrees and for various purposes. Languages are variously classified according to an assortment of criteria. There exist a number of holistic and partial typologies of languages based either on purely linguistic or on social criteria.

How are classifications useful? Being familiar with typologies of and distinctions between languages organises the knowledge of languages and their important properties. Systematising knowledge on multimodal linguistic means of communication leads to a deeper understanding of multilingualism and is instrumental for taking informed decisions in various language-related situations.

Further reading

Fenlon, Jordan and Erin Wilkinson (2015), 'Sign languages in the world', in Adam C. Schembri and Ceil Lucas (eds), *Sociolinguistics of Deaf Communities*, Cambridge: Cambridge University Press, pp. 5–27.

Chapter review

Fill in the table by (1) using material from the chapter, and (2) giving your own examples, considerations and comments.

Contd

Concept/keyword	Definition or explanation	Example from the chapter	Your own example	Your considerations and comments
Word order typology				
Linguistic structural typology				
Genetic classification of languages				
De Swaan's galactic model				
Economic-related hierarchy of languages				
Lingua franca				
English as a Lingua Franca (ELF)				
English as a Multilingua Franca (EMF)				
English as a medium of instruction (EMI)				
Sign languages				
Manually signed code				
Artificial (constructed) language				

Reflective questions

1. What are the criteria for linguistic classifications of languages and for sociolinguistic classifications of languages?
2. How can social and economic classifications of languages be used?
3. What is the difference between a *lingua franca* and a dialect?
4. What is the relationship between sign languages and manually coded languages (codes)?
5. How do sign languages evolve?
6. What are the criteria and methods for grouping sign languages into families and lineages?
7. Describe the main features of sign languages (minimum five features).
8. Explain how signers and users of *lingua francas* are multilingual.

Classifications of languages

Exercises

Exercise 5.1

Categorise the languages of your area according to the genealogical classification and according to the language typology. In addition, identify other characteristic(s) specific to the language in question (such as script, stress and intonation, and means of presentation – gesture or sound).

Exercise 5.2

Categorise these same languages according to the social typologies you know.

Exercise 5.3

Prepare a fifteen-minute student conference presentation that would (a) inform the listeners of the sign -language(s) in your region, city, community or university, and (b) discuss the challenges and outline the existing opportunities and support for sign language(s) users.

Exercise 5.4

Prepare a student conference presentation of a case study describing how signers from different countries communicate in a particular situation (such as a meeting on the street, a conversation on a university campus, a visit of relatives living in another state where a different sign language is used and so on).

Exercise 5.5

Organise a student conference on the topic of 'multilingual signers'. Presentations and posters may include case studies on exceptional individuals as well as yourself, your family members, friends and colleagues, and an analysis of the life and activities of historical or our outstanding contemporaries that use(d), studied or developed signed languages.

Exercise 5.6

Prepare a twenty-minute presentation on the topic of *lingua franca*. Examples of a title might include: '*Lingua francas* of the African continent', Swahili as a *lingua franca*', 'The dilemmas of selecting a *lingua franca* in post-colonial countries' and 'European *lingua francas* of today'. You can think of your own topic for the presentation. It can also be connected with a particular *lingua franca* of your choice.

Part III
Multilingualism in society

6 Multilingualism at the societal level: basic concepts

This chapter is devoted to the concepts and issues that are most important when dealing with multilingualism across societies. It dwells on borrowings and *Sprachbund* as manifestations of language contact and the three social forms of language use: domains, speech communities and diglossia.

6.1 Language contact

People speaking various languages come into contact in a range of situations. The groups of German, French, Romansh and Italian speakers in Switzerland have been neighbours for hundreds of years, and that is how these languages are in contact. For the pupils of a rural primary school in Brunei, language contact occurs when the native speakers of their ethnic languages – Dusun, Penan and Iban – learn English using English and Bahasa Melayu, the official language of the country (Martin 2003). There are countless occasions where language contact occurs: a movement of one group to another group's territory, settling in new countries where other languages are in use, a peaceful takeover of a territory, military conflicts and conquests of one tribe or nation by another, active trade and regular business encounters, missionary activities, intermarriages, and even conversations between individuals – all these are typical situations of language contact.

In the not so distant past, language contact occurred primarily in face-to-face interactions among individuals and groups of speakers. More distant contact took place through written forms, such as documents and books in Latin and Greek. The holy books of the major world religions provide encounters with languages which are not in daily oral use. The Qur'an is written in Classical Arabic, to be read/heeded by the adherents of Islam, who routinely speak different varieties of Arabic (Egyptian Arabic, Moroccan Arabic, Tunisian Arabic) and other languages, including Farsi, Kurdish, Urdu, Malaysian, Tatar, Pashtu or Bosnian, as mother tongues. The sacred texts of Judaism are written in Biblical Hebrew and Talmudic Aramaic, which need interpretation for speakers of modern Hebrew and other languages of believers. The Bible of the Roman Catholic Church was written in Latin before the tradition was partially discontinued in the twentieth century.

New technologies, such as social media, available gadgets and internet with participatory user-generated content, Web 2.0 and incoming third-generation web, made contact between languages, through its speakers, writers, hearers and readers a default situation. '[It] is difficult, and maybe impossible, to find a language anywhere that isn't in contact with one or more other languages at any given time,' says Sarah Thomason (2010: 32), a specialist in language contact.

Language contact occurs when individuals or groups of people speaking different languages interact, and their encounters exert an influence on one of these languages or on all the languages in contact, as well as on the speakers themselves. This influence can vary greatly, depending on the intensity of contact. The intensity of language contact is contingent on a number of factors, among them the duration of contact, the number of people involved, the purpose of the contact and relative sizes of the population speaking the contacting languages. It also matters whether, and to which extent, members of the groups have been able to master each other's language. The ability of the different groups to access each other's language easily is also a factor to be considered.

Language contact situations can range from very brief casual contact to a very strong cultural pressure exerted over several generations. The influence may be gradual, subtle or abrupt; it can involve only some groups in a country or the whole population. Certainly, the kind of influence and the degree of this influence are infinitely different in countless situations of language contact.

Multilingualism deals with several facets of language contact: linguistic, social and those related to language processing in the brain. The closest language contact is, of course, the one within the head and soul of a multilingual. Neurolinguists are concerned with this type of language contact. They investigate how the presence of two or more languages is supported and processed in a human brain, and whether mastery of more than one language causes any physical changes in the brain or makes it function in a different manner. Researchers of multilingualism have paid much attention to the impact of language contact on the identity of a multilingual, the feelings, self-image and cognitive processes pertaining to the mental processes of perception, memory, judgement and reasoning taking place due to acquisition of an additional language. These issues will be discussed in more detail in Chapters 8 and 9, which are dedicated to individual multilingualism. Sociological perspectives on language contact explore how languages coexist in the same social space and time, both face to face and digitally, what their relationships are, and how this has an impact on the lives of members of these societies.

When language contact is investigated from the linguistic point of view, the interest of researchers is in a language *per se*, that is, on how the language, its lexical assets, phonology, morphology, syntax and semantics, change over time under the influence of other language(s). The field that studies contact-induced language change is called *contact linguistics*.

6.1.1 Borrowing

From the linguistic point of view, contact with another language can result in changes in all systems of the lexis, phonology and structure of a language. One of the most widespread outcomes of language contact is *borrowing*. Borrowing denotes the adoption of words, morphological forms and grammatical patterns from another language, called *the source language*, although the *receiving language* has no obligation to 'pay for the loan'. The 'most contagious' contact is borrowing from a lexical system, as we may see that *lexical borrowings*, or *loan words*, are the most evident and rich in number.

Adoption of the words of another language happens easily, even between geographically and genetically distant languages, enriching the recipient language with individual lexical items: usually nouns and verbs, but also phrases. Some Japanese words are known to many speakers of European languages: *haiku, kimono, ninja, origami, sumo, sushi, jujitsu, karate*. Languages increased their lexis by adopting words from the languages of conquered indigenous peoples. For instance, the British colonisation of North America led to borrowings from Algonquian languages, such as *skunk, moccasin, wigwam* and others, into American English. The names of states like *Illinois, Ohio, Michigan, Wisconsin* are also derived from Native American languages. Australian English adopted words like *kangaroo* and *boomerang* from the Aboriginal languages of Australia. The Arabic language contributed to other languages the words *gazelle, giraffe, harem, hashish, sirocco, sultan, vizier, bazaar, caravan*, and via contact with the Spanish language in times of conquest came *alcove, algebra, zenith, algorithm, almanac, azimuth, alchemy, admiral*.

Borrowed words, also called *loan words*, are adopted into recipient languages with different degrees of assimilation: that is, they can conform partially or totally to the phonetical, graphical, morphological and semantic standards of the receiving language. Thus, some words are accepted into a recipient language without any changes, while others are modified to greater or lesser extent in their pronunciation, spelling or meaning. For example, the word *rendezvous* came from French into English and Russian practically intact in pronunciation but changed its original meaning somewhat. The English words *cocktail, jazz, film, tweed* retained their meanings in many languages. The words *vodka, borscht, apparatchik* from Russian; *tobacco, toreador, sombrero, macho* from Spanish; and *cliché* and *brioche* from French, sound and mean the same in many tongues.

Although borrowing typically occurs from the dominant, more prestigious language into the less prestigious and dominated, there is mostly a mutual impact on the donor and recipient languages, and word borrowing happens in both directions. In colonial India, the English language was enriched by words from Sanskrit such as *yoga, avatar, karma*; from Dravidian came *curry, mango, pariah*, and from Hindi, *bandanna, bangle, bungalow, jungle, maharaja, nabob, pyjamas, shampoo, thug, jamboree*. An interesting example of borrowing from Japanese to English and back (from English to Japanese) is the word *pokemon* – pocket monster.

Morphology borrowing is the transfer of grammatical morphemes (inflection, derivation and function words) from the source language to the recipient language. The diminutive Russian suffix -chik has made its way into Hebrew, resulting in words like bahurchik – bahur – young man, boy + chik (compare Russian пальчик). The suffixes of foreign origin from French (*-age, -ance/ence, -ate, -sy*), Greek (*-ist, -ism, -ite*) and Latin (*-able/ible, -ant/ent*) are found in English. The factors affecting linguistic borrowing are intensity and frequency of contact, and the prestige or power attached to the donor language in the opinion of the borrower.

While lexical borrowing may occur even when contact between the two language communities is not frequent or at a considerable geographical distance, *structural borrowing*, on the other hand, occurs only when there is a more intense language contact.

Structural borrowings – that is, the adoption of phonological, morphological or syntactic features from another language – are the signs of very close contact between the source and recipient languages. This actually suggests a very deep penetration of the system of one language into the other, which requires a really good knowledge of the 'donor' language on part of the recipient language speakers, as opposed to very superficial knowledge required in case of a semantic borrowing like *ciao* from Italian or *hi* from English. Structural borrowing involves the adoption of individual constructions, such as an adjective comparison or case marking from the source language. The most frequently borrowed grammatical category is that of connectors. For Vietnamese, for instance, Chinese is the source from which Vietnamese borrows reflexive and conditional markers (Matras and Sakel 2007).

Language and culture are inseparable, and language contact can result in borrowing a foreign concept and creating a new descriptive term for it. Pima Indians' new creations 'wrinkled buttocks' for elephants and 'having downward tassels' for oats are good examples (Haugen 1950).

6.1.2 Sprachbund

An extensive and prolonged contact between the neighbouring languages, even those which are genetically unrelated, leads to the appearance of similarities in the linguistic structure of these languages. This process is called *language convergence*. When languages converge, they begin to share more and more properties, such as pronunciation, grammatical structures and word order. A linguistic area across adjoining speech communities in which a group of language varieties show significant mutual agreement and overlap in form is called *Sprachbund*. The languages which share a number of common phonological, morphological or syntactic features may not be related or are distantly related. Thus, the similar features in these languages appear due to contact and borrowing, rather than due to belonging to the same language family. The Balkan *Sprachbund* that includes Albanian, Macedonian, Greek, Romanian, Bulgarian, Croatian and Serbian is an exemplary case. For instance, the feature of posing the definite article after the root of a word (post-posed definite article) can be found in Bulgarian (Slavic branch of Indo-European family), Romanian (Romance branch of Indo-European family) and Albanian (a distinct language of the Indo-European family which does not belong to any other existing branch):

in Bulgarian	*voda* (water)	*voda-ta* (noun + article)
in Romanian	*lup* (wolf)	*lupu-l* (noun + article)
in Albanian	*shok* (comrade)	*shok-u* (noun + article)

The next sections of this chapter deal with the basic concepts of societal multilingualism: speech community, domain and diglossia.

6.2 Speech community

The notion of a *speech community* (sometimes also 'language community' or 'linguistic community') is fundamental for sociolinguistics and the sociology of language. Of all existing categories of human coherence, like class, ethnicity or territorial and economic characteristics, the speech community is 'the most important kind of social group', according to Leonard Bloomfield (1933: 42). It is also a fascinating notion. On the one hand, it looks simple and useful, and therefore attractive to both scholars and people not specialising in language and societal issues. On the other hand, it is as elusive and abstract as the concepts of 'language' and 'dialect': there is no consensus on its boundaries and what a 'speech community' is. Let us look at the development of this important concept in more detail in order to understand why that is so.

Different scholars emphasise various aspects of this concept as being the most important. The simplest understanding of a speech community is that all who speak the same first language, or dialect, represent a speech community. From this viewpoint, the aggregate of people who speak French in France, Jamaica, African countries and Canada would constitute a language community, even though they are geographically dispersed and may not interact with each other. This means that every language, big or small, has its own community of speakers, who are united by the fact that they inherited the same language by birth or adoption. Among the members of large speech communities defined in this way are 1.5 billion users of English. Of these, only about 360 million people speak English as their first language (Lane 2021). There are also millions of Mandarin Chinese native speakers, roughly 917 million in 20 countries; Spanish, with 460 million native speakers in approximately 44 countries; Hindi, with 341 million native speakers; and Arabic, with 315 million native speakers. Other languages, such as Hadza spoken by the 800 nomadic hunter–gatherer Christians in Tanzania (Marlowe 2010), boast considerably smaller communities of speakers. François (2012: 86) reports the average figure of 550 speakers per language in the Torres and Banks Islands of northern Vanuatu, with 200 speakers of Lehali (François 2012: 103) and 280 Hiw speakers (François 2012: 98). Sign language communities include Deaf and hearing speakers of a particular sign language variety (Fenlon and Wilkinson 2015).

The members of a speech community share not simply the language but also, importantly, linguistic norms (Labov 1972: 120–1) and expectations about the use of this language, attitudes and values, in other words, a common understanding of when and how it is appropriate to speak this language and a shared interpretation of what is said. The members of such a group are in habitual contact (see Mesthrie et al. 2009: 37).

Like many other concepts important for multilingualism, the notion of speech community evolved from a monolingual perspective, where one language, a mother tongue, was taken as a point of departure. Thinking about language community within monolingual paradigm has its roots in the ideologies that accompanied and assisted in the development of nation-states, starting from approximately the end of the eighteenth century.

By this time, and from then onwards, the European polities started turning away from monarchies and empires, which embraced many ethnic groups, into nation-states. A nation-state is a state, or country, that has defined borders and territory, and typically consists of citizens of the same ethnicity and religious beliefs who share cultural values. The term 'nation-state' represents the principle that each nation lives within the geographical boundaries of its own state. The principle 'one nation – one language' was pursued, as it was most instrumental in uniting a nation in which the citizens shared a strong national identity. Only a handful of countries – for instance, Japan and Iceland – may now be seen as matching the 'one nation – one language' principle, due to their very strong sense of national identity and shared language, but even these countries are starting to open themselves to a wider acceptance of additional languages.

Although the monolingual view on language arrangements in nation-states still holds today, most countries of the world now either belong to traditionally multi-ethnic polities or embrace immigrants or minority groups. Therefore, it is often the case that the country and its national borders do not coincide, and the monolingual perspective does not really suit the reality. Consequently, very few speech communities now coincide with the borders of countries. There are many examples of one language and ethnicity being spread over several countries. Think, for example, of the Arabic language, spoken in about 47 countries. To add to the confusion, many African languages are closely related. De Swaan (2001) cites Mwartha Musanji Ngalasso (1990), who studied the Kikongo language in one river-town, Kikwit, and noted about twenty languages currently in use which are more or less similar to Kikongo. It is problematic to define accurately where one language/language community finishes and another starts.

The boundaries of each speech community are also difficult to define because it is practically impossible to identify precisely, numerically or in any other way the extent to which members of the community share values and linguistic norms. It is also problematic to decide which level of sharing and common understanding and which level of language proficiency suffice for speakers to be included in a community. Therefore, a speech community is a generalised notion representing all the members of the groups speaking a particular language.

Despite the difficulty of giving a perfect definition of a speech community and the impossibility of a precise delineation of the borders of speech communities, the notion itself is very useful for the study of language use in society, and for disciplines such as the sociology of language and sociolinguistics.

The concept of the speech community, although abstract and relative, is fundamental for a social study of language use because it is based on a social dimension as opposed to having a purely linguistic focus. The concept of a speech community provides a framework that connects the language and the people speaking it in one unit. Having such a unit in place, we can then discuss and analyse linguistic groups within and beyond polity borders.

Gumperz defined a speech community as follows:

> We will define it as a social group which may be *either monolingual or multilingual*, held together by frequency of social interaction patterns and set off from the surrounding areas by weaknesses in the lines of communication. Linguistic communities may consist of small groups bound together by face-to face contact or may cover large regions, depending on the level of abstraction we wish to achieve. ([1968] 1971a: 463, italics added)

This definition of a language community makes it possible to apply it even to very small groups of people, as well as acknowledging multilingual speech communities. The criteria for considering a group a speech community require them to share specific regular features of language use.

Thus, the notion of a speech community applies to big and small, rural and urban, natural geographical and political, and online speech communities of whatever size and composition. It equally applies to Francophone and Flemish communities of Brussels; to the local, recently evolved speech community of Turkish–German adolescents that uses a deviant variety of the urban ethnolect in Berlin (Dittmar and Steckbauer 2013); to communities of whistle language users – Silbo Gomero of the Canary Islands or the Mexican Mazatecs; and to nomadic communities of the Roma people in the UK, Spain, France and Russia, which use the Roma language in each community separately, or all of them as one community.

Multilinguals can be, and often are, members of a number of speech communities. Alternatively, multilinguals may indeed constitute a multilingual speech community in cases when they share two or three languages, along with the norms and assumptions associated with each of these languages. Such a group of people would constitute one multilingual speech community if, crucially, the members also share the emergent features that express the use of several particular languages in specific connection to each other and their roles in this particular society in a similar way.

6.3 Diglossia

The phenomenon of *diglossia* was brought into the spotlight in 1959 by Charles Ferguson in his article of the same name. The classic understanding of diglossia is the coexistence and alternating use of two historically and structurally related language varieties in a speech community. The use of each variety is clearly defined by social convention, and different varieties of the same language are employed on different, mutually exclusive, social circumstances and occasions.

Ferguson defined a diglossic situation as follows:

> A relatively stable language situation in which, in addition to the primary dialects of the language (which may include a standard or regional standards), there is a very divergent, highly codified (often grammatically more complex) superposed variety, often the vehicle of a large and respected body of written literature, either of an earlier period or in another speech community, which is learned largely by formal education and is used for most written and formal spoken purposes but is not used by any sector of the community for ordinary conversation. (Ferguson 1959: 336)

Ferguson called the former variety the *Low* (*L*) variety and the latter the *High* (*H*) variety. A classic example of diglossia referred to by Ferguson, and many others, is found in the Arabic-speaking world. In each Arabic-speaking country two varieties of Arabic are in use. On the one hand, there is the High, or Al Fusha variety, employed in formal situations, such as religious occasions, political speeches, news broadcasts and lectures, as well as in written discourse. On the other hand, there is the Low, demotic variety: that is, the local vernacular (Egyptian Arabic, Kuwaiti Arabic, Lebanese Arabic and so on) which serves as the medium of everyday communication. While the latter is acquired naturally as the mother tongue, the Fusha – literary or 'written', 'formal' Arabic – requires formal schooling.

Joshua Fishman (1967) extended the concept of diglossia from Ferguson's definition by applying it to the alternating use of completely different languages. Fishman's essential criterion for a diglossic situation was that, in such situations, language varieties exhibited a clear separation of social functions, '*compartmentalisation*', and for him typological relatedness was irrelevant in this connection. He suggested the following four ways in which individual monolingualism, individual bilingualism and societal diglossia (in his broader definition) operate in communities:

1. with both bilingualism and diglossia (for example, Guarani–Spanish bilingualism in Paraguay)
2. with diglossia but without bilingualism (for example, the use of classical and colloquial Arabic in Egypt)
3. with bilingualism but without diglossia (for example, German–English bilingualism in Germany)
4. (very rare) with neither diglossia nor bilingualism (for example, monolingual parts of the USA).

6.4. Domain

The concept of the *domain* of language behaviour was put forward by Joshua Fishman ([1965] 2000). In his early seminal work 'Who Speaks What Language to Whom and When?', Fishman analysed multilingual settings in order to establish the rationale behind the language choice of bilingual speakers. He found out that, in stable bilingual contexts, the use of one language rather than another in certain situations is not accidental but rather customarily associated with specific settings, topics and groups of interlocutors. He called such a specific setting a *domain* and defined it as a 'cluster of social situations typically constrained by a common set of behaviour rules' and as a 'social nexus which brings people together for a cluster of purposes' (1965: 75; [1965] 2000: 94).

Fishman identified five domains: 'family', 'education', 'employment', 'friendship' and 'government and administration'. Each domain is associated with a specific field of experience and specific roles of participants, and is appropriate to its language variety and language behaviour. Domains are settings where interlocutors make their language choice, conditioned by a particular locale and the events and subject matter associated with this domain. The domain of education, for example, is associated with institutions such as nurseries, schools, universities, events requiring the use of official language, fairly formal speech, and communication around the issues of learning, teaching, scientific disciplines, class and extracurricular events.

Additional domains, both broader and more specific types of situations, were subsequently distinguished. Languages one habitually chooses for greeting people in the street, conversing in a café over a cup of coffee with an acquaintance, buying goods in local stores, or dealing with the shoemaker and hairdresser belong to the domain of 'neighbourhood'. The domain of 'religion' has to do with religious institutions and missionaries, involving typical locations such as temples, mosques and synagogues, along with a set of 'proper' issues for conversation and prayers. Some languages are normally selected for these particular physical settings and social milieux. The Russian Orthodox Church traditionally uses Church Slavonic as a liturgical language. Recent immigrants from Korea to Ireland, members of the

Dublin Korean Church, a Christian denomination which meets at a venue made available to it by the Irish Presbyterian Church, use Korean in church services as the regular language in this domain. In the work domain, though, these immigrants, who have full-time commitments in a restaurant or supermarket, are expected to choose English, and indeed do so (Singleton et al. 2013a).

A domain is a generalisation. Domains refer to typical institutions, events and topics to talk about, and roles of interlocutors, and in this way regulate the choice of language out of two or more that can be used in multilingual settings.

Bernard Spolsky (2009: 3) pointed out that the participants in the domain are labelled by their social roles and relationships rather than as individuals.

> In the family domain, participants are labelled with kinship terms, like father, mother, brother, sister, aunt or uncle, grandfather or grandmother, or other appropriate roles such as maid or babysitter. In the school domain, the typical roles are teachers, pupils or students, or principals. In the workplace, they are bosses, employees, foremen, clients and customers. In the government domain, they are legislators, bureaucrats and citizens. Any individual of course may fill different roles in different domains, with conflicts sometimes obvious – how do I speak to my son at work if he is also my employer? (Spolsky 2009: 3)

The concept of domain is an abstraction. As such, it allows the construing of general regularities from actual language choice. Domain analysis, as suggested by Fishman, permits the elucidation of language choice-patterns in various institutional contexts in a multilingual society: literally, who speaks which language to whom and when, in multilingual communities.

> Domains are defined, regardless of their number, in terms of institutional contexts and their congruent behavioral co-occurrences. They attempt to summate the major clusters of interaction that occur in clusters of multilingual settings and involving clusters of interlocutors. (Fishman 1972: 441)

Summary

This chapter contains the description of basic phenomena and corresponding concepts that are essential in dealing with societal multilingualism. The processes and outcomes associated with language contact, such as borrowing and *Sprachbund*, are both linguistic and sociolinguistic in nature. Speech communities, diglossia and domains are well-known ways of describing how languages are arranged and how they operate in multilingual societies. Understanding these concepts facilitates an understanding of language choices by individuals and groups and of language practices in general.

Further reading

Ferguson, Charles (1959), 'Diglossia', *Word*, 15, pp. 325–40.
Fishman, J. A. (1965), 'Who speaks what language to whom and when?', *La Linguistique*, 2, pp. 67–88.

Fishman, Joshua (1967), 'Bilingualism with and without diglossia; diglossia with and without bilingualism', *Journal of Social Issues*, 23(2), pp. 29–38.

Thomason, Sarah Grey ([2001] reprinted 2004 and 2005), *Language Contact: An Introduction*, Edinburgh; Edinburgh University Press, pp. 15–21 (Chapter 2, 'Contact Onsets and Stability').

Chapter review

Fill in the table by (1) using the material from the chapter, and (2) giving your own examples.

Concept/keyword	Definition or explanation	Example from the chapter	Your own example	Your considerations and comments
Language contact				
Borrowing				
Sprachbund				
Speech community				
'One nation – one language'				
Diglossia				
Low (L) variety				
High (H) variety				
Domain				

Reflective questions

1. What kind of language contact is in place in the village of Kupwar in India? In this village, due to a long history of interaction between the speakers of languages belonging to different families – Marathi (Indo-Aryan), Kannada (Dravidian) and Hindi–Urdu (Indo-Aryan) – the structure of the languages they speak is so similar that some claim it is possible simply to replace the lexical items from one language with the other if you already speak another language.
2. Explain what it means when we say that the notions of 'domain' and 'speech community' are generalisations.
3. Describe various types of borrowing. Give examples of borrowings into the languages other than English that you know.
4. Is the concept of language community relevant in the contemporary world? If it is, in what way? If your opinion is that it is not relevant any more, please give your arguments and support them.

Exercises

Exercise 6.1

Prepare an e-poster on a multilingual speech community you live in or know of.

Exercise 6.2

Organise a class conference on diglossia. It may include presentations on diglossic situations with Arabic in various countries, standard and Swiss German in Switzerland, and Katharevousa and Dimotiki in Greece. Conduct a class discussion after all the presentations, and using it as a basis, formulate written conclusions about diglossia. These may relate to the role and meaning of diglossia in various communities or its challenges for education and teaching languages. Provide a conclusion for the paper by suggesting not less than three ways to cope with the challenges of diglossia.

7 Societal multilingualism: multilingual countries and regions

This chapter continues the theme of societal multilingualism in various parts of the world. Bilingual and trilingual countries, as well as countries with thousands of tongues in use, have diverse provisions for their languages and speakers. The chapter begins with an account of the typical ways in which communities become multilingual, then briefly outlines the most common language roles in countries and organisations, discussing multilingual arrangements on different continents. All this can help us to find answers to the questions: what are the meaningful characteristics of multilingual countries and spaces? What makes multilingual countries similar and what are their differences?

7.1 How do countries become multilingual?

One way for a country to become multilingual, dating back to ancient times, is through conquest and colonisation. King Darius the Great of Persia (522–486 BCE), noted for the administrative genius with which he governed his vast empire of conquered territories and populations in Asia, Africa and Europe, was also known as the ruler who instituted the usage of official languages. The Elamite language was employed in the government offices at Susa, which was then the seat of government. Later, following the conquest of Mesopotamia, Aramaic supplanted Elamite in this enormous country. Scholars disagree on whether the role of 'Imperial Aramaic' was as an official language or as a *lingua franca*, but what is beyond doubt is that it became the dominant language in the empire. The need to recognise one language as the official one underlines the fact that, at that time, along with one dominant language, multiple other languages were in use in the Achaemenid empire. The cuneiform inscriptions carved at that time and known as the Behistun Inscriptions testify to the active role of multiple languages in the empire. The inscriptions located on Mount Behistun, near the city of Kermanshah in western Iran, consisted of three versions of the same text, written in three different cuneiform script languages: Old Persian, Elamite and Babylonian.

Although the ancient Egyptian and Roman empires each had one unifying language – Egyptian (an Afro-Asiatic language spoken at that time) and Latin, respectively – they were *de facto* multilingual due to the fact that they embraced different territories whose populations still retained their own languages. The Roman army, for example, drafted soldiers and generals who came from countries outside Italy: Africa, Gaul, Germany, the Balkans, Spain and the Middle East. For this reason the Roman military forces included Sarmatians, Arabs, Armenians, Persians, and Moorish and Gallic horsemen, all speaking their own languages. Josephus, the first-century Roman Jewish historian, in his description of the Roman army in *The Jewish War* (c. 75 CE[1]) mentions how, before fighting, the centurions had asked the troops three times in *their own language* whether they were ready to fight. And the soldiers cheerfully answered, also thrice: 'Yes, ready!'

A second reason why countries and areas become multilingual is that they have several languages in circulation because different ethnic groups have been living side by side in these territories for many centuries. Contemporary Switzerland, which is considered the oldest and most stable multilingual country in Europe, is a good example. There are four official languages in the Swiss Confederation: German, French, Italian and Romansh. This is because the German-speaking population had a common language border with the Romansh-, Italian- and French-speaking people for centuries.

The third way for countries to become multilingual is migration. This is especially productive in the current world of globalisation. North America, Canada and Europe have received huge influxes of immigrants. Major migrations have taken place in other continents too for a variety of reasons.

In 2015, at least 350 languages were reported as being spoken in U.S. homes.[2] These include the indigenous Native Americans' languages such as Navajo, Dakota, Cherokee and Zuni; new American languages, such as African American Vernacular English and Gullah; and Austronesian languages such as Hawaiian and Samoan, as well as heritage languages and immigrant languages. The main immigrant languages spoken by millions of American citizens are Spanish, Chinese (Putonghua and Cantonese), French, German, Tagalog, Vietnamese and Italian, along with Dutch, Finnish Arabic, Russian, Welsh, Yiddish, Khmer (Cambodian) and Swedish.

The effect of migration on making places and countries multilingual is particularly noticeable in places that traditionally were perceived as monolingual or, at most, bilingual. Consider Ireland, where, traditionally, one language – English – was used by most of the population in their daily lives, and only about 5 per cent are bilingual in the official Irish and English. Since the turn of the millennium, a significant influx of immigrants, with Lithuanian, Latvian, Zulu, Polish, Mandarin, Russian, Arabic or German as their mother tongue, came to live in the country, thus turning it perceptibly multilingual.

7.2 Roles and status of languages in multilingual countries and organisations

Each country regulates the status of its languages in one way or another. Usually, there is a particular configuration of official and other variously recognised languages used *de facto* and *de jure*. The most common language statuses are as follows.

An *official language* is understood as the language of the majority, used in courts, parliament and administration, and common in all other spheres of life in a given

---

1. CE – current era (AD, Anno Domini, in other notations).
2. <https://www.cnbc.com/2015/11/04/at-least-350-languages-spoken-in-us-homes-new-report.html> (last accessed 2 September 2021).

polity. There can be more than one official language in a country. The status of official language is very much sought after by ethnic groups that do not enjoy it because this legal status opens up further opportunities, including teaching the language at school, writing important documents in this language, translation into it, and developing ethnic culture.

It also happens that the legal status of an official language is granted to minority indigenous languages to emphasise the symbolic significance of this language to the country and deference to it, even if this language is not widely spoken. This is the case with the Irish language in Ireland, spoken natively by about 3–5 per cent of the population, and the Māori language in New Zealand, which is spoken by fewer than 5 per cent of the population. In these two cases, the status of official language signals the commitment to encourage its teaching and use. In other cases, elevating indigenous or immigrant languages to the status of official languages may indicate good intentions, or it could be the result of long-term lobbying, occasional unrest or open challenges by interested groups.

Beyond the country level, multilingual corporations and supranational organisations such as the United Nations (UN) and the European Union (EU) may also have official languages. The EU,[3] an economic and political union comprised of twenty-seven member states, operates as a multilingual organisation and promotes multilingual policies. The EU has twenty-four official languages. Since the 1990s, the EU has increasingly begun to underline the major role that languages and multilingualism play in the European economy. It encourages all its citizens to learn and speak several languages.

Official languages of the European Union

Bulgarian
Croatian
Czech
Danish
Dutch
English
Estonian
Finnish
French
German
Greek
Hungarian
Irish
Italian
Latvian
Lithuanian
Maltese
Polish
Portuguese
Romanian
Slovak
Slovenian
Spanish
Swedish

A *national language* is another term referring to a country's main language. It typically denotes a language or languages which has/have close connection with peoples living in a particular territory or within particular territorial bounds, and is considered representative of this nation or nationality. The nomination of a national language is understood differently in different countries; it can describe a dialect or another language variety connected to the national identity of the polity, or indicate languages spoken as first languages in the territory of a country.

Some jurisdictions have more languages and others fewer languages that are accepted as official, national or state languages; for others, recognition on a regional rather than a national level is deemed appropriate.

A *majority language* is typically understood to be spoken by the majority of a country's population and is typically the official language of a sovereign country.

A *minority language* can roughly be defined as a language spoken by a minority of

---

3. <https://europa.eu/european-union/about-eu_en> (last accessed 24 May 2020).

the population of a territory. The populations speaking these languages are called linguistic minorities. Still, the notion of 'minority languages' and the linguistic reality in which such languages exist are not straightforward. Such languages are present in most countries in large numbers. The term minority languages embraces regional, tribal, immigrant and indigenous (also called *autochthonous*) languages, spoken by greater or smaller numbers of people. There are minority languages which count millions of speakers, such as the Marathi language that has 90 million speakers and regional status in India, Wu Chinese with 77 million speakers and no official status, and Cantonese with 70 million speakers and regional status in Hong Kong and Macau.

There are minority languages which were termed '*lesser-used languages*', such as Friulian, spoken in Italy by about 600,000 users and in several other European countries, Canada, the United States and South America (see Fachin 2006); Ulster-Scots (Avery and Gilbert 2006); Kalmyk, a Mongolian language, a minority tongue in Russia but one of the state languages of the Republic of Kalmykia, a subject of the Russian Federation (see Kornusova 2006); and Kashubian, a West-Slavic language spoken in the province of Pomerania in northern Poland by some estimated 350,000–500,000 speakers (see Wicherkiewicz 2006).

Special kinds of minority languages include European minority 'unique' languages used in one state – Irish, Welsh, Frisian – and those spread over more than one state (Basque, Catalan). These are often minority languages by status and are used by a people which has not migrated from its homeland and is not a settler or colonial population. These languages are not dominant in any state, and each of them is in contact with stronger majority languages in each respective region – English in Ireland and Wales, Spanish in the Basque Country and Catalonia, and Dutch in Friesland.

A language native to a region and spoken by indigenous people is called an *indigenous language*. It is often a minority language and is used by a people which has not migrated from its homeland and is not a settler or colonial population. Indigenous languages enjoy different status and receive various kinds of treatment from their countries and enthusiasts: for example, Gaelic (Irish). In 2007, Irish became the twenty-first official language of the European Union; the teaching of it in Ireland is a matter of constant attention on the part of teachers and academics (see, for example, Ó Ceallaigh et al. 2018). More often than not, the indigenous languages are not localised to specific countries and do not map on to country borders. Due to colonisation, borders were drawn according to criteria that did not include representation of the reality of indigenous language use.

One and the same language may be a majority language in one country or region, and a minority language in another. Finnish is an official language in Finland and a legally recognised minority language in Sweden. Russian is the major language of the Russian Federation, used in Eastern Europe and communities around the world, and has the status of an unrecognised minority language in the EU. English displays a remarkable contrast in its social roles: the global language on the one hand but a minority language in Québec, Canada, on the other. Recognition of additional languages as official is one more trajectory of a country joining those considered multilingual. Under the Franco regime in Spain (1936–76) the Catalan, Galician and Basque languages were totally forbidden and the only official language of the Spanish state was Castilian Spanish. After the restitution of democracy in Spain, all languages spoken in Spanish regions were recognised as official within their own respective communities.

For decades, the interest in majority languages was pursued along with studies and discussions on minority languages: their status and vitality, access to them, education through a minority or lesser-used language, language policy and the rights of speakers (see, for example, Lo Bianco 1987, 2017, 2020; Zuckermann 2020).

7.3 Diversity of multilingualism

A hypothetical traveller flying across the world would encounter a limitless variety of multilingual countries. They share many characteristics but also noticeable differences. How similar are multilingual areas? Why do multilingual countries differ so much? The elements constituting the phenomenon of multilingualism – speaker, language and environment – persist across time and space. That being said, they keep transforming and interacting. In other words, the same but ever-changing elements generate a different kind of multilingualism each time: that is, different varieties of social practices. Specific histories and contexts diversify societal multilingualism in different geographical locations, and multilingual social arrangements vary from state to state and continent to continent, leading to the appearance of what Flores and Lewis (2016: 98) called 'sociopolitical emergences' – multilingual areas, spaces and countries.

7.3.1 Measures of linguistic diversity

In order to measure the level of linguistic diversity in geographical regions, countries or cities, the *Language Diversity Index (LDI)* is employed. It was suggested by Greenberg in a paper published in 1956. The LDI of a country aims to establish a numerical value for what can also be called language richness in a given geographical area. It is computed with the help of eight measures (indices), based on the probability of two speakers sharing or understanding the same language. It is supposed to indicate the degree to which two people can have different mother tongues in a given country. On a scale ranging from 1 and 0, the extreme pole 0 indicates that everyone speaks the same mother tongue and no diversity exists, while the opposite extreme, an index of 1, can denote that everyone speaks different languages and no two people have the same mother tongue in a particular country. The index, understandably, may change over time; some years ago, the LDI of Liechtenstein was calculated as 0.092; that of Cyprus, 0.444; Senegal, 0.778; and Lithuania 0.404.[4]

It may be useful to record not only the number of languages used within the borders of a polity, but also the density of languages in a region. *Ethnologue* informs us that, as of 2020, the highest density (concentration) of languages was found in Vanuatu, where 110 living languages are spoken over a geographical area of 12,189

---

4. SIL (2017), *Ethnologue*, 20th edn. Available at <https://www.ethnologue.com/ethnoblog/gary-simons/welcome-20th-edition> (last accessed 15 August 2017).

square kilometres (4,706 square miles); that translates into one language per every 111 square kilometres (43 square miles).[5]

Harmon and Loh (2010, 2018) looked at language diversity through the lens of biodiversity, seeing nature and culture as having evolved in similar ways. They attempted to assess the trends in language diversity in different world regions, and with this in mind created an Index of Linguistic Diversity (ILD)[6] comparable to the Living Planet Index (LPI) used for measuring biological diversity in species population. They reported that both species populations and speakers of languages were declining at similar rates, about 30 per cent since 1970, linguistic diversity having declined rapidly in the Americas but more slowly in Africa, Australasia and Eurasia (McRae et al. 2014).

7.3.2 How multilingual countries differ from each other

Correlation of individual and societal multilingualism in multilingual countries
The use of a number of languages in a region or a country does not mean that it is populated either by monolinguals each using their mother tongue or by equally multilingual people using all the dialects and languages of this area. A variety of arrangements can be found in different countries in terms of how the multilingualism of a country or an urban hub correlates with the individual multilingualism of its citizens.

There are officially monolingual countries in which individuals are mostly monolingual but there are also greater or smaller pockets of bilingual and multilingual speakers. An example of a largely monolingual society with multilingual speakers is Argentina. Spanish is the *de facto* official language and is predominant across the country. But Argentina also recognises about forty other languages, among them Quechua, Araucano and Guarani, as regional languages; German is spoken by a few hundred thousand Argentineans of German ancestry; and there are a small number of Welsh speakers.

In some multilingual countries many individuals do not have to switch between multiple languages on a daily basis. Consider Belgium. Its capital, Brussels, is an officially bilingual region with French and Dutch recognised as official languages. This city's linguistic situation would be more accurately characterised in terms of community bilingualism, with the recognition that many individuals living there do not use both French and Dutch in their everyday lives, but rather function in one or other of these languages.

Switzerland is yet another excellent illustration of a country that is rightly considered multilingual, but in which only a small share of citizens have a real need to use three languages. They live in the trilingual canton of Graubünden, where German, Romansh and Italian are the official languages. For many of its citizens, it is possible to lead monolingual or bilingual lives due to the principle of territoriality, on which the political and administrative division of the Swiss Confederation relies. In relation to language arrangements, this means that each of the twenty-six Swiss cantons

---

5. <https://www.ethnologue.com/faq#node_121341> (last accessed 4 July 2020).
6. Not to be confused with Greenberg's Linguistic Diversity Index (LDI, 1956).

has legislative and administrative autonomy, and most of them could be described as monolingual units. A single language (such as Italian in Ticino, and German in Zürich, Glarus, Lucerne, Nidwalden and Obwalden) is recognised as official in most cantons, and must be used in all domains of social communication. Only a few cantons are officially bilingual: Bienne and Fribourg, as well as the federal capital of Berne, which have French and German as official languages. Citizens in Switzerland do not need to know all four official languages of the country. They can do well using one official language of a given canton. At the same time, for those in each language community who are speakers of languages other than the official language of a canton, separate educational facilities have been made available.

While the Swiss can choose their languages freely, government employees, especially those working in the bilingual cities and cantons, and people employed by big business, banks and insurance companies, are required to be fluent in French and German. As in other European states, English is used as an international language in Switzerland. In addition, as in many parts of the world, increasing numbers of immigrants speak their native languages – Serbian/Croatian, Portuguese, Spanish, Turkish, Tamil, Arabic, Russian, Chinese, Thai and Macedonian – as their home languages. Thus, in historically multilingual Switzerland with its four official languages, there are populations which are *de facto* monolingual, bilingual or multilingual to different extents.

Proximate and integrative multilingualism
When multiple languages coexist side by side in communities and territories, and the speakers primarily use their own languages at the expense of other languages of the community, this is called *proximate multilingualism*. Manifestations of proximate multilingualism range from indifference to languages other than one's own to some interaction and occasional language contact.

Another form of societal use of many languages is *integrative multilingualism*. Today, it proliferates, often spreading to territories formerly characterised by the proximate form owing to the globalisation processes of migrations and technological advance. The term integrative multilingualism denotes the situation where people not only encounter other languages of the milieu but habitually use them actively. The proximate and integrative forms of multilingualism are at opposite extremes of a continuum; between them there is a range of intermediate forms – less integrative and more integrative.

Challenges and issues
It is rare for perfect peace to prevail among numerous tongues, for the relationship between languages in contact is rarely totally harmonious. The societal arrangements of languages in a country are in flux, whether this is abrupt or gradual, and whether it occurs as the result of changes in a political system, or as a consequence of the activities of interest groups, or in recognition of changes in populations due to an influx of new residents.

Multilingual countries face challenges, some of which are common for most multilingual communities and others are specific to each of them. Among the common issues are, for instance, an uneasy decision-making with regard to the number and selection of languages officially recognised by a country. In cases where the choice is towards fewer languages being allowed to have an active role in a polity, what would happen to the other unrecognised languages, and how would this impact the society in question? If multilingualism is pursued, should all the languages, or only some of them, be accommodated in a country, and what should the principle of selection be? To what extent and in which capacity should the selected languages be involved in the country's institutions and activities? Among the most hotly debated issues are languages encouraged in social domains and in education in view of economic, time and spatial constraints in an organisation or in daily life. On the one hand, multilingual urban and other spaces are enthusiastically encouraged and built. On the other hand, virtually every language-related decision in a multilingual community brings with it political, demographic and cultural changes, let alone expenditure (Pons and Jiménez Weese 2021).

In education, the questions painstakingly considered in all countries are: how many languages and which languages should be taught at school or used as an additional community language? How to accommodate several languages in a school curriculum? If included in school curricula, would a certain language be a separate discipline or a means of instruction?

Along with the common features and similar concerns of multilingual countries, the dissimilarities and peculiar features of multilingual settings are no less remarkable. Each particular community's sociolinguistic setting is defined and modified by an unlimited number of factors, and various patterns of societal multilingualism are at work in different parts of the world. To illustrate this variety, two big multilingual areas are briefly described below.

7.3.3 Multilingual regions and countries: Africa and India

The regions of Africa and India have historically been known as highly multilingual.

Africa

Africa is a heavily populated continent with more than a billion inhabitants and about 2,140 living languages (*Ethnologue* 2020[7]). Hundreds of ethnic groups normally each have their own language or dialect, and these belong to one of the major language families indigenous to Africa: Afro-Asiatic, Nilo-Saharan, Niger–Congo, Khoisan or the Austronesian language family. Languages brought to the continent by colonial policies are French, English, Arabic, Spanish, Italian and Portuguese, which belong to the Indo-European language family. The ethnic groups speaking between 1,500 and 2,000 languages[8] are spread unevenly throughout the fifty-four sovereign states and four non-sovereign territories.[9] The number of speakers of many languages in Africa is counted in millions: Arabic – 100 million native speakers

---

7. <https://www.ethnologue.com/region/Africa> (last accessed 28 May 2020).
8. <https://www.nationsonline.org/oneworld/african_languages.htm> (last accessed 16 August 2021).
9. <https://www.worldometers.info/geography/how-many-countries-in-africa/> (last accessed 16 August 2021).

and 30 million secondary speakers; Berber – 40 million speakers, mostly in North Africa; Hausa – 24 million native and 15 million secondary speakers; Yoruba – 21 million native and 5 million secondary speakers; Igbo – 20 million native and 5 million secondary speakers in West Africa; and Swahili – 10 million native and 80 million secondary speakers in East Africa.

Most African states are multilingual to varying degrees. The countries often cited as outstandingly multilingual are Nigeria, which has about 514 languages, and Cameroon, known for its distinctive cultural diversity and counting over 260 national languages.[10]

The sociolinguists of Africa have long insisted that, despite having clear similarities to the rest of the world, African multilingualism is very special in many ways, and has been developing into its present state for centuries (Brann 1981; Makoni and Meinhof 2003; Anchimbe 2007; Banda 2020). The extreme diversity in the causes and forms of multilingualism in both urban and rural regions in Africa caused the authors of a recent book to use the term 'multilingualisms' – in the plural (Di Carlo and Good 2020).

Nothing should be taken for granted when considering multilingual countries. African sociolinguistic reality can defy any assumptions that Westerners might have about languages in a society. As pointed out by Makoni and Meinhof (2003: 6), a speaker of a particular language might be regarded as a native speaker, even if that person does not speak the mother tongue fluently, but has mastered the cultural and often religious practices of the community.

Language identity often does not coincide with ethnic identity in both rural and urban Africa (Di Carlo and Good 2020). For centuries, the use of indigenous (autochthonous) languages was in constant flux. It was caused by sustained migration, ongoing intertribal and interethnic marriages, the slave trade, and the desire for settlement in peaceful and fertile regions. In post-colonial times, the use of particular languages has been influenced by the unprecedented rapidity of migration and urbanisation, for various reasons: regional political military and interethnic conflicts, displacements due to slavery, arbitrary territorial changes under colonialism, and expanding industrial exploitation of natural resources (Anchimbe 2007: 3).

Brann (1981) notes that there are many cases where ethnic groups live in symbiosis. Either they are bilingual, or one has adopted the language of its host whilst retaining its ethnic identity, such as the FulBe in Nigeria, who have adopted Hausa as their second or often their only language.

Among the indigenous languages of Africa there are a few major ethnic languages which rose to become national or state languages in the 1970 and 1980s. Among these are *lingua francas* for East and Central Africa, Swahili and Lingala, new mixed languages, pidgins and creoles, as well as major ethnic languages spoken not only by their ethnic population as a mother tongue, but also by a great number of the population as a second language. Hausa in Nigeria and Wolof in Senegal are examples. Local varieties of world languages are also singled out as representative languages for African states. The multiple other indigenous languages, which are in the posi-

---

10. <https://www.worldatlas.com/articles/what-languages-are-spoken-in-cameroon.html> (last accessed 28 May 2020).

tion of second-order languages, have to make room for them by retreating to be only used for communication within ethnic groups, sometimes by assimilation into the major languages or, in other cases, by extinction. Examples of extinct languages are Bodo, which used to be spoken in the Central African Republic, or Goundo, in Chad.

As a rule, Africans speak not only their mother tongues fluently but also several other genetically diverse language varieties, and the elites speak one or more European languages, mostly English and French. The European, non-indigenous languages were fused into the complex picture of African multilingualism in addition to the centuries-long, often conflict-ridden interaction between several diverse ethnic groups and their languages.

Arabic is widely used in North and sub-Saharan Africa (Ghana, Sudan, Egypt, Algeria, Morocco, Tunisia and Libya) due to the reach of Islam and the concomitant spread of language in about the seventh century CE and possibly earlier. The impact of the seventeenth-century colonisation of South Africa by the Dutch is still reflected in the culture and languages of this country. Afrikaans, one of the languages spoken natively in South Africa, is firmly based on Dutch dialects of those times (Kamwangamalu 2004; Heeringa 2015); there are also borrowings from the Bantu and Khoisan languages.

Portugal's colonisation of African territories left Portuguese as an official language in several states, such as Angola, along with multiple national languages like Kikongo, Kimbundu, Mbunda, Chokwe and Oshiwambo. In Mozambique, where the number of individual languages is believed to be over forty,[11] Portuguese is a national or official language. Other languages that are spoken in Mozambique include the indigenous Swahili, Makhuwa, Sena, Ndau, Shangaan (Tsonga), Lomwe, Makonde, Chopi, Chuwabu, Ronga, Kimwani, Zulu and Tswa, as well as immigrant languages (Arabic, Chinese) and foreign languages (English and French).

German has retained its presence on the continent since the late 1800s: in Namibia it is a recognised regional language, along with Afrikaans, Damara, Herero, Rukwangali, Silozi, Setswana and Oshiwambo, while official status is granted to English.

By the end of the nineteenth century, most of the other regions and states were brought under the rule of France and the British empire. Therefore, African countries are commonly divided between those that are labelled *Anglophone* (speaking English and also having a cultural background associated with English) and countries referred to as *Francophone* (speaking French and having a cultural background primarily associated with the French language).

The decolonisation processes started in the 1940s and unfolded during the 1960s and 1970s. African states had to choose an official or national language. This was important both for administrative use and for definition of their country's new identity. In many states the language(s) of the former colonial power remain as official languages: for example, English in Kenya, French in Burkina Faso, and English and French in Cameroon and Rwanda. The 'received' languages are convenient links for conducting government and planning administrative functions. Political and emotional considerations played a great part, too. The European languages

---

11. <https://translatorswithoutborders.org/language-data-for-mozambique> (last accessed 2 September 2021).

are perceived as useful for international contacts in science, technology, business and education. They are effective as *lingua francas* for any kind of dealings between African countries. The ex-colonial languages are not perceived as connected with any particular ethnic group and thus can be used as a neutral code in the complex and sensitive African reality, which carries a potential for conflict between states and tribal groups. Among the colonial languages, English has experienced a notable boost in recent decades, also as the vehicle of personal and communal economic progress.

Language-related controversies in Africa refer mostly to two issues:

1. The multiplicity of tribal languages and their role in society and education. This issue involves disputes about which and how many indigenous languages should be taught in schools and in higher education, and encouraged for use by communities. It also relates to how this choice of preferable languages, among the scores of other tribal tongues, can be instrumental in the search for a new identity for individuals, multiple ethnic groups and entire states in Africa.
2. The status and role of 'colonial' languages as opposed to indigenous languages of the particular area in Africa.

The special type of multilingualism existing in African contexts 'is characterized by the coexistence of oral and written, foreign and indigenous, official and non-official, pidginized and non-pidginized languages used for distinct and less-intervening purposes' (Anchimbe 2007: 9) More recently, Banda (2020) has characterised the current multilingual situation on the continent, and in particular in Zambia, as an intense language contact, fluent and complex, where all languages, minor or major, official and non-official, have roles to play. Along with the shared features in language use, language policies and language-related challenges, each African state or territory faces its own issues evolving from the peculiarities of its ethno-social history and fundamental values.

India

The Indian population of 1,353 billion[12] (as of 2018) speaks about 6,600 languages, which belong to at least four language families. Recently, scholars singled out two more language families for India: the Tai-Kadai language family of about seventy-six languages, including Thai and Lao, and the Great Andamanese language family represented by ten languages (Abbi 2018), thus bringing the total to six language families. The languages of the Indo-European family are spoken by approximately 70 per cent of Indians. About 22 per cent of the Indian population, mostly those living in the south and in isolated areas in the north, speak Dravidian languages, such as Tamil, Telugu, Kannada and Malayalam. The rest are speakers of languages belonging to the Austro-Asiatic or Tibeto-Burman families.

This huge number of languages includes the official language of India, 'Hindi in the Devanāgarī script'; widespread English, which has the status of 'associate language';[13] and twenty-two so-called 'scheduled languages' – that is, languages

---

12. <https://data.worldbank.org/country/india> (last accessed 28 May 2020).
13. <http://www.languageinindia.com/april2002/officiallanguagesact.html> (last accessed 16 August 2021).

recognised in the 'Eighth Schedule' of the constitution. It is believed that over 96 per cent of the Indian population speak one of these twenty-two scheduled languages as their first language and that they are written in thirteen different scripts. Languages, both scheduled and non-scheduled, spoken within the borders of any of India's twenty-eight states may be granted official status within the borders of a given state for the purposes of regional government.

The language report of Census 2011 showed an extreme language diversity at both individual and community levels. The mother tongue of each member of a household need not necessarily be the same.[14] Individuals are at least bilingual, and many are multilingual in the sense that they have at least partial competences in several languages which they use in a range of situations and encounters in everyday life. The transparency and fluidity of boundaries between languages (Khubchandani 1997) help speakers move between various patterns of language use in their social interactions and in various domains of their daily life, 'to glide from one language to another' (Annamalai 2008: 228). Individual multilingualism (plurilingualism) is perceived as a norm in India, rather than something out of the ordinary. This does not mean, though, that all the languages of a multilingual are completely mastered by him or her. Some languages are known better than others, while some are used only orally and in very specific situations or with a limited vocabulary sufficient for a particular kind and place of conversation. A much-cited illustration of the everyday language repertoire of an Indian merchant is given by Prabodh Bechardas Pandit (1972: 79) and demonstrates how India lives in a multilingual mode of communication:

> A Gujarati spice merchant in Bombay uses Kathiawadil (his dialect of Gujarati) with his family, Marathi (the local language) in the vegetable market, Kacchi and Konkani in trading circles, Hindi or Hindustani with the milkman and at the train station, and even English on formal occasions.

A special feature of Indian multilingualism is that the speakers of languages which are widely distributed across India, or speakers of languages with few users, tend to preserve and perpetuate their language varieties. Thousands of mother tongues, mostly minority languages, are typically maintained throughout the years because of the fundamental values peculiar to language use in India. India is noted for maintaining the home language across generations, even when the population migrates to another linguistic area (Pandit 1979), and for having the largest number of home languages.

Contact between communities presupposes at least some knowledge of neighbouring languages. Efforts were made to reduce the heterogeneity of the population in each state and gradually make linguistic borders fit better with administrative ones. Still, the administrative division of the country does not always parallel its linguistic borders. For some states, deciding on their official language is relatively easy because it is possible to single out the majority of speakers of one language from one language community. Such is the case with Gujarati in the state of Gujarat and Punjabi in Punjab. Other states and union territories have no simple linguistic

---

14. <https://censusindia.gov.in/> (last accessed 28 May 2020).

> 'Regional and minority languages are found in most of the countries of the world, but while sharing some basic characteristics in their functions, they are infinitely different in various multilingual communities. In India, the "scheduled languages" of India, although "state languages" in a real sense, are more robust than the regional languages used to be in Europe, but not nearly as robust as the national state languages in contemporary Europe. They are more fluid, more varying over time, more differentiated according to social status (there are marked caste differences, but also occupational and class variations), more penetrable by other, "higher" languages (such as Hindi and English). They tend to shade imperceptibly from one region to the next, from one version into another, so that, say, a Hindi dialect in the northwestern zone of the Hindi area may be completely unintelligible to a speaker in the southeastern part, and yet, the two are connected by a chain of adjoining, mutually intelligible dialects,' notes De Swaan (2001: 63).

majority. The state of Jammu and Kashmir is of a remarkable linguistic diversity, its principal languages being Urdu, Dogri, Kashmiri, Pahari, Punjabi, Ladakhi, Balti, Gojri and Dadri; there are also numerous languages and dialects with smaller numbers of speakers. Another example of a heterogeneous population with a large number of languages within the borders of one state is Pondicherri (Puducherry), where the official languages are French, Tamil, Malayalam and Telugu, while English is used for communication between districts. It is typical that a state contains a mixture of speakers of many languages rather than speakers of one or two languages. If we arrange the states according to their diversity, one of the smallest states of India, Goa, would take first place as it has the highest percentage of minority-language speakers at present – 48 per cent, with the largest minority group among them being Marathi speakers, who comprise 33 per cent of all the minority speakers in this state.[15]

Major regional languages (vernaculars) are accepted nationally, while other languages are accepted as dialects of particular regions. The noticeable differences in the domains of use, functions and prestige of languages make some researchers speak about the hierarchical nature of multilingualism in India, characterised by a double divide: one between the elitist languages of power and the major regional languages (vernaculars), and the other between the regional languages and the tribal ones (Mohanty 2010:131). Indeed, English and Hindi, and to an extent a few other regional languages, are obviously more conducive to achieving career, academic and business goals, and provide easier access to education. English remains the language used by the educated minority all over India. It is now closely associated with wider social and political aspirations and is starting to be available to those for whom it used to be inaccessible.

In 2010, David Graddol noted a conspicuous trend of English becoming an accessible asset for the underprivileged classes and lower castes, and in rural areas. A touching and material manifestation of this trend is the initiative to build a temple in Banka village in the northern Indian state of Uttar Pradesh to worship the Goddess of the English language. The Dalit, formerly called 'untouchables' and considered to be at the bottom of the traditional Hindu caste system, who are still marginalised,

---

15. Numbers taken from Graddol (2010).

believe that English will help them climb the social and economic ladder (Pandey 2011).

Multilingualism in India has its own face, which Ajit Mohanty describes as follows:

> [t]he uniqueness of Indian multilingualism goes beyond the simple presence of many languages in different activities. The complex social–psychological and socio-linguistic relationship between languages and their speakers and the role that many languages play in the life-space of individuals and communities give a very special character to Indian multilingualism. (Mohanty 2010: 133)

Summary

It would be an over-simplification to think of multilingual countries and communities only as territories or groups of people where two and more languages are used. There are numerous multilingual communities: cities, countries, tribes, and transnational and supranational organisations. They became multilingual through a variety of ways and share similarities, but at the same time are different in many respects.

The number of languages present in a country is significant but it is far from being the only characteristic of multilingual countries. The origins of multilingualism, number of linguistic lineages and typological divergence of language varieties a region, as well as the roles and statuses assigned to languages in a country and the patterns of individual multilingualism coupled with the country's history and culture, play a role in the emergence of a particular and unique kind of multilingualism in each location.

Reality shows us that it would be next to impossible to distribute multilingual countries neatly into individual types or to predict exactly the kind of multilingualism to be developed in any specific country over the long term or near future. We may conclude that each multilingual setting is multilingual in its own way.

Further reading

Banda, Felix (2020), 'Shifting and multi-layered dominant language constellations in dynamic multilingual contexts: African perspectives', in Joseph Lo Bianco and Larissa Aronin (eds), *Dominant Language Constellations: A Perspective on Present-day Multilingualism*, Cham, Switzerland: Springer, pp. 75–93.

Eberhard, David M., Gary F. Simons and Charles D. Fennig (eds) (2020), *Ethnologue: Languages of the World*, 23rd edn, Dallas: SIL International. Available at: <http://www.ethnologue.com> (last accessed 12 August 2021).

Graddol, David (2010), *English Next India: The Future of English in India*. London: British Council.

Chapter review

Fill in the table by (1) using material from the chapter, and (2) giving your own examples.

Concept/keyword	Definition or explanation	Example from the chapter	Your own example	Your considerations and comments
Proximate multilingualism				
Integrative multilingualism				
Majority languages				
Minority languages				
Official languages				
National languages				
Regional languages				
Titular languages				
Language Diversity Index (LDI)				
Francophone and Anglophone				
Multilingual rural areas				

Reflective questions

1. List the ways that countries become multilingual. Give your own examples.
2. How are multilingual countries similar? How are they different?
3. Identify similar features of multilingualism in the multilingual countries of India and Africa (either think of Africa as a multilingual continent or choose one state).
4. What is the difference between the terms 'official language' and 'national language'?

Exercises

Exercise 7.1

Describe in some detail a multilingual country of your choice. Trace the historical changes in the multilingualism pattern of that particular country. Single out the specific features of multilingualism there. Be prepared to present your work in front of the class (or in a tutorial) and take questions from your co-students.

Exercise 7.2

Speak/write about the problems in your multilingual community. Describe your own/a multilingual community, mentioning its origin and history, and outlining the community–individual axes, the composition and number of languages. List and mention the nature of the challenges. Outline the future of the multilingual community as you see it and sketch the urgent measures you would suggest undertaking to improve the sociolinguistic situation in the community you are describing.

Exercise 7.3

Design a poster or an e-poster that would describe and map:

- the majority and minority languages in your community
or
- the official languages and/or the titular languages of a country of your choice.

Exercise 7.4

Prepare a conference presentation. In it, report on a multilingual region, country or community of your choice. Use tables and figures to describe the quantitative data.

Exercise 7.5

Find on the internet an interactive map of a region or country to show the languages used there, or design your own. Deliver a presentation to your classmates.

Part IV
Individual multilingualism

8 Individual multilingualism: psycholinguistic and cognitive dimensions

In the previous chapters, we discussed the societal, geographical, political and cultural aspects of multilingualism and referred mostly to groupings and speakers' communities. This chapter deals with several dimensions of *individual multilingualism* and touches upon the cognitive, emotional and physiological characteristics that brand a multilingual individual. The chapter aims to emphasise the unique features of tri-multilinguals by comparing them to bilingual individuals and considering their linguistic behaviour, language acquisition, ways of communication, and capacities across their lifespan and in various health conditions.

8.1 Who are the multilinguals?

As was already noted in the first chapter, in recent decades, concerns have emerged about the correctness of treating bilinguals and multilinguals as totally similar language learners and users. Since a lot in education, social interaction and even medical treatment, directly and indirectly, depends on knowing the characteristic features of those we teach, deal with or treat, the question of whether bilingualism and multilingualism are the same or different is indeed an important one. Furthermore, as of today, multilinguals constitute a sizable part of the world population and recognising their particular qualities and behaviours is vital for education, social interactions of all kinds, and care of the young and older, healthy and not so healthy populations. In this book, the term multilingual refers to individuals who use or acquire *three or more languages*.

8.2 Special features and language behaviour of multilinguals

Researchers have found *differences* between multilingual speakers and those who use two languages. Which divergences between the two have such studies established? Initially, researchers noted the more evident *quantitative dimension*: one's vocabulary grows with the addition of words from a third language. Besides, with the appearance of the L3 system, formerly unknown ways of expressing grammatical meaning and new linguistic and cultural concepts which do not exist in the first two languages are obtained. Further studies in a range of disciplines have demonstrated that the quantitative changes appearing with the transformation of a bilingual to a trilingual are not as minor as they had previously seemed because they convert into critical *qualitative differences* between bilinguals and multilinguals. This is how multilinguals obtain unique emergent qualities.

8.2.1 Complexity and emergent qualities

The qualitative change that ensues with adding one language to the previous two is more meaningful than its quantitative counterpart. Multilinguals develop new features that are specific only to them and are not observed in mono- and bilingual speakers. In the complexity theory, the phenomenon that occurs when something new arises and has properties that its parts do not have on their own is termed *emergence*. Multilingual users are, formally speaking, complex emergent systems.

Complex systems differ in the level of their complexity. How to discriminate between lower- and high-complexity levels? Higher complexity is associated with high degrees of *integration* and *differentiation*, and multilinguals exhibit both. Trilinguals display higher metalinguistic awareness than bilinguals (Jessner 2006), which implies a higher degree of knowledge and cultural integration. The fact that cross-linguistic interactions in trilinguals are more numerous, diverse and profound than in bilinguals also indicates a higher degree of integration.

Sophisticated differentiation is seen in the daily practices of multilinguals who keep separate their three linguistic systems, including pronunciations, accents and lexes, and who are reported to have an advanced ability to make appropriate linguistic choices. Multilinguals exhibit high differentiation when they activate or deactivate their languages, 'knowing' from an early age when and with whom to speak which language (Hoffmann 2001b). Integration and differentiation in multilinguals' language use increase exponentially as compared to bilinguals, thus testifying to high complexity levels in tri- and multilinguals.

Why be concerned with levels of complexity? Because different levels of complexity mean that the outcomes of dealing with complex systems (such as individual multilingual speakers and their efforts to acquire languages, or an entire educational system in a country and its efficacy) can be predicted with various degrees of accuracy, or not at all. Consider the following points. Based on two things, we attempt to make predictions with some confidence. The behaviour of systems determined by two variables (say, two languages) is considered complex but predictable, at least theoretically. Starting with systems involving three variables (as with three languages), the outcome is considered inherently uncertain, influenced by spontaneous inner and extrinsic factors. In other words, becoming trilingual crucially raises the complexity of learning and using one's languages (see more on the complexity of multilingualism in Aronin and Jessner 2015: 280–2). From this, it follows that one should always bear in mind the complex and changeable nature of multilingual individuals, and the highly variegated trajectories of learning, using, conjoining and interacting between their languages and personal lives.

8.2.2 Features of linguistic and learning behaviour

The higher level of complexity associated with multilinguals underlies and explains the qualitative differences between bilinguals and multilinguals. Below some of them are described.

François Grosjean (1989, 2001) came up with the fruitful concept of *language modes*. He defined a language mode as the 'state of activation' of the speaker's languages and processing mechanisms (Grosjean 1998: 136). While a monolingual can activate one language – for example, Swedish (one language mode) – a bilingual with, say, Swedish and English can choose between three modes – speaking Swedish, speaking English or, in cases where an interlocutor knows the same two languages, speaking Swedish and English. A trilingual individual can enact seven language modes and a quadrilingual eleven. Note that the number of modes rises progressively with the addition of another language to the repertoire of a language user:

- one language – 1 mode
- two languages – 3 modes
- three languages – 7 modes
- four languages – 11 modes.

The choice of language mode is determined by the situation, topic of conversation, and the language knowledge of those participating in the communication. Socially, language modes are about the ability of an individual to function in monolingual, bilingual, trilingual and highly multilingual contexts.

De Angelis, in her 2005 study of non-native lexical transfer, pointed to the *distinctive learning behaviour* of multilinguals, 'a type of behaviour that speakers of two languages do not display' (2005: 14). Based on her findings, De Angelis concludes that 'the interaction between non-native languages cannot be assumed to be governed by the same principles that govern the interaction between the native and one non-native languages' (De Angelis 2005: 14).

Similarly, Kemp (2007) found out how multilinguals use *language learning strategies*, which also turned to be quite different from the strategies that the learners of the second language use. The results of the study led Kemp to believe that they 'may mean that, compared to L2 learning, augmentation in number and frequency of strategies used, occurs to a greater extent during the acquisition of the third language, increasing more gradually in additional languages' (Kemp 2007: 257).

In the area of pragmatics, Safont-Jordà (2012) discovered 'quite a different pattern' in the use of politeness strategies by a child in the third language, English, as opposed to the previously used Catalan and Spanish (Safont-Jordà 2013: 112). At about the same time, studying the acquisition of syntax, Berkes and Flynn (2012) found that the performance of the L3 study group in relation to relative clauses was undeniably better than that of the L2 group and postulated that the 'results would indicate that enhancement took place in the learners' syntactical knowledge due to multilingual experience' (Berkes and Flynn 2012: 10).

Collectively, these and other studies point toward a threshold effect that is already present in the acquisition of a third language. Multilinguals display distinctive features not only when acquiring but also when using their languages.

8.2.3 Extent of language skills used by multilinguals

Tri- and multilinguals do not normally use each of their languages to the full. People who master two languages to a comparable extent are called *balanced bilinguals*, and they do not constitute the majority among bilinguals. Decades ago, Grosjean underlined (1998, 2001) that being bilingual does not necessarily mean knowing two or more languages equally well. An individual may have different degrees of proficiency in each of his/her languages and use them at different times, in different situations and with different purposes. *Balanced trilinguals* are less common than balanced bilinguals. Equally high proficiency in all the languages of a multilingual is neither a societal expectation nor a reality. In each language, some specific skills and not others are required to be mastered to different levels. Edwards (2019: 155) explains that '[c]ommon sense dictates that multiple fluencies are rarely equally developed within the individual; it would be uneconomical to "over-develop" certain language skills'. Multiple language users distribute language functions between their many tongues, thus remaining fully competent speakers, listeners and communicators in their own right, and unique in their own way. The partial use of language skills that allows a user to communicate using a language across particular domains that s/he can communicate in is called *functional capability*. It is a real-world and common way of using multiple languages employed by individuals. The degree of functional capability in each of the multilingual's languages is a matter of intention and ability of an individual and language proficiency requirements in a particular society or organisation. Multiple fluencies and the functional capability of a speaker/user of more than two languages rest, to a great extent, on the private inner workings that take place in a multilingual: cross-linguistic interactions and processes occurring in the brain.

8.2.4 Cross-linguistic interactions

Monolinguals have only one language to master. Bi- and multilinguals experience aspects connected with the interaction of their languages. While acquiring and using more than one language, individuals compare them, translate, code-switch, and experience positive and negative transfer from one code to another. With multilinguals, the interlingual phenomena occur between three and more languages and therefore are not only of binary nature. The cross-linguistic interactions between three codes are much more diverse, complex and intricate than those between only two languages. The recent developments in cross-linguistic influence (CLI) research have revealed one more distinctive feature of multilingual language use: in addition to the traditionally studied mutual influence of a native language on a second one, a new kind of interaction, that which takes place *between non-native languages*, becomes possible in trilinguals.

Both positive and negative transfer in multilinguals does not necessarily mean a transfer from the L1; rather, it is associated with several languages and the multiple complex interactions of various degrees that take place concomitantly. In addition to rich interactions across various subsystems, such as phonetics, orthography semantics, syntax, morphology and pragmatics, cross-linguistic interaction also presupposes a transfer of experiences, emotions and strategies. As a result, heightened *metalinguistic awareness* – the ability to focus on the systematic elements of language and the ability to think about language in an abstract way – is a key component of *multilingual competence* (for example, Jessner 2006, 2008).

Due to a higher level of complexity associated with multilinguals, it is more complicated than with bilinguals to determine the most important conditions for triggering or constraining the occurrences of cross-linguistic influence. The triggers discussed by both bilingual and multilingual researchers are:

1. *Language distance*: more precisely, the similarity between languages. This has been consistently found to be the foremost trigger of the transfer. Research indicates that learners' language production and comprehension are markedly influenced by the language that is most similar to the target language, especially if proficiency in the source language is high, and if there has been recent exposure to it. With trilinguals, one should consider the language distance between three pairs of languages (L1–L2; L2–L3; and L1–L3) and also the mutual impact of the language distance between pairs or groups of close languages, such as English and French, or linguistically distant languages, such as Chinese or Korean.
2. It is worth noting here that a learner's individual perception of language distance, called *psychotypology*, which does not necessarily match linguists' definitions of typologically close or distant, may also trigger the transfer of skills, words and grammar patterns to the target language. Evidence of psychotypological dimensions in L3 learning was reported in the 2009 study by Ó Laoire and Singleton, where languages from three different language families, English and German (Germanic family), Irish (Celtic family) and French (Romance family) were involved. Their study of the two groups of English speakers who also knew Irish and were learning either French or German has demonstrated the complexity and intricacy of the participants' cross-linguistic consultation under the impact of the psychotypological factor. The participants, native speakers of English with Irish as their L2, acquiring French, drew synonyms and antonyms from their L1, as they 'seemed to be influenced by recognition of lexical closeness of English and French' (Ó Laoire and Singleton 2009: 99), while those with English and Irish, studying German, exhibited signs of influence from Irish, their L2, where the similarities of German and Irish were evident – namely, in word order in subordinate clauses – but not concerning the morphology in prepositional phrases, which are not obvious enough to learners.
3. There is also some evidence that despite the similarity, whether real or perceived, between the source (often L1) and target language (L3), learners draw from non-native languages (L2). In such cases, cross-linguistic interaction is explained as being stimulated by what is variously called *L2 status* or the *foreign language effect*. It refers to the 'tendency of L3 language learners to activate the first foreign language' (Hufeisen and Jessner 2019: 73). One of the explanations for this phenomenon is that association with the foreignness attributed to an already known non-native language makes a language learner prefer this language (L2), even if it is not well mastered, as a source of information for the next non-native language rather than L1 (Hammarberg 2001: 23).
4. One more CLI trigger is *recency of use*: how recently a language was last used (Hammarberg 2001). Most multilingual speakers know that the languages used recently tend to influence language production to a greater extent than those that go unused for a long time.
5. *Proficiency* in the target language and in languages that serve as source(s) for transfer is another strong factor for cross-linguistic interactions (De Angelis and

Dewaele 2011). Studies report how low or high proficiency in a language correlates with triggering or constraining interlingual transfer. As the proficiency in L3 rises, the cross-linguistic influence from L2 weakens (Hammarberg 2001).

8.2.5 Multilingual brains

Proficiency in various languages plays an important role for multilinguals from various points of view. On the one hand, as was already mentioned above, the use of several languages by a multilingual in a community does not necessitate equal and perfect mastery of all the skills in all the languages. Sometimes, just a basic communication ability in one of the multilingual's languages may suffice. On the other hand, the level of proficiency affects the healthy multilingual speaker's brain organisation and is important in recuperating after brain-damage events.

While all languages are believed to be active and to operate concurrently in both highly proficient and also differently proficient multilinguals (Kiran and Goral 2012), the level of proficiency influences the degree to which similar areas of the brain are recruited when processing languages. Some neurolinguists posit more overlap of multiple languages within subjects with higher proficiency and an early age of acquisition (Andrews 2014).

The studies by Green (for example, 1998), Paradis (for example, 2004) and other later research have shown how proficiency plays a role in determining the order and extent of the linguistic outcomes of brain impairment after strokes or incidents. In particular, different recovery rates in each language were observed in patients who had different proficiency levels in their languages before the damaging event. Parallel recovery might be expected in patients who enjoyed high proficiency levels across their languages before the aphasia-producing incident. Better recovery is reported for the languages that patients use more often (see, for example, Andrews 2014; MacLoddy et al. 2019).

Advances in the technology used in imaging techniques has boosted studies in the fields of clinical neurology and neurolinguistics. While research on language-related disorders in multilinguals continues (see, for example, Kiran and Goral 2012; Goral and Conner 2013), current and vibrant neurolinguistic work has *moved from a focus on language pathologies* (mainly aphasias), which was traditional in the twentieth century, *to the study of healthy individuals*.

The study of the organisation and functioning of three and more languages in the brain received significant impetus when the global scientific community arrived at an understanding of multilinguals as a distinct category of individuals who are important in their own right: hence the recent trend of *distinguishing between the bilingual and the multilingual brain*. Certain unique properties of multilinguals were noticed, particularly regarding early language representation, grey-matter density and speed of lexical retrieval (Higby et al. 2013). This, in turn, stimulated a particular interest in tri- and multilinguals, and several important traits of multilingual brains were discovered.

It was found that multilinguals recruit the *executive control* system somewhat differently from users of less than three languages. Executive control of the cognitive processes is currently a salient topic. Bialystok, Craik and Luk (2012) defined executive control as 'the set of cognitive skills based on limited cognitive resources for such functions as inhibition, switching attention and working memory'. Executive control is manifested in the ability to manage, coordinate and sustain information-processing activity over time, to avoid concurrent activities if needed, and to interrupt and then resume processing activities. Control in cognitive processes is important for managing linguistic conflict, and supports multi-tasking and sustained attention. Language-switching habits are among the areas where trilinguals express their abilities in executive control. Some trilinguals, labelled *non-switchers*, were found to be less distracted by irrelevant stimulus information, consistently performed better and faster in tests, and demonstrated better self-monitoring abilities and better efficiency than others dubbed *switchers*. Switchers are thought to possess weaker control and non-switchers, stronger control (Festman and Mosca 2016). Comparing multilingual speakers to other multilinguals, rather than comparing multilinguals to bilinguals, is a new and important development in research on the multilingual brain.

The issue of *switching costs* in multilinguals presents another fascinating question that remains to be answered, and cannot yet be fully explained using the same methods as those employed for bilinguals. Switching cost is expressed in the time (measured in milliseconds, or ms) needed for a reaction: that is, for switching from one language to another. The size of the language-switch cost depends on the direction of the switch (L1–L2 or L2–L1). Studies investigating switching between two languages found that longer reaction times (higher switch costs) were needed for switching from a weaker language (usually L2) to a more dominant and strong language (usually L1). This is called *asymmetrical switch cost*. The phenomenon, a lag in the reactivation of L1 when switching from L2 to L1, is explained by the need to inhibit the dominant L1 more intensively when producing words in the less dominant language L2. In balanced bilinguals, the switch costs are symmetrical.

With regard to the *trilingual phenomenon of switching costs*, the situation is more complex, less clear and harder to explain. The data received to date concerning multilinguals' switching costs defy the simplistic expectations built on experience with bilingual switching. We can expect trilinguals to need a longer response time when switching from one language to another simply due to the increased amount of data (languages not used at the moment) they have to suppress. But this is not always the case. Costa et al. (2006) and Costa and Santesteban (2004) reported the tendency of switch costs to disappear, at least when multilinguals are equally proficient in their languages and use them in similar ways. Mosca (2019) describes multilinguals' controlling system as 'strategic' and 'flexible', meaning that it adjusts languages' activation levels, depending on potential conflict situations, such as the typological closeness between languages.

Finally, many neuroscientists now accept the fact of *individual variation* in the neurological presentation of languages in the brain. In earlier neurolinguistic and clinical studies, this diversity was neglected as researchers attempted to categorise the diverse multilingual data into a more or less uniform framework. Today, variation across subjects in individual brains is accepted as a norm and data on the multilingual brain are increasingly interpreted with individual variation in mind (Andrews 2014).

Once multilinguals have gained qualities not found in bi- and monolinguals, does that mean that they become different when they learn additional languages? A frequent question from both laypeople and linguists is whether an individual becomes a different person while speaking different languages. Eminent researcher of multilingual individuals John Edwards puts it like this: '[t]here is some evidence that language choice may implicate different aspects of personality: informants are liable to give slightly different pictures of themselves, depending on the language used in interviews and on questionnaires'. And, '[t]he fact that different social settings and variations in language-affect linkages lead to different patterns of self-presentation clearly does not imply separate personalities, although it does suggest an enhanced repertoire of possibility' (Edwards 2019: 139).

8.3 Multilinguals in conditions of health and decline

During their lives, multilinguals experience language(s) acquisition, maintenance and loss, and these processes occur concurrently and discretely in different life periods and under various conditions (Herdina and Jessner 2002; Andrews 2014: 27). To use words that are part of the wedding ceremony, people live through their lives with their languages 'in sickness and in health, in joy and sorrow, through the good times and the bad'. In this section, we discuss what happens to individuals' language practices, proficiency and linguistic abilities when they age, become ill or stay healthy.

8.3.1 Multilinguals throughout their lifespan

Early and late multilinguals

The terms *early* and *late* when applied to multilinguals imply perceived differences in proficiency and language behaviour, depending on the age at which they acquire their languages. The exact ages at which one is considered an 'early' or 'late' multilingual vary. A team of neuroscientists (Wattendorf et al. 2014) investigated sentence processing in early and late tri-multilinguals with the help of functional magnetic resonance imaging (fMRI). Their participants were adults between twenty-two and thirty-five years old, of similar educational backgrounds and highly proficient in three languages (these included German, English, French, Italian, Swiss-German, Catalan and Indonesian). Participants in this study were divided into two groups, depending on whether they learned a second language (L2) early in life before the age of three years[1] and were labelled *early multilinguals*, or after the age of nine and were called *late multilinguals*. All the participants in this study had learned a third language (L3) after the age of nine years.

The researchers found that, in both early and late multilinguals, the brain areas that are commonly involved in sentence processing were activated (Wattendorf et al.

---

1. The age of three was defined as a benchmark due to the belief that bilinguals can already master basic language skills in two languages at this age, and that by three the underlying cognitive functions are mature (Meisel 2008). Other authors define multilinguals as early by age four and late after age ten (such as Perani et al. 1998).

2014: 57). That being said, comparison of the groups of early and late multilinguals revealed during the tests that early multilinguals and late multilinguals had higher neuronal activity in different areas: *early* in the prefrontal and cortical areas, and *late* in the left posterior superior temporal gyrus (pSTG) (Wattendorf et al. 2014: 59–60). In contrast to late multilinguals, early multilinguals displayed significantly higher neuronal activity in certain areas of the brain, but this happened only during the processing of the early acquired languages (L1 and L2) (Wattendorf et al. 2014: 55).

The researchers suggested that early language experience has a pervasive influence into adulthood and that the engagement of language control in adult early multilinguals appears to be influenced by the specific learning and acquisition conditions during early childhood (on early childhood conditions see the section on trilingual families in the next chapter).

Age and additional language acquisition

Language development does not end in early age or even in midlife. It is a life-long process, which goes through periods of acceleration or backward development or halts. It is normal for some of the multilinguals' languages to be used more intensively during certain periods of their life while others go to the back burner. Travel, long stays and residence in another country bring various languages to the forefront.

If individuals do not become multilingual in their early years, they might do so later in life, both at school and in informal settings. Muñoz and Singleton (2019: 223), summarising many years of research on age and multilingualism, assert that '[i]n the appropriate conditions [...] learners of all ages may become successful multilingual individuals'. The learning environment, personal cognitive abilities, attitude and motivation are among the crucial factors here. The effect of age on language acquisition varies according to the particular learning context, individuals' capabilities, aptitude and goals in additional language mastery. Researchers note that an early start in language is justified under sufficient exposure to the target language. In another kind of setting, such as those typical of foreign-language learning situations where input is limited, older beginners were found to be more efficient learners. The proficiency of older learners and those who started learning their additional language earlier was compared when they were at the same age. The former were reported to catch up with those who started young, despite having had fewer hours of instruction.

The impact of multilingualism in situations of healthy ageing and disease

As multilinguals age, they, like all other people, experience physical changes. Vision, hearing, memory, learning and verbal knowledge, especially word retrieval, may decline. Cognitive science does not see language as a separate skill or capacity in our cognitive system. Kees de Bot and Sinfree Makoni (2005), who investigated the relationship between language and ageing, pointed out that ageing is an overall process touching the whole person physically, cognitively and emotionally. Researchers emphasise high individual variation in age-related changes; age impacts the human body and cognition in different ways for different individuals (Oxford 2018).

Cognitive reserve

Fortunately, the human brain has an ability to maintain cognitive functions despite lesions or insults. This phenomenon is known as *cognitive reserve*. Cognitive reserve represents the brain's resilience, and this is very helpful as cognition is expected to be damaged due to ageing or accidents that cause decline of the neural structure. In practice, individuals with higher brain reserve can continue to live their lives normally and still function adequately, even in the face of brain atrophy and increasing damage.

An illustrative example of cognitive reserve in action is the story of Sister Mary from the so-called 'nun' study (Snowdon 1997). We can appreciate the gap between the neuropathological damage to and behavioural resilience of Sister Mary's mind in the description of the case by de Bot and Makoni (2005: 57):

> She became a trained teacher in the course of her career and was teaching full time till she was 77 and part time till she was 84. After her retirement she remained active in the community. She died at the age of 101.7 years. She had had her last functional assessment just eight months prior to her death and was assessed as being cognitively intact (27 out of 30 on the MMSE [Mini-Mental State Examination]). Post-mortem analysis of her brain showed abundant neurofibrillary tangles and senile plaques, which are normally associated with dementia. In that sense she was a good example of the possible compensatory mechanism of linguistic ability for brain damage.

More languages naturally provide more communication opportunities, and with age, individuals who use three and more languages tend to accumulate a wide variety of experiences, including life-long experience in language learning. While the extent of the input of language learning is not yet disentangled from the various types of life experiences that are believed to lead cumulatively to strengthening of cognitive reserve, it is undoubtedly significant. In addition to the acquisition of languages, the activities that are considered to enhance the cognitive reserve include higher education, engagement in intellectually stimulating leisure activities and physical exercise, occupational status and a dense social network (Scarmeas and Stern, 2003; Freedman et al. 2014; Colcombe and Kramer 2003).

The *impact of the number of languages* known to a person was found to matter in terms of delaying the onset of dementia symptoms. Howard Chertkow and his colleagues (2010) put the kernel of their findings right into the title of their article: 'Multilingualism (but not always bilingualism) delays the onset of Alzheimer disease'. The results show that speaking two languages may delay the onset of dementia only in immigrants, while an overall protective effect requires proficiency in at least three or four languages. Another team of neuroscientists conducting a collaborative investigation involving speakers of twenty-one to twenty-five first languages in Canada and India reported the remarkable impact of the number of languages spoken on the delay of onset of dementia in the following way: 'Monolinguals were diagnosed 5 years earlier than bilinguals, 6.4 earlier than trilinguals and 9.5 years earlier than those speaking four and more languages' (Freedman et al. 2014: 12). The researchers also discovered that those who spoke four or more languages were diagnosed at a significantly older age than those who spoke one or two languages.

Along with the tangible general positive effect of knowing more languages, multilingualism alone is insufficient to guarantee the postponement of dementia. Being an immigrant or a resident also makes a difference in the onset of brain deterioration, depending on the particular context and languages. In immigrant populations in both of the countries they studied, the protective effect of bi-/multilingualism was less expressed (Freedman et al. 2014: 11). Other findings from this study also included the fact that the protective effect of bilingualism was not found in native-born Canadians who spoke English, whereas French speakers in the Canadian monolinguals' sample were diagnosed 5.3 years earlier than the English speakers (Freedman et al. 2014: 12).

The study by Kavé et al. (2008) was devoted to the effect of multilingualism on the cognitive state of the 'oldest old'. The data drawn from a representative sample of the Israeli Jewish population with a mean age of 83.0 years demonstrated that cognitive state differed significantly among the groups of self-reported bilingual, trilingual and multilingual individuals. Interestingly,

> [t]hose who reported being most fluent in a language other than their mother tongue scored higher on average than did those whose mother tongue was their best language, but the effect of number of languages on the cognitive state was significant in both groups, with no significant interaction. (Kavé et al. 2008: 70)

The researchers believe that the number of languages a person masters throughout their lifespan constitutes a facet of their cognitive reserve. Multilingualism is thus considered to be a source of *neuroplasticity*, the brain's adaptation to life experiences.

Summary

This chapter is devoted to multilingual individuals: those who acquire and use three or more languages. Tri-multilinguals are similar to, but also significantly different from, bilinguals in a number of ways. Ordinary daily observations, experiences and research reveal special features of multilinguals, characteristic of their linguistic behaviour, language acquisition and ways of communication.

Tri-multilinguals do not simply use or acquire 'one more' language, as it might seem. A multilingual identity is far from being a mere sum of three or more monolinguals contained in one body. The chapter has shown that the additional language transforms the person significantly, to the extent that s/he acquires so-called 'emergent' features that are not present in a monolingual or bilingual. The unique characteristics of users of multiple languages, speakers and listeners, in their own right, do not make them 'better' than others. Instead, they allow multilinguals to display cognitive and linguistic behaviours specific only to people using three or more languages.

Multilingual individuals are remarkably diverse. 'Early' and 'late', 'balanced' and 'unbalanced' multilinguals, 'switchers' and 'non-switchers' are only some of the categories. In this chapter, we have provided an overview of a variety of multilinguals on the basis of their age, abilities and living conditions.

We also referred here to the distinctive features of multilingual individuals in cognition, and employment of skills in each of their languages, language modes and cross-linguistic interactions. Multilinguals in general possess distinct abilities and can perform functions that either are not performed by mono- and even bilinguals, or are performed to a different extent. For example, they were found to diverge from mono- and bilinguals in cognitive processing, particularly in control mechanisms. Recent studies of older populations empowered by advanced imaging technologies have demonstrated that the number of languages known to a person influences their later life and can delay the onset of dementia.

Overall, the data on multilingual individuals from psycholinguistic, neurolinguistic and applied linguistics research testifies to high individual variation in language behaviours, communication and the neurological presentation of languages and their functioning. Being multilingual appears to be generally beneficial across all ages in terms of widening the horizons, sharpening metalinguistic awareness and strengthening cognitive reserve in older age and brain damage.

Further reading

Andrews, Edna (2014), *Neuroscience and Multilingualism*, Cambridge: Cambridge University Press, pp. 68–102 (Chapter 3, 'Neuroscience applications to the study of multilingualism').

Muñoz, Carmen and David Singleton (2011), 'A critical review of age-related research on L2 ultimate attainment', *Language Teaching*, 44(1), pp. 1–35.

Chapter review

Fill in the table by (1) using material from the chapter, and (2) giving your own examples and reflections.

Concept/keyword	Definition or explanation	Example from the chapter	Your own example	Your considerations and comments
Multilingual				
Individual multilingualism				
Language mode				
Multicompetence				
Brain reserve				
Switching costs				
Cross-linguistic interaction (CLI)				
Proficiency				
Early and late multilinguals				
Functional capability				

Individual level: psycholinguistic and cognitive

> **Reflective questions**

1. Who are the multilinguals? Provide your own definition and give examples.
2. What are the special features of multilinguals that distinguish them from monolingual and bilingual language users?
3. What is special in the learning behaviour of multilingual individuals?
4. Which criteria would you use to classify multilinguals? Do you expect the list of criteria for multilinguals to be more extended than that for bilinguals? Why?
5. What is the current focus of interest in cross-linguistic influences? Why is looking at L1–L2 interaction alone not enough?
6. List and describe the triggers for cross-linguistic transfer.
7. What is the role of proficiency in linguistic transfer and recovery from a brain damage incident?
8. How is age associated with becoming a successful multilingual individual?
9. How important is the number of languages known to a person?

> **Exercises**

Exercise 8.1

Speak or write about the implications of distinguishing between bilinguals and multilinguals in research, education and language learning. Discuss your ideas with your coursemates.

Exercise 8.2

Discuss the unique features of multilinguals. Can you think of additional special characteristics of multilingual individuals?

Exercise 8.3

Visualise the unique features of multilinguals in any way you find appropriate: a drawing, photo/photos, collage or three-dimensional craft object.

Exercise 8.4

Represent your ideas on the implications of distinguishing between bilinguals and multilinguals in research, education or language learning on a poster or e-poster.

Exercise 8.5

Organise an exhibition of visualisations representing multilinguals. The exhibition, whether real or virtual, can include pictures, collage, patchwork, installations or other representation. Supply each item with a label containing a title and a concise description.

9 Individual multilingualism: social dimensions

Social factors, such as policies, educational affordances and community perceptions of what is normative and what is outside the norm, underlie individual multilingualism. Social assumptions lie behind our self-image and influence how we present ourselves to the world, our individual choices and the outcomes of multilingual life journeys. Despite the distinctive features and behaviours characterising them, multilinguals are far from being a homogenous group. This chapter starts with the description of multilinguality, the identity of multilinguals as it is shaped by social reality and seen though academic discourse. Then it proceeds to a discussion of some salient categories of multilingual individuals and traces ways of becoming multilinguals in a family and in society.

9.1 Multilinguality – the identity of a multilingual

9.1.1 Expansion of the identity concept

The twentieth century and especially recent decades witnessed a substantial rethinking of what identity is. If we cast a glance back in time – to the medieval world, for example – we see that individuals were mostly defined by the race, ethnicity, religion, profession, gender and class they belonged to, and people did not see themselves as independent from society. Everyone was a member of a community with a fixed role to play as part of a group. Awareness of individuality and of personal freedom, as understood today, came much later.

Modern global tendencies brought with them a focus on personal identity as consisting of multiple facets, each of them important and worthy of attention. Today, in addition to a person's family role, his/her other characteristics, including professional, economic and leisure interests, formerly considered unworthy of public and academic attention, have come under the spotlight. Accordingly, current interest in multilingual identity includes not only linguistic skills, but also, necessarily, the cognitive, psychological, cultural and physical resources that are tightly knotted together in multilinguals' lives.

One more novelty in understanding identity is the recognition of change in social norms, whether in terms of worldview, religion, behaviour or appearance. Interest in the unconventional and non-traditional is also a sign of our times. In multilingualism, too, groupings and individuals that used to be categorised as peripheral and non-central, in various senses, and whose needs were disregarded, started to be identified as requiring public and academic attention. The novel dimensions of identity that have a particular bearing on multilingualism are opening out into the realm of technology and into the physical environment: body and setting, including things, events and spaces.

Technological impact on multilingual identity

A technological revolution has drastically changed our life. Constantly upgraded and ever more sophisticated communication devices, information and communication technologies and second-generation internet, or Web 2.0, encourage collaborative interactive networking. Some artificial intelligence (AI) features are already being implemented as part of a Web 3.0, currently in development, such as smart home appliances using wireless networks and the internet of things (IoT). All these expand the range of personal options for acquiring information and connecting with people: first of all in English, and increasingly in other languages.

A transformation of linguistic practices has taken place in several directions: in terms of a boost in communication and information opportunities, and of learning and maintaining languages. Belonging to a variety of groups and communities across time and space has become a norm of current life for many. Languages have become available for learning with the appearance of online linguistic resources such as thesauri or multilingual dictionaries, and sites and applications to support language learning, and an e-learning environment for studying several languages. Digital infrastructures are increasingly being developed that deal with minority languages, aiming to document the lexicons of endangered and less-resourced languages and to provide linguistic tools for maintenance, acquisition or improvement of skills in these tongues. Thus one's identity can be enriched by learning, or at least knowing more, about one's heritage language. With much more multilingual input, technology makes stimulating interactions possible for multilingual identities. This does not mean that all these technology-related changes bring only positive results for an individual. Kramsch (2014) juxtaposes positive and allegedly negative impacts of technology. The latter include a multiplicity of identities blurring oral and literary genres (such as email, Skype and blogs). She feels '[t]he very technology that promised to give all learners access to any foreign culture and its members is exacting its own price: shallow surfing of diversity instead of deep exploration of difference' (Kramsch 2014: 46).

Things and activities that were unimaginable to earlier generations have prompted some scholars to suggest that we have mutated into 'informatic' beings (Tofts 2003), and that the nature of contemporary humans has altered from that of people from classical antiquity, the Renaissance and the Enlightenment, who lived in an era prior to this hi-tech advance. Tofts explains:

> The intimacy of the human–computer interface, as intuitive to quotidian experience as speaking and writing, has meant that it is largely irrelevant to distinguish technology from the social and cultural business of being human. At a deeper, metaphysical level, this intimacy with the virtual space of the network, which extends our ability to be present elsewhere, to be here and there at the same time, has altered some of the defining parameters of human nature. (Tofts 2003: 3)

Whether we agree with this view or see it as a bit of a reach, one thing is clear: technology-induced modifications in contemporary human life impact multilinguals by making them dependent on particular conditions for languages that are available or not available on the internet,[1] but undeniably expand and enrich their identity as well.

Multimodal dimensions of multilingual identity

In other spheres of human existence beyond the technological, a number of intriguing new facts showing manifold dimensions of identity have been discovered. Cognitive studies and anthropology, substantiated by interdisciplinary studies in cultural neuroscience, neurophilosophy and neuroarchaeology, have evidenced the *indissoluble connection of cognition, body and material world*. This novel understanding of human nature underlines multilateral relationships between the human brain, body and culture, and deliberates on the inseparability of thought, action and material things (see, for example, Wolfe 2014; Neidich 2014; Malafouris 2009, 2013; Capra and Luisi 2014).

In 1998, philosophers Andy Clark and David Chalmers offered their answer to the question 'where does the mind stop and the rest of the world begin?' They claimed that cognition is not limited only to the brain. According to them, environment plays an active role in driving cognitive processes, and things serve as cognitive extensions of the human body: the 'human organism is linked with an external entity in a two-way interaction, creating a coupled system that can be seen as a cognitive system in its own right' (Clark and Chalmers 1998: 11).

Under 'external entities' we list communities, milieu and places, including urban and rural spaces and material culture. External symbols, a kind of extended memory record, allow humans, unlike other creatures, to support cognitive profiles called 'exograms'. They are complementary to the brain's memory traces, internal symbols called 'engrams' (Donald 1993: 745). John Sutton maintains that 'external elements may play a role different from, but complementary to, the inner ones' (2010: 205), and Lambros Malafouris, in his book *How Things Shape the Mind* (2013), shows how things have become cognitive extensions of the human body.

Thus, the margins of identity expand from the brain and 'soul' to the body and the environment of the multilingual. The implications of this spill into day-to-day life and communication of various kinds, and into language teaching and language policies. The feature of 'affective understanding' that many things possess is conducive to mutual understanding and cooperation, and better organising social spaces, and is only one among many repercussions of our awareness of the expansion of multilinguals' identity.

Multilinguals exist in a wider and richer environment than ever before, both real and virtual. Their world includes diverse people with their languages, social conventions and rules, their culture and their historical past, all of which together make

---

1. For example, texting, in languages that do not yet have programming support, which takes place using Latin/English script, or the availability of autocorrect programs, text recognition and predictive text functions at a later date than for internationally more dominant languages (Bedjis and Maaß 2017).

up the colourful and rich context for one's life. We can conclude that the most recent findings have shown that the identity of multilinguals has many more facets and deeper interrelations with the surrounding world than was thought before. For that reason, the multilingual individual has to be viewed from a more comprehensive and complex perspective, and more factors have to be taken into consideration – all of them together, in concert.

9.1.2 Multilinguality

The term *multilinguality* has two shades of meaning: one refers to the simple fact of being multilingual; the other conveys a wider sense of what it means to be a learner and user of three or more languages. Each multilingual can be described by their own multilinguality. Multilinguality is the intrinsic characteristic of a multilingual, an identity largely, but not entirely, defined by their languages.

The term is an extension of the terminological refinement derived from the works of Hamers and Blanc ([1989] 2000), who distinguished between bilingualism as an individual attribute – for which they coined the term *bilinguality* – and societal bilingualism – for which they retained the term bilingualism. Along the same lines, Aronin and Ó Laoire (2004) proposed the term *multilinguality* in distinction to '*multilingualism*' as a societal phenomenon and as a characteristic of multilinguals, different from *bilinguality* and from the kind of identity that is typical of monolinguals. Their definition of multilinguality included mastery of several languages 'at any level of proficiency, including partial competence and incomplete fluency, as well as metalinguistic awareness, learning strategies and opinions, preferences and passive or active knowledge on languages, language use and language learning/acquisition' (Aronin and Ó Laoire 2004: 17–18).

Beyond the fact that a person knows, uses or is in the process of acquiring more than two languages, the concept of multilinguality necessarily includes *everything that causes and accompanies* that knowledge and these acquisition processes. The notion of multilinguality also embraces *everything that results from* using and learning several languages, both in the present and in the future as a potentiality.

Language constitutes one of the most defining attributes of an individual's identity because human language incessantly provides informational, cognitive and emotional input, and through this input transforms a person each minute. The impact of a language is not one-time or only present-time; it begins from the first days of life and continues steadily during the life course through education, encounters and activities. Therefore, the core of multilinguality is an individual set of active languages complemented by dormant or unused languages of a linguistic repertoire. Around them, metalinguistic awareness, learning strategies and opinions, preferences and further language acquisition, as well as the entire life path, develop.

That being said, multilinguality is far from being a purely linguistic characteristic of an individual; it is more than one's 'linguistic identity'. Multilinguality incorporates various other human aspects or dimensions, which may be physiological and psychological (such as physiological abilities of articulation, age, gender, memory, personality type), educational (such as studying in a multilingual school or university, taking language courses, acquiring an additional language in another country), economic (having a status or job where mastery of an additional language or languages is required) and social (social ties and influences, reference groups). These facets interact and combine to shape one's multilinguality at any given period of one's life. Incoming influences constantly modify personal multilingualities. These include, among other things, the idiosyncrasies and peculiarities of the communicator, individual specificities, such as physical abilities of articulation, or use of an alternative means of communication, or particular perfect or partial skills (see Section 9.3 on polyglots and exceptional multilinguals in this chapter). Therefore, we can say that multilinguality is brought into being by an interplay of social and personal factors, and displays itself through the physical, cognitive, cultural and social qualities and characteristics of an individual (Aronin and Ó Laoire 2001). This remarkable interplay between multiple facets of identity renders multilinguality a whole, not divided or separated into distinct subidentities.

Each person's multilinguality is shaped as special by legacies of historical events and family history, embedded assumptions, and social opportunities that one can foresee and perceive as plausible or real. As such, multilinguality is very personal and transpires through particular linguistic and cognitive behaviour, career choices, social opportunities and lifestyles.

Multilinguality is dynamic. The circumstances of one's life – growing up in a trilingual family where family members speak three different languages to a child, studying in another country, being in the company of speakers of one of their languages – form and frame multilinguality through constant flow and change. Often, being members of several discourse communities, multilinguals share their values and assumptions to a differing extent, mixing them in a variety of ways. The range of accompanying emotions and affective states rises and fades, stimulated and modified by languages – and by events carried out through languages.

In theoretical terms, the concept of multilinguality belongs to a holistic ecological perspective (see more on methodologies and research perspectives in Chapter 11). In Figure 9.1, multilinguality is represented by Danuta Gabryś-Barker as an ecosystem. From such a perspective, multilinguality is a psychological notion, in that it describes an individual. It also relates to sociolinguistic enquiry as it points to the social status, opportunities and involvement of an individual. Investigating multilinguality, one has to regard the social milieu as an important influence, and consider the societal consequences of language learning and use. Summarising the description of multilinguality, we define it as an individual characteristic, based on one's linguistic assets, enabled by abilities, developed by experience, and expressed through actions, perceptions, attitudes and personal life scenarios, both real and possible.

9.2 Trajectories of becoming multilingual

9.2.1 Simultaneous and successive patterns of acquisition

Like bilinguals, multilinguals can acquire their languages either simultaneously (at the same time) or successively (one after another). *Simultaneous* and *successive multilingualism* are bred in a family and often guided by parents. Would-be multilinguals

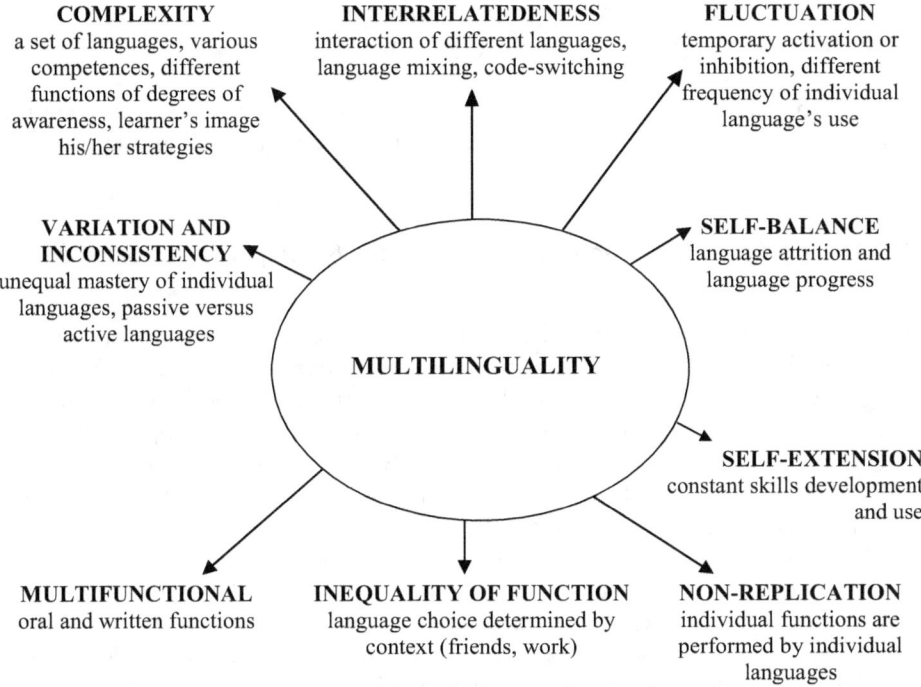

Figure 9.1 Multilinguality as an ecosystem (Gabryś-Barker 2005: 35, reproduced with permission).

have an extensive choice of scenarios to master their languages. If a bilingual can either acquire both languages together, or learn them one after the other, a child for whom three or more languages are available in his/her close milieu can start with three languages simultaneously; learn L1 first, adding L2+L3 later; or, on the contrary, commence language acquisition with two languages simultaneously and complete the learning with L3. And these are not all the possibilities. An important variable for any pattern of language acquisition is the age of acquisition (AoA).

9.2.2 Hoffmann's typology of trilinguals

In 2001, Hoffmann offered a typology of trilinguals, based on the circumstances and the social context in which children become users of three languages. The following five groups of multilinguals were singled out:

1. trilingual children who are brought up with two home languages which are different from the one spoken in the wider community
2. children who grow up in a bilingual community and whose home language (either that of one or that of both parents) is different from the community languages
3. third language learners: that is, bilinguals who acquire a third language in the school context

4. bilinguals who have become trilingual through immigration
5. members of trilingual communities.(Hoffmann 2001a)

Apart from social conditions for individual tri- and multilingualism (in a country and a community), family is one more decisive factor in producing multilingual individuals.

9.2.3 Becoming or not becoming multilingual: challenges and choices of multilingual families

It is clear from the above that family language provisions are important for children's linguistic future. One may assume that once the parents have three or more languages available in a family, they easily pass on all these languages to their children. However, contrary to popular assumptions, it transpires that the opportunities that are present both in wider society and in a family, and that allow children to become trilinguals, do not always lead to a child actually becoming trilingual. In fact, not all children growing up in trilingual families become tri-multilinguals; rather, many of them are ushered into their lives as bilinguals or monolinguals.

Why does this happen? Suzanne Barron-Hauwaert (2003, 2004) researched bilingual and then trilingual families from different parts of the world. She points out that 'The world of the trilingual family is similar, yet different to the bilingual family. The languages cannot be equal and have more of a link to a particular place and time, such as school or activities' (2004: 156). Andreas Braun and Tony Cline (2014), who studied trilingual families in England and Germany, have explained the complications of raising children trilingually, and outlined the conditions under which attaining this aim becomes more likely. Their research shows that family trilingualism does not come easily, and that it may be more difficult under some conditions than under others. Especially in countries that, historically, are 'mainly monolingual', such as Germany, England, Russia and Japan, parents face difficulties in maintaining three languages in a family. Due to the community language having a much stronger influence than the family languages, parents in immigrant families may drop one or two of their additional languages at home in favour of the community language. Multilingual parents are sensitive to the perceived 'low' status of heritage and home languages, and to the 'high' status of official and national languages; considerations of practicality dictate that languages such as English, French and German open doors for their children to education, employment and grant opportunities. For social and economic reasons, a native-like proficiency in these languages is often desired. Add to this the mundane but powerful fact that maintaining three languages in a family represents quite an effort, and we understand why parents might give priority to only one language, or at most two, thus sacrificing home languages. Braun and Cline (2014: 91) reported that only 5 out of the 70 trilingual families that were interviewed in their study attempted to maintain three languages in their family and used three languages with their children equally. The choice not to develop the potential of their family's additional languages is legitimate and is a matter for each family.

Other parents in Braun and Cline's (2014) study used a variety of strategies to ensure that their children continued to develop trilingually, in spite of the obstacles.

Trilingual families that insist on maintaining their languages are faced with the need to design a working and reasonable family language strategy. While the mother and father in a bilingual family may use a 'one parent – one language' (OPOL) strategy,[2] which is known to be quite successful, parents of a trilingual family are not as conveniently placed to fit three languages into their daily routine. The language input distribution becomes a challenge, as it requires careful planning and the involvement of extended family members, friends and community.

Grandparents play a decisive role in maintaining additional languages in a family. In Braun and Cline's study, when grandparents spoke a community language – say, English in England – they could communicate in it with their grandchildren. In this case, the chance to maintain additional languages in the family and raise new multilinguals diminished. The study showed that, in order to raise a child trilingually in a mostly monolingual community, parents and children have to put in a significant effort and hard work to keep up a deliberate language maintenance strategy. Braun and Cline advise parents to seek additional support by way of enrolling a child in an international or multilingual school, or by employing a nanny. However, for a child born into a community in which the use of several languages is so widespread that it is perceived as natural and normal, the chances that they become a tri-multilingual are higher than in a mainly monolingual society. Still, in such settings too, it is important for parents to make informed choices.

9.3 Various categories of multilinguals

9.3.1 Polyglots

Polyglots, or 'super-linguists' as they used to be called, traditionally attract curiosity. Polyglots can be defined as individuals who prominently speak more languages than others, even more than 'average' multilinguals. Throughout history, the exact number of languages that makes a person a polyglot in the eyes of others has been variously defined as six-plus or eleven-plus, but outstanding multilinguals are believed to have enjoyed high proficiency in many more languages than that. Many polyglots known to us were royals and rulers, perhaps because their lives and attainments were closely watched and often noted in writing. The annals of history bring us the names of Mithridates, King of Pontus, who is said to have been a fluent speaker of the languages of all the twenty-five nationalities of his vast empire (Russell 1863: 9). Aulus Gellius (as quoted in Russell 1863: 10) testifies that the King practised communicating 'with each and every' of his subjects in person and directly without interpreters, 'with as much correctness as if it were his native dialect'. Lady sovereigns, such as Cleopatra, Zenobia and Christina of Sweden, have also distinguished themselves in languages. Cleopatra's extraordinary attainments included speaking Ethiopian, the language of the Troglodytes (probably a dialect of Coptic), the languages of the Medes and the Syrians, and also Hebrew and Arabic; in addition, she was said to have understood many more.

---

2. OPOL – 'one parent - one language' – is a strategy for raising children bilingually. It requires each parent to speak just one language with the child.

In the late medieval period, reviving intellectual activity and historical events gave a new impulse to the study of languages. We know of Frederic II, who was fluent in Latin, Greek, Italian, German, Hebrew and Arabic; Ibn Wasil, an ambassador to Manfred, the son of Frederic II, who lived in Italy in 1250 and was familiar with the Western Tongues; and the learned Rabbi Maimonides of Cordova, at the beginning of the twelfth century, who, in addition to mastering many Eastern tongues, 'was also thoroughly familiar with the Greek language' (Russell 1863). At the Carolingian court of Charlemagne served Alcuin, an English scholar, clergyman, poet and teacher; in addition to the modern languages which he must have picked up in various kingdoms during his expeditions with the Emperor, he was also familiar with Latin, Greek, Hebrew and Arabic.

As an example of remarkable proficiency recorded in historical documents, Russell (1863: 16) relates the story of Roderigo Ximenes, Archbishop of Toledo:

> An example of, for the period, very remarkable proficiency in modern languages is recorded in the history of the Fourth Lateran Council, 1215. Roderigo Ximenes, Archbishop of Toledo in the early part of the thirteenth century, a native of Navarre, but a scholar of the University of Paris, was one of the representatives of the Spanish Church at that Council. Ximenes addressed to the Council a long Latin oration in defence of the claim of Toledo; and, as many of his auditory, which consisted both of the clergy and the laity, were ignorant of that language, he repeated the same argument in a series of discourses addressed to the natives of each county in succession; to the Romans, Germans, French, English, Navarrese, and Spaniards, each in their respective tongues. Thus the number of languages in which he spoke was at least seven, and it is highly probable that he had others at his disposal, if his auditory had been of such a nature as to render them necessary.

We know less of commoners who were super-multilinguals in the past. Russell labelled commoners known to have linguistic talent as 'uneducated linguists'. These people, among whom were dragomans or interpreters, couriers and servants, acquired their outstanding language skills in fluent communication in several languages by various means. Two remarkable examples which we find in Russell's book (1863: 21) are a *valet-de-place* described by the Austrian General Baron von Zach (1747–1826), who, being ignorant of the grammar of his own language, could speak nearly all the European languages with the greatest ease and correctness. Another celebrated commoner was a dragoman who lived on the island of Corfu in the first part of the sixteenth century and was known by the name of Genus Bey. The fascinating story of his life includes being carried away by pirates and then sold as a slave in Constantinople. His trajectory brought him to Egypt, Syria and other Eastern countries, where he acquired proficiency in multiple languages, both those of the East and those of the West. When Genus Bey was finally noticed by Suleiman the Magnificent, the Sultan appointed him his First Dragoman, with the rank of Pasha. Contemporaries and historians described this distinguished polyglot as an extraordinary man, who 'knew perfectly no fewer than sixteen languages, viz: Greek, both ancient and modern, Hebrew, Arabic, Persian, Turkish, Moorish, Tartar, Armenian, Russian, Hungarian, Polish, Italian, Spanish, German, and French', and was 'the first man of his day for speaking divers sorts of languages, and of the happiest memory under the Heavens' (Russell 1863: 19).

But the most celebrated person whose outstanding linguistic skills were tested multiple times and marvelled at by his colleagues, visitors and those who just happened to meet him, and who still attracts special attention in our own times (Russell 1863; Watts 1859; Erard 2012), is Cardinal Giuseppe Caspar Mezzofanti (1744–1849). The abilities of this legendary polyglot were 'so immeasurably above even the highest of these names in the department of language, that, at least for the purposes of comparison with him, its minor celebrities can possess little claim for consideration' (Russell 1863: 121).

According to various accounts, Mezzofanti, a citizen of Bologna, mastered and variously used between thirty-eight and fifty-eight languages, among them Greek, Latin, Spanish, Hebrew, Arabic, French, German and Swedish. He acquired, in his school and later years, Magyar, Bohemian or Czechish, Polish and even 'the Gypsy dialect', mastered in the years of the military campaigns that were fought between 1796 and 1799 (Russell 1863: 154). Working in public hospitals and attending the poor and sick in their homes, Mezzofanti learned the tongues and dialects of those he met. In this way, Flemish, the Sardinian dialect, Persian, Turkish, the Cornish dialect, Welsh, Armenian and languages of Western Africa, as well as the Algonquin he knew best, were added. In Angolese, for example, he composed pieces for recitation at the academic exhibition of the Epiphany more than once.

No doubt Mezzofanti's extraordinary gift was conferred on him by his personal abilities and enhanced by his life circumstances, but these alone do not fully account for his outstanding polyglotism. He devoted a great deal of time to learning languages, sometimes in ways that most people would find extremely boring. He took every opportunity to talk with native speakers, and to translate, read and consider languages. Michael Erard, a linguist and journalist who undertook an investigation of past and present polyglots when visiting the library in Bologna where Mezzofanti used to work, found stacks of flashcards in many languages, most of them written in the Cardinal's own hand (2012).

Erard also tracked some other outstanding contemporary polyglot individuals. Among them is Erik Gunnemark, who was remarkable for his ability to translate from forty-seven languages, and was said to need dictionaries for only twenty of them. Another polyglot in our own time is Alexander Arguelles from Berkeley, of whom Erard writes that he learns and maintains multiple languages by 'subjecting himself to an unforgiving schedule, keeping spreadsheets that record the hours and minutes he spends on each one'. Erard (2012) sets out the number of hours dedicated by Arguelles to his native language and to the other fifty languages he has targeted:

> Of 4,454 hours of language study Arguelles did over a period of 456 days, he spent 456 hours on his native language, English, and also 456 on Arabic, and then a descending number of hours on the remaining 50 languages on his spreadsheet.

Only a few of these historical and contemporary multilinguals have extraordinary abilities (Edwards 2019: 147). Most of their outstanding success in learning languages comes from the following features, which are shared by many: memory – if not excellent, then at least simply good; systematisation and organisation of learning, coupled with determined – sometimes close to obsessive or compulsive – persistence and tenacity; and frequent and continuous work. These examples of outstanding polyglots reveal that there is no magic or superhuman ability behind their stunning results; rather, their success rests on hard work every day, and on tedious or dull practices where as much time and energy as possible are invested with skill to fit this routine into their daily life, and where enthusiasm and strong motivation are key.

9.3.2 Other exceptional multilinguals

More categories exist of language users who excel 'in the language department' (in Russell's terms). They are either assisted by their outstanding nature or encouraged in the daily use of several languages and communication codes by their life circumstances. In the following section, we will refer to so-called 'savants' and to people who are deaf or hard of hearing.

'Savants'

The word 'savant' comes from French and means 'learned person'.[3] The currently used label 'autistic savant' was introduced by Dr Bernard Rimland in 1978 to refer to an individual affected with a neurodevelopmental disorder, mostly on the autism spectrum, who, alongside the significant challenges that the disorder brings, displays extraordinary skills in one specialised field. Contrary to popular belief, not all autistic individuals are blessed with outstanding abilities; savants constitute about 10 per cent (Treffert 2009). Savants may have a very low IQ, and problems with saying the most basic sentences, tying their shoes, working out the change in a monetary transaction, or driving. They appear to live in their own world and have difficulty in forming relationships with others. These challenges may considerably limit the chances of autistic savants to live independently, but along with that, or despite that, 'savants' have an 'island of genius' which 'stands in marked, incongruous contrast to the overall handicap' (Treffert 2009: 1351). Savants may demonstrate extreme abilities in music, complex mental calculations at a great speed, art or language' and for this reason are sometimes called 'handi-capable'.

Among the prodigies of this kind who are alive today is Daniel Tammet (born in 1979), a 'high-functioning' autistic savant and a Fellow of Great Britain's Royal Society of Arts (elected in 2012). Tammet knows ten languages and perceives words and numbers as shapes and colours. He is the author of several international bestsellers, one of which, *Born on a Blue Day*, has been translated into twenty-four languages.

The skills at which savants excel are generally related to memory. Due to the proneness of 'savants' to repetitive behaviour, task repetition and practice, such traits as memory, repetition and inclination to orderliness make them similar to polyglots and this can explain their linguistic skills.

---

3. See, for example, <https://www.merriam-webster.com/dictionary/savant> (last accessed 17 August 2021).

Deaf and hard-of-hearing language users
A description of unique multilinguals would not be complete without mentioning deaf and hard-of-hearing language users.

Contemporary life encourages deaf and hard-of-hearing individuals to use not one – and often not just two – but several language codes. In their early years, deaf children may be confronted with various home sign systems, sign languages and manual sign codes, such as Manually Coded English (MCE) or Sign-Supported English (SSE), and are exposed to highly variable linguistic input via their hearing and deaf peers, parents, neighbours and teachers. Hearing parents, siblings and other family members, as well as teachers, often study sign languages in addition to the auditory ones that they normally use. When a more dominant or acknowledged sign language is taught at school, then a child may be bilingual in two sign languages. In addition to the variety of sign language that is in use at their school, workplace and location in the community or country, Deaf[4] community members make regular use of the languages used in technology and the media. Deaf people also need to be proficient in the spoken languages and acquire literacy skills in reading the languages of the country and community they live in – for example, English or Irish in Ireland to read documents, newspapers and books. Sign and spoken languages in the same community are linguistically unrelated and have different grammatical structures at their core, sometimes with a significant linguistic distance between them (see more on sign languages in Chapter 5). Thus, Deaf community members make regular use of not only natural sign languages, but also, to varying degrees, the language of the majority hearing culture in its spoken, signed and written forms – and are thus multilingual individuals.

Summary

In this chapter we underscored the societal dimensions of individual multilingualism. It is society, and its development level and discourse, that define how the public, government and science see multilingual individuals. Individual multilingualism is highly underwired socially; even investigations of individuals that might appear to have nothing to do with societal research, such as neuroscience or the identity of multilinguals, do have societal linkages and meaningful implications.

The contemporary public and academic vision of identity has expanded to embrace many aspects that were previously deemed unfit for exploration. Technologically modified environments, new mobility trajectories and super-diversity, among other things, have brought deep changes to the very nature of contemporary identity, especially a multilingual one. The identity of a multilingual is not limited to their linguistic identity, but necessarily and naturally expands to embrace social, physiological, cultural and material dimensions. Multilinguality is a concept that represents all these facets of a person. The multilinguality of each individual is unique. That being said, one may categorise multilinguals into abstract or real groupings.

---

4. As described in Chapter 5, when the word 'Deaf' is written with a capital letter, this is to signify the status of the Deaf Community as a multilingual group, like any other minority language community in its own right, and as a subculture within the majority hearing culture.

Some multilinguals are polyglots, who have mastered an extraordinary number of languages. Another category of individuals with outstanding linguistic abilities are the so-called 'savants', persons with autism or a similar condition who, at the same time, are blessed with the gift of superior linguistic ability. The Deaf normally use several language varieties, encompassing auditory, gesture and codes. Especially successful multilinguals, including polyglots and 'savants', seem to display common personality traits that include having a good memory and a propensity for insistent practice and organisation.

'Ordinary' multilinguals, who constitute a sizable portion of the world's population, undergo dynamic language-related experiences from early childhood throughout their entire lifetime. Growing up in the appropriate wider context of a country and community has been found to be conducive to the acquisition and maintenance of several languages. Early language experience, which is normally determined by family language provisions, has a powerful influence into adulthood. However, not all multilingual families realise the potential for the trilingual development of their children, for this requires not only beneficial societal settings, but also substantial effort on the part of parents and children to maintain the three languages. Scholars agree that learners of all ages may become successful multilingual learners, given the appropriate conditions.

In order to teach, treat and deal with multilinguals realistically and confidently in education, business, healthcare and other spheres, it is necessary to accept their utmost diversity and the constant change that each multilingual identity undergoes. Instead of looking for absolute rule-bound regularities in a multilingual's cognition and sociolinguistic behaviour, it is preferable to focus on general patterns of linguistic behaviour and their unique qualities and abilities.

Further reading

Braun, Andreas and Tony Cline (2014), *Language Strategies for Trilingual Families: Parents' Perspectives*, Bristol: Multilingual Matters.

Todeva, E. and J. Cenoz (2009), Multilingualism: emic and etic perspectives', in E. Todeva and J. Cenoz (eds), *The Multiple Realities of Multilingualism: Personal Narratives and Researchers' Perspectives*, Berlin: Mouton De Gruyter.

Chapter review

Fill in the table by (1) using material from the chapter, and (2) giving your own examples and reflections.

Concept/keyword	Definition or explanation	Example from the chapter	Your own example	Your considerations and comments
Individual multilingualism and society				

Contd

Concept/keyword	Definition or explanation	Example from the chapter	Your own example	Your considerations and comments
Facets of multilingual identity				
Multilinguality				
Simultaneous multilingualism				
Successive multilingualism				
Exceptional multilinguals and 'ordinary' multilinguals				
Polyglots				
'Savants' and their linguistic abilities				
The Deaf as multilingual individuals				

Reflective questions

1. How does the realisation of vast margins of identity in time and space relate to daily life? To education? To language teaching? To work in multilingual teams and organisations?
2. How can the study of polyglots and exceptional multilinguals contribute to the knowledge about individual multilingualism?
3. Which criteria would you use for classifying multilinguals?
4. Suggest (a) the possible trajectories and (b) required conditions for becoming a multilingual for children that you know and who live in different communities or countries.

Exercises

Exercise 9.1

What are the benefits and challenges of being a polyglot?

Exercise 9.2

Do you support the choice of multilingual parents not to pass on all their languages to their children? Discuss the issue from the point of view of the community and the country, and from the point of view of the individual and the family.

Exercise 9.3

Make a short video in which you describe your multilingual family and report on the strategies that have been or are used to maintain several languages.

Part V
How we experience and study multilingualism

10 The ways we experience, treat and use languages

Ordinary language users and scholars investigating societies and languages witness an enormously vibrant sociolinguistic reality. In these bustling times of glocalisation (global + local), people's identities and entire communities have changed. Accordingly, the ways that we experience, treat and use languages have altered too. Today, it is increasingly typical for the essential functions of communication, cognition and identity marking to be performed by selected sets of languages, rather than by a single language. The tasks and functions carried out by named languages restructure, reshuffle and alternate, redefining languages' appellations according to their roles and importance in novel and particular situations.

This chapter considers sociolinguistic phenomena, current understanding of which has taken shape comparatively recently. It details new developments in language practices, by referring to language repertoires, Dominant Language Constellations and translanguaging. It also exposes the current roles and corresponding nominations of languages in their various contexts, and emphasises the material culture of multilingualism as a dynamic and powerful modality contributing to the diversity and multimodality of multilingualism.

10.1 The way we treat languages – language nominations

Thousands of languages, previously spoken in limited territories, have spread around the world and made most countries conspicuously multilingual. In addition to national or official languages with fixed status in a state, various cohorts of speakers use multiple languages. Majority and minority populations variously employ languages of high standing, regionally important languages, and also languages that used to be ignored or disregarded. Many language varieties have acquired new social roles. Pidgins, dialects or so-called lesser-used languages have gained recognition and legitimacy, to various extents. All these languages perform different tasks and can be variously meaningful for different segments of the population and for different countries. Languages are now visible and 'densely' located across contemporary polities. A need has emerged to mark the role and place of each language for individuals and societies – and this is what language nominations do.

10.1.1 What are language nominations?

We are not surprised when we hear someone called 'mother', 'father', 'relative', 'director' or 'principal'. Each of us has a number of social roles, and stable terms exist that specify family and community roles. We are used to habitually categorising people in such a way. This allows us to situate a person immediately in a wider social context and communicate with him/her accordingly. Something similar happens to languages when we speak or think of them.

Special terms for languages are called *language nominations*. For example, in the phrase 'Russian is my *mother tongue*', 'mother tongue' is a language nomination. Language nominations are specific appellations which are assigned to various named languages and dialects (such as Spanish, Norwegian or Russian), according to their perceived role for particular individuals or communities. Language nominations serve as additional labels to the proper language names, and include 'official language', 'majority language', 'indigenous language' and 'immigrant languages'.

A single named language can be characterised by numerous language nominations. Consider Danish. The proper name 'Danish' is often substituted by the language nominations 'an official language' and 'a national language', describing the function that Danish carries out in Denmark. Danish is also a 'minority language' for Danish communities in Norway, Sweden, Spain, the United States, Canada, Brazil and Argentina, and a 'home language' for around 15–20 per cent of the urban population of Greenland. Another example would be French, an international language, the national language in France and an official language in Canada. English is a 'mother tongue' and a '*de facto* official language' in the United Kingdom, a 'minority language' in Malta, one of the official languages in Canada and a 'link language' in Sri Lanka. Each such additional label serves to describe precisely and to indicate the role of a particular named language for specific communities and individuals under particular circumstances.

10.1.2 How do language nominations emerge?

There are a number of ways. The most straightforward means of discovering nominations attached to particular languages in a country is to search for language nominations in state documents. The Canadian Official Languages Act (1969) made English and French the official languages of the country.

In addition, language nominations have been increasingly proposed in recent decades by sociolinguists and applied linguists to address specific practical situations, often in connection with varied issues in politics, education and healthcare. For instance, the 'heritage language' nomination was selected from a number of options by language professionals in North America in response to the upsurge of interest on the part of grandchildren of immigrants in the languages of their forebears. The term serves a practical purpose because it allows educators to develop a basic definition of a 'heritage language learner', who is different in important ways from the traditional foreign language student. 'Heritage language learner' refers to a language learner who is raised in a home where a non-English language is spoken, who speaks or at least understands the language in question, and who is to some degree bilingual in that language and in English (Wiley 2001). 'Less commonly taught languages' (LCTLs) (Kondo-Brown 2012) is a nomination for foreign and heritage languages in the context of the USA.

A number of language nominations – including 'regional language' and 'minority language' – were worked out for better management and protection of minority languages. The European Charter for Regional or Minority Languages, issued by the Council of Europe in 1992, aimed to ensure more favourable provisions concerning the status of regional or minority languages, the legal status of persons belonging to 'minorities', and recognition of the regional or minority languages as an expression of cultural wealth. This charter contains exact definitions of regional and minority languages.

Finally, there is a customary way of evolving language nominations by way of popular coinage. Such nominations as 'mother tongue', 'home language' and 'native language' carry emotional connotations and advertise the value and role currently assigned to a given language by a particular community. They traditionally bear connotations of origin, permanency and inseparable emotional ties. Conversely, the language nomination of 'foreign language' points to distance from one's way of life and culture and a usefulness for particular purposes, such as tourism or reading (Aronin and Singleton 2010; Aronin et al. 2011).

10.1.3 How expedient are language nominations?

At present, numerous nominations exist, some of which are used routinely, and others of which are put forward anew or modified by language users, researchers and official bodies across the world. Compared to earlier times, the number of language nominations has conspicuously increased in recent decades. Quite a few habitual nominations have changed their meaning and scope. An illuminating example of such a conversion is the appellation of *mother tongue*. This has ceased to be as default and straightforward as it used to be when it unquestionably referred only to one language. Currently, a noticeable number of people can claim they have two, or even more, mother tongues; others would need some time to decide which of their languages deserves such a nomination.

Still other nominations have been clarified, and their meaning has been narrowed in order to be used in specific fields of activities. For example, in education today it is important to distinguish between English as a Second Language (ESL), English as a Lingua Franca (ELF) and English as a Foreign Language (EFL). In the context of writing syllabi, courseware and textbooks, determining the number of teaching hours for a certain language at school, and selecting appropriate vocabulary and grammar (Cook 2013), each of the nominations presupposes different aims, ways of dealing with languages, and outcomes (see Chapter 4). The distinction between the *second* and the *third language* is crucial when it comes to experiment design in applied linguistics. The processes of second language acquisition (SLA) and third language acquisition (TLA) entail divergent ways of teaching and learning languages, and necessitate quite dissimilar approaches to bilingual and multilingual learners.

The heightened utility of language nominations for the daily life of language users and societies, as well as for understanding current language practices, can be appreciated from the following points:

- *Language nominations point to the functions* of languages in a community or organisation, *and by this define the boundaries of each language's use.* While an official language is used freely across a country or a state in banks and offices, schools and theatres, and is encouraged and supported in both written and oral forms, through media of all kinds, non-official languages do not fully enjoy these benefits. Other languages may have limited circulation and opportunities, which sometimes leads to social movements, such as demanding that a government grant a language or a dialect the nomination of 'official'. While disputes around a nomination being attributed to a language in a country might seem superficial, as it is only a 'label' that is in question, in reality the issue goes deeper than merely words. Language nominations do not just signify the status of a language projected on to its speakers; also at stake are financial, educational and cultural opportunities for the speakers of this language, along with ethnic revival and even political adjustments.
- The number and assortment of language nominations referring to a particular language make evident *the role and importance of this language* for a country, community, organisation, family and individual. For example, in Israel, English is not an official language *de jure* (Hebrew and Arabic are) but it is often called the country's *de facto* official language. It is also a *second language* and a *foreign language* for many, and a *mother tongue, home language* and *heritage language* for a section of its citizens, and thus is one of the *minority languages* in the country, as well as being a language of work (for foreign workers, for example) and a *language of academia*.
- Language nominations also *reflect a range of perceptions regarding languages* on the part of those who speak them, and on the part of those who may appraise or deal with languages and their speakers. The attitude to a language may change, and language nominations reflect such changes. Consider the nominations for the 'colonial' or 'received' languages, applied to English, French, Portuguese and German in the African context. They carry connotations that involve a historical, political and emotional load. Stripping English, French and German of their former official status, in some African countries, indicates the sensitivity of matters connected with languages and their status in society. *De facto* use of such languages for day-to-day communication, within states and between states, demonstrates current changes in demands and awareness of languages. Annamalai (2006) notes that the view of the English language among many Indians has gone from associating it with colonialism to associating it with economic progress, and English continues to be widely used 'until such time as all non-Hindi States had agreed to its being dropped' (Official Languages Act, 1963; as amended, 1967).
- Language nominations *formally indicate* the role of particular language *for a person* and *often convey a subjective evaluation* of a given language or a dialect. Subjectively, some Arabic language native speakers distinguish between the two diglossic varieties and define Al Fusha, the written 'formal' variety which requires formal schooling, as their second language, and Ammiya, colloquial Arabic, as their mother tongue.

How we experience, treat and use languages

- *Discussions of language nominations indicate and bring to the fore new language-related challenges facing society.* Their modifications also *disclose emerging processes in society* which might go unnoticed. For example, the debates on heritage language evidence the global trend for ethnic revival.
- The global proliferation of language nominations in numbers, and the intensiveness of their use in social practices (not just the existence of nominations), are novel phenomena. Such a development is specific to the post-modern conditions of current multilingualism. Another major recent transformation connected with languages relates to the way languages are *used*.

10.2 The way we use multiple languages: language repertoire and Dominant Language Constellations

As in the case of language nominations, the novelty associated with the use of multiple languages by individuals and by groupings does *not* lie in the fact of use in itself, rather in *how* languages are used today. The mastery and deployment of many languages are traditionally associated with the concept of *language repertoire*.

10.2.1 Language repertoires

The notion of language repertoire is based on a metaphor that underlines the idea of stock inventory and selection. 'Verbal repertoire' has been interpreted by John Gumperz (1964: 137–8) as the sum of various skills in a single language and the term has since been used by linguists 'to refer to the broad stock of speech styles, registers, varieties, and languages people know' (MacSwan 2017: 187). With the recognition of bilingualism, the concept came to include more than one language, as 'an individual's particular set of skills (or levels of proficiency) that permit him or her to function within various registers of (a) language(s)' and the 'totality of linguistic varieties shared by the group as a whole' (Schiffmann 1996: 42; Pütz 2004: 227). The current understanding of language repertoires has extended, so that they may comprise various language skills in any number of languages.

Language repertoire is an important and useful concept in sociolinguistics. It can be imagined as an asset, resource or a store of language varieties and language skills, possessed by an individual or a group. With contemporary media and technology making languages more available for learning and use, the list of potential linguistic skills and abilities grows to become theoretically unlimited and we can speak of the global extension of repertoires.

Now, how do we use our linguistic riches in daily routine? A single language is clearly insufficient for carrying out all the tasks of contemporary life. Using the *entire* language repertoire on a daily basis, with all its skills and varieties, is not plausible. Given its size and the human being's constraints in terms of time, effort and energy, language repertoire in its entirety does not serve as a linguistic 'unit of circulation'. In our day-to-day lives, we customarily employ only a portion of our language repertoire. This set of the most important languages which are predominant in an individual's daily usage is called a *Dominant Language Constellation*.

10.2.2 Dominant Language Constellations

The concept of Dominant Language Constellation (DLC) was proposed by Aronin (2006, 2016) to represent the cluster of selected languages which, functioning as a unit, perform the most vital functions of human language for an individual or for a community. For a person, a DLC is a group of his/her most expedient languages sufficient to maintain life in a multilingual environment at a particular period.

While the repertoire of multilinguals may encompass skills and registers in five, six, seven, eight or more languages, DLC contains only the active, most vital, part of one's language repertoire, typically three languages that together ensure the performance of the functions of human language. These would often be a local language, a country's official language and an international language: for example, Faroese/Danish/English in Denmark and Polish/German/English in Germany. Usually, several DLCs that are in use by particular populations in a state characterise its various inhabitants. Consider the multilingual contexts of Zambia, where seventy-two indigenous languages are spoken, seven of which have been designated official (regional) languages: Bemba, Nyanja, Lozi, Luvale, Tonga, Kaonde and Lunda (Banda 2020). Typically, Zambians speak at least four languages, with multiple and multilayered DLCs operating across individual/household, community, regional and national boundaries (Banda 2020).

DLC is a unit

The languages of the DLC cluster are not separate languages in a strict sense. The linguistic qualities and social functioning of a language are not the same when it is used in a constellation, as compared to when it is used separately in monolingual mode. Carrying out all language functions that human language is responsible for together, the languages of the DLC form one workable language unit. Therefore, a DLC is not just the sum of the languages constituting it; it is an entity that possesses characteristics beyond the sum of its parts. The interaction of three or more languages operating in concert gives DLCs their dynamism as they co-evolve in a variety of diverse contexts and times.

DLC maps

A convenient visualisation of the use of languages is possible using so-called 'DLC maps'. These show both the languages of language repertoire and those of a DLC cluster. The DLC map in Figure 10.1 gives an account of the use of languages by a typical Russian speaker in Israel.

DLC is adaptable and dynamic

In response to changing day-to-day reality, DLCs are adaptable and dynamic. Languages of the repertoire, even if long unused or dormant, may be called into service by events in individuals' lives and thus shift to a DLC. Among such socially conditioned or personal events can be migration, the start of studies, especially in another country, marriage or specific life projects provoking the need for specific languages. The opposite, when a language moves out of a DLC cluster, is possible too. The functions of a multilingual's languages can be reassigned; a growing

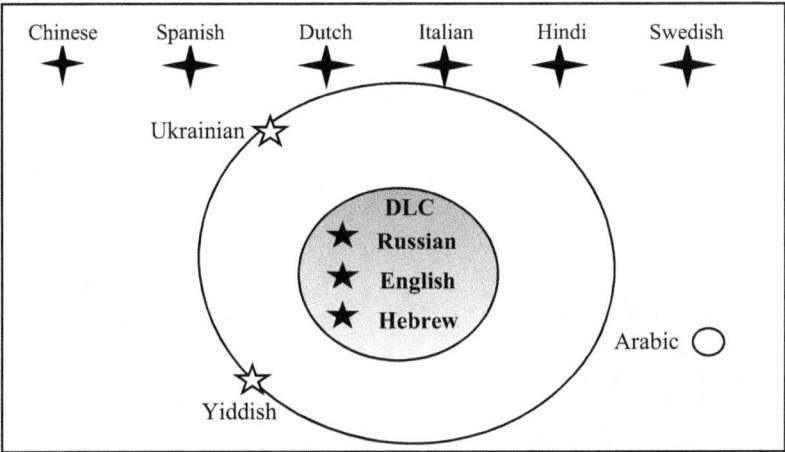

Figure 10.1 The Russian-speaking community in Israel: language repertoire and Dominant Language Constellation. Key: five-point stars show languages in the language repertoire. Circle planets denote repertoire languages of which users have weaker knowledge or which are seldom used. Four-point stars mark languages a person is exposed to in their close environment and often understands – whether as separate words and phrases, or more. This can be either a heritage language in a family or a language often heard due to social proximity, whether by wish or by circumstance.

confidence and ease in the use of one language, accompanied perhaps by less use of another language, intensive study of yet another language of one's language constellation and constant, steady use of the other – this is the natural dynamics of multilinguality.

How a DLC adapts to important personal life events is described by Sarasi Kannangara (2020). In this study, the dynamics of her personal DLC of Singhalese/English/German is demonstrated by DLC maps in varying contexts across a time span as driven by different personal aims and social environments (see Figure 10.2).

We can see how the two most important languages for Sarasi during the nursery and preschool stage – English and Singhalese – keep their importance and presence in her life over many years, but their actual use oscillates, depending on the situation and country she lives in. Compare, for example, the most recent years (Figures 10.2c and 10.2d). Singhalese occupied 40 per cent of all language use for Sarasi during her university education years, but only 5 per cent in her current (2017) life. The use of German goes up from 40 per cent to 70 per cent in recent years, and the use of English from 20 per cent to 25 per cent. As compared with early childhood (Figure 10.2a), in later life (Figures 10.2b, 10.2c and 10.2d) her linguistic repertoire grows substantially and includes Tamil, Sanskrit, French, Japanese and Hindi at varying levels of language skill.

Languages of a DLC are not arranged in any built-in hierarchy
Celebrating the existence of multiple languages in society, and their diversity, is a popular research topic in current multilingualism. That being said, scholars note

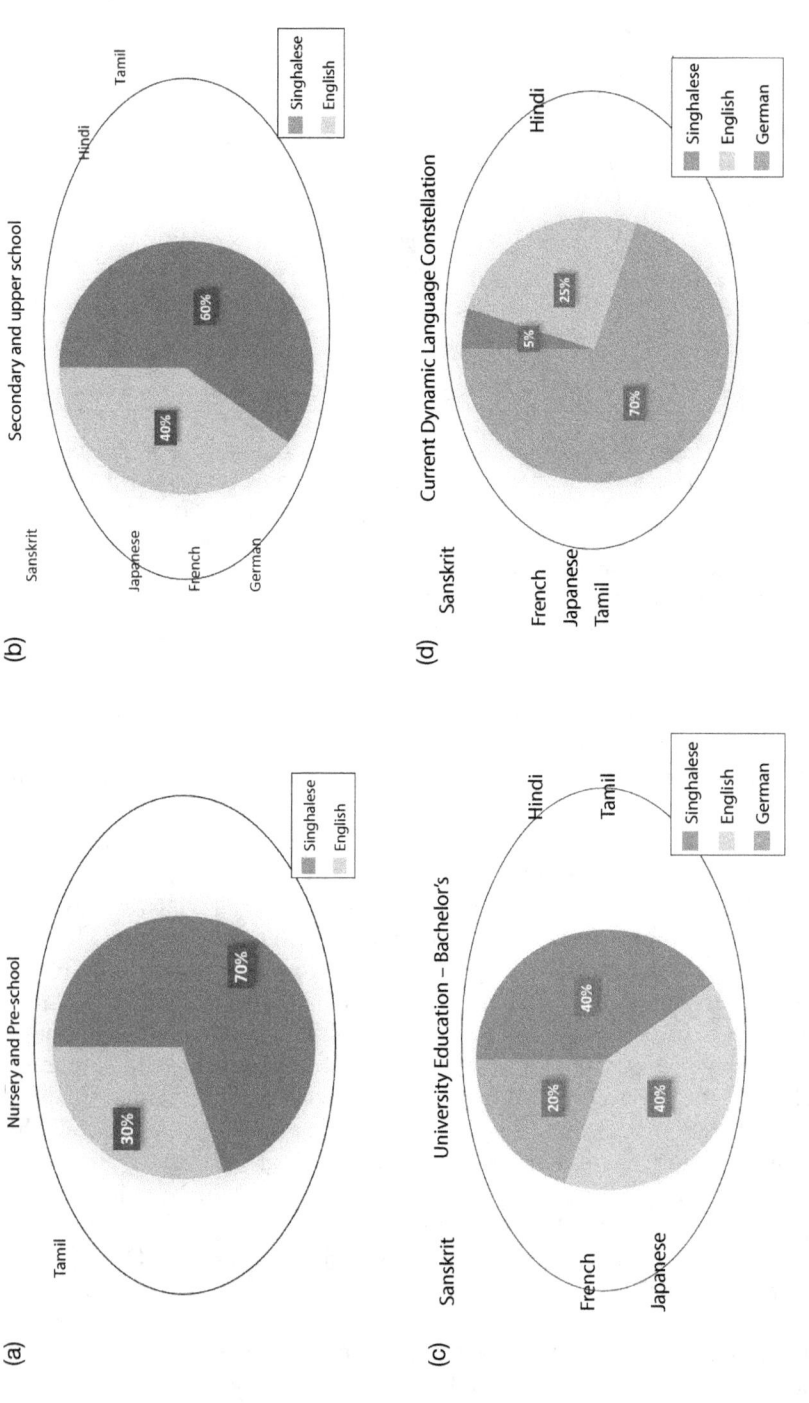

Figure 10.2 Selected Dominant Language Constellation maps (after Kannangara 2020, reproduced with permission). (a) Nursery and preschool. (b) Secondary and upper school. (c) University education – Bachelor's. (d) Current Dynamic Language Constellation.

the sharp hierarchy in value accorded to different named languages in education and communities (Lo Bianco 2020, 2019). In this respect, the DLC perspective represents an exception because a DLC pattern does not arbitrarily assign one language a status above the others in any of its configurations; that is, the unit is not intrinsically hierarchical. The non-hierarchical structure of a DLC does not mean that each language has an equal role, enjoys the same amount of time in use and evokes the same emotional attachment on the part of its user, or that each language of a DLC is mastered to the same proficiency level. Rather, within a unit of DLC, different languages and skills play different roles and have various weights in various aspects of their use. Some of an individual's languages that meet in one DLC may be mastered at the native or passing-for-a-native level; others can be characterised as manipulated with incipient proficiency only. In different DLCs, languages are 'arranged' in various configurations where numerous determinants, such as proficiency in each language, the amount of time it is used or emotions currently experienced by a speaker towards that language, may put one language to the fore and others on the back burner.

The 'pecking order' of languages in a DLC is not arbitrary, but rather is defined by current needs and actual situation. A DLC does not prompt the user, teacher or researcher to label languages as 'bigger' or 'smaller', more important or less important, and does not even over-emphasise the nominations of mother tongue, L1, L2, L3 or Ln. It is owing to the non-hierarchical structure that, in examining a particular DLC situation, a researcher or a teacher chooses any language as a point of departure and can focus on any aspect of the DLC that they deem worthy of close examination.

The absence of an arbitrarily in-built hierarchy of languages in a DLC involves language policy issues. It allows a departure from default assumptions and beliefs that stem from the status of languages in society. It is particularly expedient for minority languages, and important for multilingual countries with an especially challenging choice of languages for education. Language policy specialists working within a DLC framework, as well as language enthusiasts, ensure the priority in acquisition and use of language(s) that they deem currently important for their community.

DLC is multimodal

Thinking about the languages of a DLC, we remember that brain, body, material environment, culture and milieu are involved in each of them (see Chapter 8). A DLC embraces languages in their multiple modalities of virtually all possible aspects: written and aural, a range of signs, pictures, images, video, spatial and material resources.

10.3 The way we experience languages

10.3.1 Translanguaging and code-switching

Like DLC, *translanguaging* recognises the linguistic realities of the twentieth century and brings to the fore the pattern of using several languages concurrently. The conception of translanguaging is in tune with other accounts of current multilingualism cumulatively labelled by Pennycook as the 'trans-super-poly-metro movement' (2016), in that it places the focus of interest on *speakers' practices* as they are situated in social spaces, and not on languages.

What is translanguaging?
The term *translanguaging* denotes fluid language practices when a speaker goes beyond the boundaries of named languages. Instead of using one mainstream language, as is a traditionally accepted norm of appropriate use of languages in social and educational settings, the translanguaging speakers freely and creatively employ languages at their disposal.

García and Li Wei (2014: 20) use the term 'translanguaging' 'to refer to both the complex language practices of plurilingual individuals and communities, as well as the pedagogical approaches that use those complex practices'. Both formal and non-formal educational programs have been developed with the aim of allowing children to use their language assets to the full. In pedagogy, translanguaging is encouraged as a scaffolding practice and as a legitimate teaching and learning resource in a range of modalities. Educators distinguish between students' translanguaging and teacher-directed translanguaging as a deliberate pedagogical practice. Translanguaging is especially amenable for multilingual children and learners of additional languages, especially at the beginning of their multilingual journey.

Translanguaging reminds us that human thinking is not limited to only one modality of language in its conventional sense of speech and writing. The action and social practice of translanguaging also involve situationally selected visual, auditory, kinaesthetic and other *multimodal* means and channels of information.

From a sociolinguistic perspective, translanguaging is a dynamic process, consisting of fluid and free language practices in which multilingual speakers express themselves by navigating complex social settings through strategic employment of multiple languages. From such a viewpoint, multilinguals are seen as performing expert language practices rather than doing so because they are foreign or ignorant, and because their languages are 'incomplete' or 'broken' (Hesson, Seltzer and Woodley 2014: 3).

An illustrative example of such flexible and original creative practices comes from Li Wei (2018). He describes how ordinary English utterances are reappropriated for communication between Chinese users of English, resulting in the creation of words and expressions with entirely different meanings:

> Smilence = smile + silence, referring to the stereotypical Chinese reaction of smiling without saying anything.
>
> Chinsumer = a mesh of 'Chinese consumer', usually referring to Chinese tourists buying large quantities of luxury goods overseas. (Li Wei 2018: 11–13)

The creations look English and broadly adhere to the morphological rules of English, but with Chinese twists and meanings that would be understood only on condition of understanding the sociopolitical context in which these expressions occur, and of being familiar with the history of Chinglish, and the particular subjectivities of the people who created and use these expressions. An important feature of translanguaging activity is that, in addition to using the assets of more than one language concomitantly, it also involves creativity in fusing sociohistorical and cultural nuances. That is why Li Wei argues that terms such as *code-mixing* and *code-switching* do not fully capture instances and the phenomenon of translanguaging (Li Wei 2018: 11–13). What is code-switching, then?

What is code-switching?
Code-switching has been extensively studied for several decades since about the 1950s, originally from a linguistic perspective and then in the area of applied linguistics. Code-switching[1] can be very generally defined as the alternating use of more than one language, dialect or any other variety of language (code) in one conversation. Although the major attention is placed on bilingual and multilingual code-switching, monolingual speakers also switch between styles or dialects of one language. Code-switching occurs when speakers of two or more languages switch or mix their languages within a single speaker's turn or between speakers' turns. When speaking in a selected (base[2]) language, they may substitute a word or a phrase in another language.

In the first and partially in the second stages of societal awareness of languages (see Chapter 3) code-switching in speech was mostly perceived negatively, being explained as a compensatory strategy for insufficient knowledge of a base language, and for limited vocabulary and syntactic constraints. More recently, other stimuli for code-switching have been recognised, thus causing it to be seen as a natural behaviour in interaction with other bilingual and multilingual speakers. In the multilingual stage of societal awareness of languages, code-switching is considered a norm for multilingual speakers. Many researchers now admit that code-switching commonly takes place in multilingual contexts, not simply due to a lack of knowledge of a particular language, but for various communicative functions, such as establishing rapport between interlocutors, expressing solidarity or claiming identity, and excluding others who do not speak this language from a conversation. Baker and Jones assessed code switching as 'a valuable linguistic strategy' (1998: 58), especially in the circumstances of immigration/migration, being in a foreign situation, cooperation with foreign colleagues, or the initial stages of bilingualism. Consider these examples of code-switching from and to various languages:[3]

(1) Gracias for the lovely gift. Está awesome! (Spanish + English)
(2) Are we eating chez ta mère demain? (English + French)
(3) Nó còng đang celebrate cái sinh nhật. (Vietnamese + English)

For a literary–historical example, we can also recall the many instances of code-switching that pervade Leo Tolstoy's 1869 novel, *War and Peace*. The characters

1. Similar and close terms are 'code-mixing' and 'code-meshing'.
2. Base language with reference to code-switching – a language in which one is speaking, a selected language (Baker and Jones 1998).
3. These examples are taken from the site <https://owlcation.com/humanities/Code-Switching-Definition-Types-and-Examples-of-Code-Switching> (last accessed 22 April 2020).

representing the Russian aristocracy of the beginning of the nineteenth century speak French and Russian among themselves, habitually shuttling not only between these two languages, but occasionally into others. Typical of this are the utterances of Anna Pavlovna Scherer, a wealthy St Petersburg socialite, maid of honour and confidante to the dowager Empress Maria Feodorovna:

> (4) 'Soyez tranquille, Lise, you will always be prettier than anyone else,' replied Anna Pavlovna (Tolstoy n.d.: 15)
>
> (5) Prince Andrew looked Anna Pavlovna straight in the face with a sarcastic smile.
>
> '"Dieu me la donne, gare a qui la touche!" They say he was very fine when he said that,' he remarked, repeating the words in Italian: '"Dio mi l'ha dato. Guai a chi la tocchi!"' (Tolstoy n.d.: 29)

Code-switching or translanguaging?

Thinking in terms of switching or mixing codes usually implies adherence to the traditional view of language as a discrete system. Many of the linguistic and SLA theories and views on bilingual education, especially in its assessment and pedagogical routines, draw on an understanding of named languages, such as Turkish, Russian or Swedish, as separate structural and cognitive entities and distinct sets of skills. In their turn, translanguaging scholars maintain that named languages are not discreet systems in reality, but are only considered as such on the basis of nation-state ideology which is 'tied to ethnicity, territory, birth or nation' (Pennycook 2006: 67).

Theoretically, translanguaging represents a move away from longstanding traditional views on what 'language' is. In contrast to code-switching scholars, translanguaging academics see named languages as a social construct and the 'inventions of social, cultural and political movements' (Makoni and Pennycook 2007: 2). They maintain that translanguaging is part and parcel of everyday social life and believe that, in order to communicate, speakers select and deploy features from a unitary linguistic repertoire (Otheguy et al. 2015; García and Li Wei 2014).

This disagreement, expressed in different positions with respect to translanguaging, constitutes one of the most salient current discussions related to multilingualism. The implications for taking one or the other view (translanguaging or code-switching) are far-reaching, ranging from concerns of practicality to economic, political and educational decisions and their serious consequences.

In the course of debates that were conducted with in-depth examination of the issue in multiple domains, ranging from linguistics to educational practice and the field of social inquiry, some clarification and harmonising of the views is taking place. MacSwan advocates 'the existence of discrete languages and multilingualism along with other "treasured icons" of the field including language rights, mother tongues and code-switching' (2017: 169). He takes a nuanced stand, acknowledging the positive role of translanguaging in pedagogy and using it as a lens for language policy. That being said, MacSwan distinguishes grammars from linguistic repertoires and agrees that bilinguals, like everybody else, have a single linguistic repertoire, arguing, however, that they have a richly diverse mental grammar (MacSwan 2017, 2020). For translanguaging scholars, using the rich language assets of bilingual and multilingual children is the top priority. They argue for giving students the affordances to expand what is truly psycholinguistically real, namely their lexical, structural, and other semiotic resources, engaging, to be sure, the importance of named languages and boundaries for schools and societies, but keeping in mind that these are sociocultural constructions without cognitive linguistic reality. (Otheguy at al. 2019: 649)

One more way in which we experience multiple languages is intercomprehension, discussed in the next section.

10.3.2 Intercomprehension/receptive multilingualism

In situations involving people from different countries, such as in business meetings, institutional cooperation and tourist encounters, there can be a number of scenarios by which to understand your interlocutor. You can invite an interpreter, switch to your converser's language, or use English or another language as a *lingua franca*. To pursue these options the speakers, or those who help them, have to display sufficient competency in these languages. If this is not the case, one more possibility is available - *intercomprehension* or *receptive multilingualism*, when interlocutors speak their respective mother tongues and one understands the other. Ten Thije (2019: 329) gives the following definition: 'Receptive multilingualism (RM) refers to the communication mode by which interlocutors use different languages and still understand each other on the basis of the passive language competencies of each interlocutor.'

A receptive type of communication has been used since at least the Middle Ages. Braunmüller (2007) described how, in the Late Middle Ages and Early Modern times, complete bilingualism in northern Europe was rather an exception and merchants deployed their passive or partial competences in other languages in trading situations. Scandinavian multilingualism is, perhaps, the most known for its intercomprehension practices from the beginning of nineteenth century between Danish, Norwegian and Swedish in areas of political and cultural cooperation. A European Commission document on intercomprehension reports that Scandinavians use their mother tongue and are understood by Scandinavians from other countries in most inter-Scandinavian situations, including meetings of the Nordic Council, where the delegates speak either Danish, Norwegian or Swedish in its plenary and committee sessions and are understood by the other delegates without interpretation. Intercomprehension is also used by Scandinavian Airlines System (SAS) on all its flights, and the cabin staff can speak either Swedish, Danish or Norwegian during flights between any Scandinavian destinations. *Mutual intelligibility* is found between the languages of Romance and Slavic language families (Doyé 2005).

The advantage of this type of communication is that both interlocutors can express themselves more precisely and articulately in a language they know better, while at the same time having a suitable understanding of the interlocutor's message. High or near-native productive proficiency in the other's languages is not required and even rudimentary knowledge of a language may be sufficient in certain situations.

Both oral and written communications can be conducted in a receptive multilingualism mode. Receptive multilingualism scholars note that the processes of understanding differ in oral and written communications. They have established that reading a text in an unknown language is often easier than hearing someone speaking an unknown language (ten Thije 2019: 332).

The term 'intercomprehension' is associated with languages that are closely related and belong to the same language family (for example, Romance, Slavic, Germanic and Finno-Ugric), such as French, Italian and Romanian, or Russian and Ukrainian (see Chapter 5 for language classifications). Such languages may be quite similar in vocabulary, grammar and pronunciation, and therefore are mutually intelligible.

Understanding labelled as receptive multilingualism is also possible between languages not belonging to the same language family, such as Russian and Estonian, or when a speaker of German understands a speaker of Spanish, on condition of some basic acquisition of another language, or at least knowledge of international lexis. In both cases, the receiving interlocutor, a hearer or a reader, exercises passive receptive skills. That being said, it is clear that the recipient has to be quite active in order to grasp the message. S/he makes more of an effort to decide on whether and how to negotiate any problems that occur between interactants, or choose a so-called *let-it-pass strategy* (ten Thije and Zeevaert 2007).

Receptive multilingualism skills allow work and communication in languages that are beyond people's language repertoires without excessive learning effort. Sometimes, speakers of one language can understand the other language without prior instruction. However, correspondences between languages are often not recognisable automatically (Hufeisen and Marx 2007). It is possible to strengthen language comprehension with the help of language awareness and special instruction in how to take advantage of correspondences between the languages involved. For this, a set of specific strategies on the side of the hearer and particular competences in receptive multilingualism are to be developed.

Due to the intensified mobility of people around the globe and a considerable increase in international communication, this additional ability of people to understand each other is exploited in various situations, such as in the Swiss army (Berthele and Wittlin 2013) or in language teaching. Didactic methods have therefore been developed that expand the capacity of people to understand, first of all, closely related languages, and distant languages as well. For instance, the EuroCom project yielded elaborate teaching methods that target receptive competences for achieving receptive multilingualism amongst related languages in Romance, Germanic and Slavic language families (McCann et al. 2002; Hufeisen and Marx 2007).

Building on the view that, once a learner has knowledge of one language, further languages in the same family are easier to learn – especially regarding receptive skills – Marx (2012) investigated how speakers of one language, German, concurrently develop reading skills in multiple etymologically related languages: Danish, Dutch, Icelandic, Norwegian or Swedish. Among other things, she wanted to know which languages might be easier to comprehend in which situations, and for which learners.

German university students with knowledge of English were asked to read a short text in an unknown Germanic language. They were guided to use their previous knowledge in and about languages, and assistance was provided by a series of seven 'sieves' or steps – techniques to see similarities between the languages. These include internationalisms, vocabulary, sound equivalences, spelling and pronunciation, syntactic structures, morphosyntactic elements and linguistically individual words.

Students had to sort through the languages involved and search for commonalities or patterns by comparing different aspects of each language to each other. For example, 'because of historical consonant shifts, the German language graphemes <t, tt> are often <d> in the other languages (and <d, ð> in Icelandic), as evidenced by German *Tag*, English *day*, Dutch and Scandinavian *dag* or Icelandic *dagur*' (Marx 2012: 469–70).

Among the practically useful findings of this study is the fact that neither the number of languages previously learned nor language proficiency seemed to correlate with intercomprehension success.

Dutch is much easier to intercomprehend than the other Germanic languages; content words appear to be easier to comprehend than function words and syntactical structures, and the time spent on reading, which is often a good measure of task difficulty, have shown the following evaluation of difficulty in reading the languages:

Time spent on task: Dutch < Swedish < Norwegian < Danish/Icelandic.

10.3.3 The material culture of multilingualism

Material culture is one more channel through which we experience languages. Objects, artefacts, places and spaces are tangible manifestations of multilingualism. Since human children grow up in the midst of the consequential socially and historically constituted artefacts and traditions (Tomasello 1999: 10), everyday things and personal belongings, such as food, clocks, memorabilia, books and furniture, and technological appliances, which accompany every step in our life, may be said to underlie language capacity. Corporeal, physical and concrete materialities are found in public spaces and are abundant in the private sphere. In a multilingual world, material culture is 'a specific blend of materialities, originating from many cultures which constitute a multilingual society' (Aronin and Ó Laoire 2013: 228).

Using materialities and living amidst them, especially those inscribed in multiple languages, we decipher meanings and express our identity. Things may evoke happy times, be a source of painful feelings or nostalgia, or be the source of a particular attachment for a person or a community. How, when, why and in what manner particular items are used, placed, moved or concealed provides valuable information regarding languages, groups and individuals. Some things are manipulated, moved or staged upfront, while others are forgotten or hidden, and yet others are not used but kept as memories. Along with spoken and written texts, the material realm is an ineluctable part of human discourse.[4]

> Material culture is the realm of physical items embracing everyday objects, such as goods and products, food and utensils, furniture, pieces of art, medications and medical devices, books and pens, and carpentry tools; it also includes roads, monuments and clay tablets from the past, and technology appliances from the present, all produced by humans and interconnected by and with local and global mindset, culture, tradition and social life.

---

4. Discourse, in a broad sense, is the entity of sequences of signs and events in accordance with specific content, shared beliefs, values, assumptions and practices.

Artefacts are active voices which represent our attitudes and behaviour; in a multilingual, heterogeneous community, they convey the particular linguistic and cultural group voice and, of course, individual voices within a certain public sphere. Consider, for example, a Tula cake, or *Tulsky prianik*, sold in the chain of 'Russian' stores in Haifa. The inscription ТУЛЬСКИЙ is in Russian and the immediate environment is multilingual: Hebrew, Arabic and Russian, Romanian, Amharic and other languages. In these settings, the cake is a multilingual item, adding to multifarious economic and political realities in the multilingual discourse of a society, and also providing additional tenors to the identity of the Russian-speaking immigrants to Israel.

Objects and artefacts safeguard the maintenance and standing of minority languages in wider society and shape the identities of minority speakers. Therefore, investigations of materialities in a variety of local, urban, educational and home settings are especially informative for minority communities. See, for example, the study by Hornsby (2018) on Lemko language and culture in Poland and the examination of Croatian contemporary culture by Oštarić (2018).

Objects that they use or live among tag people; they reveal the cultural world they belong to and open up traditions and mentalities. On the other hand, artefacts and objects often serve as instruments through which values, attitudes and beliefs are instilled. Acquiring or using certain objects related to other cultures or associated with one's heritage language may make a person feel and behave in a certain way and not another.

Materialities are used in education and in language teaching. Objects and devices evoke emotions that can change people's attitude to the languages that are being learned. Strategic use of material culture objects in language teaching stimulates the 'affective understanding'.

These and other aspects of materialities, as they connect with the experiencing of languages by cultures, societies and individuals, are explored by the 'material culture of multilingualism', a subfield of multilingualism studies (Aronin et al. 2018).

Summary

Recent decades have been marked by significant changes in the essence, spirit and manifestations of multilingualism. The novelty of the current multilingualism is felt in the way humankind evaluates, refers to and deals with the languages at its disposal. Understanding the changing roles and distribution of those roles in various communities has resulted in an increase in language nominations, and in careful attention being paid to them.

Experiencing and treating languages take place through the special patterns of their use: in units of Dominant Language Constellation, by way of translanguaging and intercomprehension, along with manipulating the material culture of multilingualism. All these phenomena emphasise the diversity and multimodality of contemporary language practices.

How we experience, treat and use languages

Further reading

Aronin, Larissa (2018), 'Theoretical underpinnings of the material culture of multilingualism', in Larissa Aronin, Michael Hornsby and Grażyna Kiliańska-Przybyło (eds), *The Material Culture of Multilingualism*, Cham: Switzerland: Springer, pp. 21–45.

García, Ofelia and Li Wei (2014), *Translanguaging: Language, Bilingualism, and Education*, London: Palgrave Macmillan.

Hammarberg, Björn (2010), 'The languages of the multilingual: some conceptual and terminological issues', in C. Bardel and C. Lindqvist (eds), *Approaches to Third Language Acquisition, International Review of Applied Linguistics in Language Teaching (IRAL)*, 48(2–3), pp. 91–104.

Wardhaugh, Ronald (2010), *An Introduction to Sociolinguistics*, Hoboken, NJ: Wiley-Blackwell, pp. 98–112 (on code-switching).

Chapter review

Fill in the table by (1) using material from the chapter, and (2) giving your own examples, considerations and comments.

Concept/keyword	Definition or explanation	Example from the chapter	Your own example	Your considerations and comments
Language nominations				
Language repertoire				
Dominant Language Constellation				
Multimodality				
Translanguaging as a social practice				
Translanguaging in education				
Code-switching				
Intercomprehension/ receptive multilingualism				
Material culture of multilingualism				

Reflective questions

1. What are language nominations? How do language nominations help researchers and stakeholders to understand language practices and language attitudes, and to influence language practices, language attitudes and language maintenance?
2. Describe the concepts of Dominant Language Constellation (DLC) and language repertoire. How are they similar and how are they different? How are they connected?
3. Are there DLC configurations that provide more cognitive, linguistic and social advantages for the individual than others?
4. How can DLC analysis be used for language teaching?
5. Is it useful to develop a hierarchy of DLC? If so, according to which criteria?
6. What does a translanguaging approach mean for multilingual education?
7. What are the practical outcomes of the research on intercomprehension?
8. How does the material culture of multilingualism render the life experience multimodal and multilingual?

Exercises

Exercise 10.1

A frequent question is 'what is the difference between translanguaging and code-switching?' What would you answer? Read the blog entry by Li Wei (9 May 2018): 'Translanguaging and code-switching: what's the difference?', at <https://blog.oup.com/2018/05/translanguaging-code-switching-difference/>.

Exercise 10.2

Relate the non-hierarchical organisation of DLC to current issues in minority languages and language rights. Think of the formats in which such a discussion is appropriate – blog, internet publications, enthusiasts' organisation and so on.

Exercise 10.3

Prepare a presentation on your own DLC or on the DLCs in your region, city, community or university. Include images or models of DLCs in your presentation.

Exercise 10.4

Deliver a presentation on translanguaging in your community: in society and in education. Provide your analysis of the impact of translanguaging on various social-communicative situations or on educational practices.

Exercise 10.5

Take part in a conference with a poster or presentation on the material culture of multilingualism. You can describe and analyse a single material culture item or the materialities of a home, or study the characteristic features of material culture in a selected multilingual community.

Exercise 10.6

Organise a student conference on the material culture of multilingualism. Write a review about the conference and post it on the appropriate media, sites or blogs.

Exercise 10.7

Set up a blog on the material culture of multilingualism. Invite your classmates and friends to post descriptions, pictures, questions and ideas on multilingual material culture, both in the public sphere and at home.

11 Methods of studying multilingualism

In the previous chapters, we dealt with many of the facts and empirical research findings reported to date in multilingualism. In order to obtain scientifically valid empirical and theoretical knowledge, scholars deploy research methodologies and analytical tools. Researchers address concepts and terms, hypotheses, classifications, methods, theories and models. This chapter provides an overview of the general methodology of research in its application to multilingualism.

11.1 Features of multilingualism research

Scientific knowledge about multilingualism underlies language-related decisions in all areas of our life. It provides the basis for government and local policies concerning languages in economics, communication and education. Furthermore, it can help resolve issues in business, demographics and the personal existence of multilinguals. Research may also offer practical guidance relating to language policy, language pedagogies, language acquisition and language assessment.

11.1.1 Characteristics of research in multilingualism

Research in the field of multilingualism complies with the foundations of research in other disciplines and has its unique traits, which are both advantageous and challenging.

Due to the variety of disciplinary roots in multilingualism, research objectives, subjects of study, scope of investigations, and methods employed, all of which may differ from one academic subarea of multilingualism to another, it is no wonder that research methodologies, methods and techniques that now comprise multilingualism research are remarkably manifold and wide-ranging.

Multilingualism can boast an impressive collective list of methods that is probably unthinkable in any other domain of knowledge. Each discipline, as a rule, draws on the research philosophies accepted in its field of origin. Each subfield of multilingualism studies has a more or less stable set of traditional research methods. Multilingualism research includes the methods of natural science, such as mathematics and computational methods, life sciences, and humanities and social sciences. For example, neurolinguistics employs the methods of neuroscience and clinical studies to determine how languages are processed in the brain. The two primary technologies used in multilingualism research that image brain function in real time (not just the structure of the brain), thereby making it possible to detect changes over time, are positron emission tomography (PET) and functional magnetic resonance imaging (fMRI). With the interests of multilingualism expanding to distant and adjacent disciplines, 'appropriating' methods of research from them has become a successful practice, enriching our knowledge of multilingualism.

The richness of interests and routes of research, as well as multiple potential sources of appropriation of methods, are some of the most significant advantages and attractions of research in multilingualism. They also generate serious challenges.

11.1.2 Challenges

First of all, researchers note a lack of consistency not only between the subfields of multilingualism but sometimes within the same subfield. Similar types of situations, populations, classes, languages and processes are often studied by researchers in different subfields of multilingualism, with diverse focuses corresponding to each particular discipline. Moreover, even within one discipline, various schools of thought may considerably diverge on crucial concepts, such as 'proficiency' or 'bilingual'.

The second cause of challenges in researching multilingualism is that many of the subject matters and concepts studied in multilingualism are challenging to capture. Areas such as 'language awareness', 'comprehension' and 'understanding' are rather non-concrete and abstract concepts, which change according to specific situations. The meaning of even basic multilingualism notions, which seem to be apparent at first, such as 'language', 'foreign language', 'second language', 'dialect', 'language community' and 'language speaker', though not abstract, is not understood in the same way by everyone.

As a result, the situation described by Weinreich, about seventy years ago, is often still valid: 'no two studies are thoroughly comparable, because the linguistic techniques employed and the sociological orientation, if any, on which they are based have been so different from one case to the next' (Weinreich 1953: 15).

Still, scholars give illustrative examples of how it is possible to navigate the multidisciplinary area of multilingualism. A classic method that arose from the social necessity to address a problem and cope with it, and that is known to all scholars of multilingualism today, is the *matched guise technique*. This emerged from the insightful mixture of at least three fields: sociology, psychology and linguistics. Developed by Elizabeth Peal and Wallace Lambert (1962) at McGill University in Canada to show the prejudices about French held by both English– and French–Canadians, the technique consists of the following. An individual who had mastered the two relevant languages – English and French, in this case – read the same message in English and French. Then participants were asked to listen to the recordings and evaluate the personality of the recorded person. It was often the case that evaluations of the same speaker reading the text in different languages differed. Lambert and his colleagues attributed the different evaluations of the same speaker to the fact that experiment participants evaluated the language groups to which they thought the speaker belonged. Lambert and his colleagues also demonstrated that these evaluations are important in facilitating or hindering second and consecutive language learning.

The third issue presenting a challenge in studying multilingualism is the necessity for understanding the distinction between methods employed in bilingualism studies and methods of investigation in multilingualism. Researchers in multilingualism, by default, employ methods that have been traditionally in use in bilingualism and second language acquisition (SLA) research. There are two implications here. The first is that the seemingly natural transfer of research methods from bilingualism to multilingualism studies supplied the field of multilingualism with an array of methods that were already tried and tested. One reason for the fact that multilingualism widely uses research methods from bilingualism is that many bilingualism research methods are indeed suitable and appropriate for investigating multilingualism too. Another reason is inertia. Theoretical differentiation between bilingualism and multilingualism is a comparatively recent development, and many researchers still use the methods and research apparatus of bilingualism without questioning its suitability. In research, the difficulty in differentiating between bilingualism and multilingualism lies in the fact that studying multilingualism phenomena requires significant practical effort to control multilingual factors in an experiment, as opposed to dealing with only two languages. It is no wonder that several interesting research questions were simply ignored in the past since they were considered insolvable because too many factors were involved. This is how Ulrike Jessner (2006: 15) explains the gradual realisation of the problems arising from mixing bilingual situations and multilingual ones:

> The growing interest in TLA [third language acquisition] and its cognitive and linguistic effects has also given rise to doubts about all experiments which have been carried out with 'bilingual' subjects who, in fact, might have been in contact with other languages, but had never been asked about their prior linguistic knowledge (see also de Bot 2004: 22). Whether this would have had an effect on the results of the experiments or not remains an issue to be discussed. It may or may not have affected the results and the conclusion drawn had this information been taken into account in the language biography of the testees in the first instance. This again depends on the kind of experiment and linguistic field in which it is embedded.

A response to this challenge is the use of methods specific to multilingualism, such as the complexity method and other new and emerging perspectives discussed in this chapter. Employing them does not exclude extensive use of traditional methodologies.

11.2 Research methodologies and types of research

In this section, we will briefly define the main terms and notions that have to do with research in general and research in multilingualism in particular.

11.2.1 Philosophies, methodologies and types of research in multilingualism

Research methods are systematic ways of examining phenomena and establishing relationships between them. *Research techniques* are specific research operations performed to obtain, classify or analyse data. Word association tests, sentence completion tests, the matched guise test, statistical manipulations, and the use of observers or audio-visual recording devices are examples of research techniques.

A combination of research methods and techniques selected to be carried out in a particular study is called the *research design*. The research design is expected to ensure integrity, logicality and a lack of bias. For each study, a researcher designs a research methodology consisting of several logically connected and relevant methods and techniques, which should lead to answers to the research questions posed. As the rationale behind each study and each particular context is different, the research designs are tailored to each study.

The *research methodology* describes the logical path of specific steps leading to answers to a research question. The concept of research methodology is broader than that of research methods. The research methodology includes methods and techniques, the choice of which is generally based on a research philosophy.

A *research philosophy* (or research approach) is a philosophical basis for a study that consists of a general attitude to research, including the underlying assumption concerning whether the 'truth' or 'reality' exists and whether we, as researchers, can find it. The principles of how to find 'real', 'correct' knowledge, which kind of data will allow us to arrive at 'the truth', how it is to be collected and analysed, and what would not be the right way to do it are also determined by following a particular research philosophy. There exists an array of research philosophies that guide research in multilingualism studies. Positivism and interpretivism, which underlie most research in several disciplines other than multilingualism, are widespread in multilingualism too.

According to the *positivist view*, reality is absolute (certain and definite), and the physical world is operated according to objective laws. Objective data and authentic knowledge ('truth', 'reality', 'meaning') can be derived from our sensory experience – visual, auditory, tactile, olfactory. The role of science is to discover facts, identify and explain regularities and make predictions. The positivist approach requires its researchers to reach authentic knowledge by isolating the phenomena in question, describing them from an objective viewpoint and verifying them via empirical evidence. The findings obtained by research based on the positivist approach should be *replicable*. This means that, ideally, valid and reliable research can be repeated as previously carried out and similar results should be obtained. Hence, there is a requirement for a clear and generally acceptable way of presenting knowledge. The treatment of data in positivism is logical and mathematical.

The *interpretivist* approach appears to be quite the opposite of positivism and is often called antipositivism. Unlike in positivism, in this instance subjective interpretations of reality, introspective and intuitional perceptions are accepted as a legitimate way of gaining knowledge. This is because interpretivists believe that there may be many interpretations of reality, with all of them describing the same reality. Researchers working in the framework of interpretivism insist on studying phenomena in their natural environment, holding that the context allows a researcher to understand the phenomena under research. Moreover, those who adhere to the interpretivist approach believe that, to gain knowledge about reality, researchers have to focus on interpretations, on what is subjectively meaningful. Therefore, interpretive studies can contain 'dense descriptions', historical accounts, personal narrations and 'vignettes'. Interpretivism often relates to various historical debates, philosophy and sociology domains.

Research types can be classified from a variety of perspectives.

A distinction is often drawn between *pure* and *applied research*. Pure or fundamental research aims to increase the understanding of fundamental principles in a field of knowledge. Pure research is based on theory related to some abstract ideas and results in the formation of a theory or generalisation. It has no specific practical purpose, such as a ready-to-use recipe for how to learn five languages in the shortest time possible. It is intended to bring neither immediate answers nor instant practical outcomes. An example of pure research in multilingualism studies is the philosophy of multilingualism (see, for example, the entry 'Multilingualism and philosophy' in the *Encyclopedia of Applied Linguistics*, Aronin and Singleton 2012).

On the other hand, applied research is problem-oriented research intended to provide a solution for a particular, often pressing, problem. Multilingualism scholars in the subfield of applied linguistics are determined to find answers to the difficulties that learners confront. For instance, Martha Gibson, Britta Hufeisen and Gary Libben (2001) wanted to know whether having a second language helped or hindered German prepositional verb production. The participants, multilingual men and women learning German as L3 and whose other languages included Armenian, Bulgarian, Chinese, Arabic, Japanese, Swedish, Mongolian and other languages, were asked to perform a pen and paper task that required filling in the correct preposition to go with the verb: for example, *hoffen* _____ (Gibson et al. 2001: 141). The questionnaires asking about the participant's mother tongue and second language(s) were analysed in connection with the data's accuracy in using the German prepositional verbs in the pen and paper task. The findings described specific inhibitory and advantageous effects of the multilinguals' other languages, structurally similar to or dissimilar from German, on the production of German prepositional verbs. The value of this applied linguistics study is that it provides information about which other background languages as L1 and L2 are advantageous and disadvantageous in respect of the production of German verbs.

Research is often described as being either *longitudinal* or *cross-sectional*. The distinction is based on whether a study is approached synchronically (*synchronic* means relating to a particular time, at one point in time) or diachronically (*diachronic* pertains to changes happening over time). A longitudinal study is a study of individuals or groups over a period of time in which researchers are concerned with the way something – for example, a learner's productive skills in L3, or the vocabulary of a trilingual child – develops and evolves over time. In such studies, repeated observations are carried out, the results of which are then compared, analysed and interpreted. Such a study can take months, years or even decades, since it allows researchers to study long-term effects and can, therefore, gauge age-related changes and intergenerational effects. One example of a longitudinal study is that of Maria Pilar Safont-Jordà on multiple language acquisition in early childhood. In two studies (2012, 2013), Safont-Jordà traced the development of pragmatic competence in a trilingual boy, Pau, who is a consecutive bilingual in Spanish (L1) and Catalan (L2), and is learning English as a third language. To see the development of the child's requestive behaviour in English, the researcher obtained data from diary notes and regular recordings of mother–child interaction at home and during short car trips over several months, from age 2.9 to 3.6 years.

Another example of a longitudinal investigation is a study by Peter Ecke and Christopher J. Hall (2012), who examined changing patterns in a multilingual speaker's tip-of-tongue (TOT) states over ten years. The subject, a multilingual whose language repertoire consisted of five languages – L1 German, L2 Russian, L3 English, L4 Spanish and L5 Portuguese – recorded more than a hundred TOT states, and analysis of the data revealed the dynamics of lexical retrieval (ease or failure of access) in L1, L2, L3, L4 and L5 in a multilingual and interaction between his languages.

A *cross-sectional* study is conducted at a single point in time. As opposed to a long-term study that notes and describes changes over time, a cross-sectional study is cross-cut or snapshot-like, investigating a situation at a particular time. In this sense, it is synchronic.

When the study involves a large number of subjects drawn from a defined population or the whole population, it is called a *survey*. An exemplary survey study carried out by Michael Clyne in Australia will be discussed later in this chapter.

The two research philosophies, the positivist and the interpretivist, are typically associated with different **types of research**: the former with quantitative research, and the latter with qualitative research.

11.2.2 Quantitative research

Quantitative research based on a positivist philosophy is carried out with the assumption that reality can be measured and counted. To understand reality, we must break it up into smaller units, or separate things, so that they can be counted and measured. Quantitative research contains numbers, proportions and statistics. It deals with numerical data or data that can be converted into numbers. This research inquiry may also quantitatively record people's attitudes to languages, their emotional and behavioural states, and their ways of thinking.

Quantitative research is regulated by principles which ensure that the research is conducted in as unbiased and neutral a manner as possible. A key aspect of quantitative research is removing researcher bias. A researcher must use tools that ensure neutrality and eliminate factors that may distract one from the intent of the research. In quantitative research, researchers normally have a theory and a distinct idea of what to measure before they start measuring it. Quantitative research results in finding a set of numbers, which are then subjected to statistical analysis. The analysis yields the findings, which can ideally be projected to additional or broader groups or populations. Quantitative research seeks generalisable results, which can be projected and applied to other populations. Although quantitative research is mostly employed in the 'hard' sciences, such as astronomy, it is also used in applied linguistics and the sociology of language. These disciplines are not as strict as 'hard' sciences. Still, all efforts have to be made to exclude or limit the bias.

Quantitative research falls into four major types:

1. ***Descriptive*** research determines and reports the way things are. It answers questions concerning the current status of the subjects of the study. Most census-type

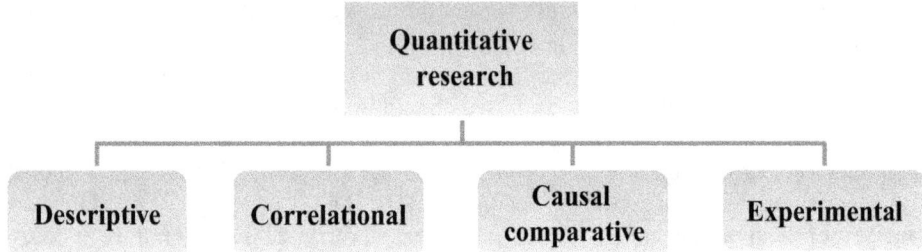

Figure 11.1 Types of quantitative research.

data can be categorised as being descriptive, in that the number of speakers of a language in a state, region or city is simply cited or described.
2. *Correlational* research aims to determine whether a relationship exists between two or more quantifiable variables. The degree of relationship is expressed by the correlation coefficient, which is a number between .00 and 1.00. Correlational research does not establish a cause–effect relationship; it merely states that there exists (or not) a correlation between the two factors.
3. *Causal–comparative* research is similar to descriptive research because it describes conditions that already exist; therefore, it is called *ex post facto* (Latin for 'after the fact'). However, unlike descriptive research, it attempts to establish the cause–effect relationship and to determine reasons for, or causes of, the existing condition.
4. *Experimental* research establishes the cause–effect relationship and makes a comparison; it is dissimilar to causal–comparative research in that, here, the variables are manipulated. In multilingualism studies, experimental methods are often used when researching the teaching of second and additional languages.

Language demography
An important kind of descriptive research mentioned above consists of studies describing the current state of languages and populations. This is called *language demography*. The focus of language demography studies is the collection and analysis of data relating to population groups' language use. Language demography observes linguistic trends and contains statistics relating to languages among populations. Large-scale data are collected through *censuses*. In addition to population counts, censuses conducted across the world are the sources from which we may receive essential information on both the distribution and the vitality of languages in regions and countries.

Censuses are generally carried out by governmental agencies at fixed intervals of time: for example, every five years in Canada, New Zealand and Austria, and every ten years in Brazil and the USA. The collected statistical information yields data on language use in different groups in multilingual societies. With the help of such data, changes and new developments, such as language shift, can be monitored and decisions regarding the necessary language education can be taken on an informed basis.

The statistics obtained from large-scale censuses still do not tell us everything we would like to know about the use of languages at home and in the wider community;

they do not provide us with details about 'how much a speaker uses the language at home' and 'who speaks what language to whom and when' (Fishman 1965). For this, we need language surveys.

Surveys, one more method of obtaining systematic quantitative information, may supply more in-depth demographic information. A survey is typically not as all-encompassing as a census. While smaller in scale, it can nonetheless yield more data on a particular language issue. In surveys, respondents are asked a number of specific questions for statistical analysis. Language-related surveys are typically aimed at revealing a speaker's first language, and their other languages, and their current language use. Both censuses and surveys ask language-related questions on country of origin, mother tongue, the language of the household and other languages used. The data on languages and populations obtained from censuses and surveys can then be analysed and compared against individual and group factors. By comparing the data on mother tongue and current language, we can learn, for example, if a language shift has occurred in a particular ethnic group or population.

Language demography data are often analysed to monitor and assess language shifts, especially in immigration contexts. This is how we have learned about the general trends in the use of languages by immigrants in their new countries. The studies of Michael Clyne provide a good example of what can be learned from statistical, demographic data on languages. In his book *Dynamics of Language Contact* (2003), Clyne gives an account of the linguistic situation in Australia, a country that continues to witness a significant influx of immigrants from various parts of the world. Clyne analysed the findings of the 1996 census carried out by the Australian Bureau of Statistics, concerning immigrant languages and their contact with English in Australia. Having studied the immigrant populations from Asia, Africa, Europe and South America to Australia for at least three generations, he made useful comparisons between generations and their period of living in the country. He concluded that the shift of the newcomers to the English language, the primary language of Australia, is inevitable (Clyne 2003: 11). But whether the speakers of other languages adopt English along with their other languages or substitute their other languages for English, how long this process takes, and whether it happens in the same way and at the same rate for all ethnic immigrant groups of all ages are important practical questions that can be explored with the help of language demography surveys.

Whether the language shift to the 'new' language occurs swiftly or whether the following generations of immigrants maintain the language of origin also depends on the successive waves of immigration supporting a language. The increased numbers of Polish native speakers brought some new opportunities to use this language in Australia. Clyne reported that the Polish group of immigrants to Australia slowed down their shift to the English language due to new immigration in the 1980s. Clyne also found some specific developments for particular groups of immigrants in Australia. He noted, for example, that in the German language enclave, which dates back to the mid-nineteenth century, the language was frequently maintained for three, four or even five generations.

11.2.3 Qualitative research

Qualitative research is often rightly associated with the interpretivist approach, but it is also related to relativist or post-modern philosophies. *Case studies, action research* and *ethnography methods* are all frequently used in qualitative research within the qualitative paradigm. Qualitative-oriented researchers do not conceal their quest's subjective nature; they base their search for knowledge on interpretations, biases and presuppositions because they believe that social reality or truth is socially constructed and there are multiple realities, rather than a single one. Qualitative research does not claim that the processes it discovers are universal, and the findings are immediately and widely applicable to larger demographic groups or communities than those who participated in the research.

Qualitative research aims to describe phenomena and explore the *meaning* of social phenomena, intentions, behaviour, culture and traditions. Qualitative researchers interpret the phenomena under investigation in particular contexts, such as why, in the process of acculturation, some immigrants might retain their languages longer than others, or what motivates parents in multilingual families to use or not to use all their languages with their children.

Data in qualitative research are non-numerical; there is no emphasis placed on comparative statistics as in quantitative research. The data qualitative research yields are multilayered, containing detailed descriptions, which among researchers are called 'rich' or 'thick' descriptions, thought to be able to capture a cross-cut of an ever-changing and dynamic reality. Although qualitative research uses 'merely' descriptions, it can eventually yield a more or less complete picture of any particular phenomenon. Questionnaires and interviews, observations, focus groups, narrative inquiry, discourse analysis, and analysis of metaphors are only some of the methods employed in qualitative research.

Ethnographic research

The origins of *ethnographic research* in applied linguistics and multilingualism lie in the seminal works of John Gumperz (for example, 1964, 1968, 1971a, 1971b, 1982a, 1982b) and Dell Hymes (1974). Interpretive qualitative research and interpretive ethnography (Denzin and Lincoln 2005; Denzin et al. 2008) have yielded several ethnographic studies within and across multilingual contexts. Those that emerged at the end of the twentieth century mostly deal with language policy and planning, language learning, and schooling (see, e for example, Zentella 1997 on Puerto Rican children in New York; Hornberger 1989 on language policy and work with Quechua communities).

Research from the last thirty years concerned with the relation of language and culture is carried out in the related fields of sociolinguistics, applied linguistics, linguistic anthropology, cognitive science and communication studies (including intercultural communication), the boundaries of which it is not always possible to establish. These multidisciplinary investigations posed new questions and have enriched multilingualism, multiple language acquisition and education research, in that they pay more attention to the cultural context and social, historical, transnational and global phenomena. *Autoethnography*, with its focus on personal experience as a method, draws together features of autobiography and ethnography. The current methodological trends encourage a focus on *subjectivity* – subjective perspectives of both researcher and researched – and on *performativity* – transformative power of language that has the effect of change (Kramsch 2014).

There are new, intensively developing lines of qualitative research, such as the *material culture of multilingualism* and *visualisations*, where specific methodology related to the study of environment features strongly.

Visualisations include drawings, pictures, photos, collage, DLC maps and material culture items existing in a multilingual environment. Visual methods gained legitimacy in knowledge production not so long ago. In earlier times, it was believed that using a visual image for scientific speculation was entirely inappropriate and irrelevant. Recently, the canon of research tools has shifted, admitting visual data and their analysis as important methodology in multilingualism and multiple language acquisition. Pondering visual images helps us to think and compare, and the visualisation of patterns may assist in the evaluation of data and bear the potential for prompting solutions to commonly occurring problems (Elmqvist and Yi 2012). Today, visualisation and tangibilisation methods are successfully used to study representations about multilingualism and linguistic diversity, the professional development of foreign language teachers, and multilingualism as a social and an individual process (see, for example, Kalaja and Melo-Pfeifer 2019; Chik and Melo-Pfeifer 2019).

11.2.4 Holistic and complexity research

There is also a third distinctive type of research, with its own philosophy and methods, that is employed in multilingualism studies – *holistic* and *complexity research*. In this approach, researchers strive to reach a complete picture of what they study, rather than examining the separated components of the phenomena, as positivists do.

Holistic and complexity perspectives explore multilingualism reality as a complex system, where each part cannot be understood as separated from its environment. From a holistic standpoint, multilingual individuals and groups, classrooms, learning and teaching practices are understood as an ecosystem. The works of Einar Haugen (for example, 1972) and Nancy Hornberger (2003) on the holistic approach to language ecology represent this perspective. The methods of complexity science are especially relevant for multilingualism. *Only* traditional methods do not consider, and therefore do not account for, multilingualism's crucial property – its complexity.

Complexity approach

The Complexity and Dynamic Systems Theory (CDST)[1] perspective is an appreciated methodology in many fields of knowledge and in multilingualism as well. Linguists, educators and language teaching specialists apply the complexity approach to the study of a new reality. Because complexity is so appropriate for multilingualism, it is described below in more detail.

1. CDST – Complexity and Dynamic Systems Theory, a unifying term for Complexity Theory and Dynamic Systems Theory suggested by De Bot (2017).

The complexity perspective presents the world as an integrated whole rather than a dissociated collection of parts. It contests the view according to which one can understand the world by breaking things down into their components and understanding them separately. Dissimilar to this traditional view, complexity thinking asserts

- that the whole is *not* the sum of its parts
- that the world around us is characterised by irregularity, fragmentariness, fuzziness and even chaos.

In opposition to traditional thinking, which did not allocate special attention to the *relationships* between the subsystems of which a system is composed, the complexity scientific vision relies on 'systemic thinking – thinking in terms of *relationships, patterns, and context*' (Capra and Luisi 2014: 243, italics added).

Complex interactions
Bossomaier and Green (1998: 7) provided a very clear illustration of complexity (as distinct from mere complicatedness). It runs as follows:

> If you roll a billiard ball across a billiard table, then any good billiards player can predict the path that it will follow. If you roll two balls, then the problem is still simply a matter of calculating each ball's path individually. However, there is also a chance that the two balls will bump into each other. Add a few more balls and the problem of keeping track of paths and collisions becomes very difficult and predicting the state of all the balls becomes well nigh impossible.

For billiard balls and the billiard table, let us substitute languages and society. What is true of the billiard balls is true of languages in terms of their contact and interaction. Instead of tables, let us think of environment – society, community, school, say, in New York, USA, and instead of balls, think of English, French, Maori, Hungarian, Moldavian, Kanada, Vietnamese or Finnish, which you may encounter there on the street or at a school. Multiple agents (billiard balls) are not only languages but also modes of their use, variety of speakers, products of their origins, linguistic abilities and needs, political and historical nuances of time and place, and so on. All this inevitably makes multilingual contact complex: complex and not merely complicated. What turns something from being merely complicated (having many elements) into something truly complex are the *interactions* between those elements; in the case of multilingualism, these involve interactions between languages, speakers and contexts, and between their minute components.

We return to Bossomaier and Green's (1998: 7–8) billiard-balls-and-table illustration.

> Suppose now that you roll (say) 100 balls around on the table. With so many balls, they will be bumping into each other all the time. The problem of computing individual paths becomes virtually impossible. Such a system is essentially unpredictable at the individual level. It is hard to record, in the sense of logging where everything is, and devoid of simple patterns.

In the same way, multiple interactions result in complexity in language teaching and learning, the practices of child-rearing, everyday linguistic experiences and numerous unique forms of multilinguality. Among other key tenets of the complexity that explain multilingual phenomena and processes are 'sensitivity to initial conditions' and 'emergence'.

Sensitivity to initial conditions
The slightest change in language use or acquisition, such as an early or late onset of study or exposure, the presence or absence of a relative speaking a language, or an encounter with a foreign film that sparks or enhances interest in a particular language – any of these and countless other 'initial conditions' may result in significant deviations from the expected mastery of language outcome. Such sensitivity to initial conditions is highly representative of all kinds of multilingualism phenomena, be it education, communication at work or language processing. In the complexity approach, sensitivity to initial conditions is known as the 'butterfly effect', modelled by the mathematician and meteorologist Edward Lorenz (1917–2008) at the Massachusetts Institute of Technology for his study of the weather.

Emergence
'Emergent' in complexity science refers to processes, structures, behaviours or properties that are the *products of the interactions* of their parts and that cannot be understood simply by understanding their parts. Emergent phenomena are more than the sum of their parts and have properties, which are the properties of the whole system or thing, but not the properties of its parts. In other words, the properties of the parts constituting the emergent phenomena are different from the properties of the whole emergent phenomenon.

The emergent phenomena, processes and structures are found in live and physical nature: these are hurricanes and sand dunes, flocks of birds and schools of fish, and communities of ants, which behave in a special way according to the rules of the flock or school and not as a single bird, fish or ant. They include bacterial infections and evolution, crowds (not the sum of individuals of which they consist, as is well seen in the crowds' unpredictable behaviour), stock markets and traffic jams. Consciousness is considered to be an emergent property of the brain.

To this list, we can add contemporary emerging multilingual societies, or 'sociopolitical emergences' as they are termed by Flores and Lewis (2016: 98). A multilingual individual is an emergent phenomenon too, since we cannot reduce such an individual to the sum of words that he or she knows, the skills mastered in the three languages, or even the knowledge and culture possessed by the person at a particular moment in time. *Emergent properties* are entirely new features, events or phenomena, which develop 'spontaneously' from the interactions of individual parts. Most existing works in which researchers have adopted a complexity perspective in studying multilingualism and language acquisition use *network modelling* and *computer simulations.* For instance, Paul Meara (2006) explored the idea of a vocabulary network, where, in the structure of a graph, words are represented as nodes, and the links between words act as arcs to connect the nodes. He built monolingual, bilingual and trilingual models, and then ran computer simulations to determine the emergent properties of interacting bilingual and trilingual lexicons. His trilingual models, for example, 'show that under certain conditions, activity in

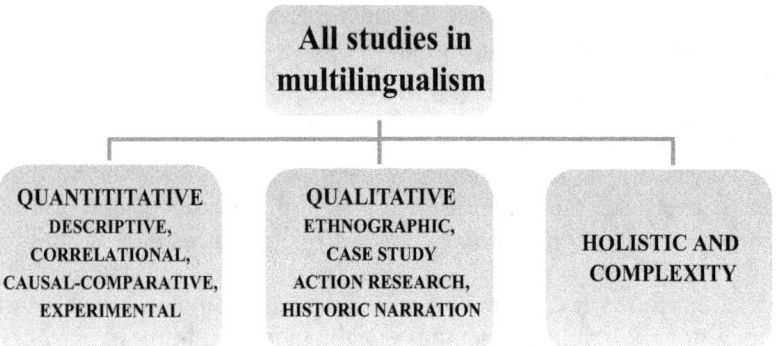

Figure 11.2 Types of research used in multilingualism studies.

an L3 can sometimes generate spontaneous reactivation of words in an L2' (Meara 2006: 642).

CDST has provided a welcome and fruitful perspective for the study of multilingualism and has been applied to the areas of second and third language acquisition and applied linguistics (see, for example, Cameron and Deignan 2006; Larsen-Freeman and Cameron 2008; Larsen-Freeman 2013, 2017; Herdina and Jessner 2002; Aronin and Jessner 2015).

11.2.5 Triangulation

It would not be right to think that research has to be either qualitative or quantitative, or based only on the complexity approach. In fact, it is often the case that a combination of qualitative and quantitative methods and techniques is used in one study, depending on the phenomena, data and context being investigated. The combination of various methods is warranted because no single method can be thought to be strictly reliable. To avoid arbitrariness and bias in interpreting the results, researchers employ *triangulation*. In simple words, triangulation is a combination of methods in the study of the same issue or phenomenon, used as a way to increase the validity and credibility of the research results. Employing a variety of data sources and several methods of data collection, or multiple research perspectives rather than one single theory, one data source or one method is expected to compensate for the weaknesses of each isolated method, source or perspective, by adding the strength of the other. It is assumed that triangulation will give researchers greater confidence in their findings and can lead to a better understanding of a phenomenon under investigation (Denzin 1978; Flick 2007). Especially promising for multilingualism is the type of triangulation called *interdisciplinary triangulation*, whereby sources, investigators, theories and methods are recruited from several disciplines (Janesick 1994). It is important to note that triangulation is not simply a combination of different data, methods and theories from a number of disciplines. For this to be qualified as triangulation, the design of a study, its logic and each method or technique should be scrupulously analysed and carefully pre-planned.

Summary

Research into multilingualism seeks answers to a great variety of individual and social issues. The methodology of multilingualism is highly diverse and cross-disciplinary, employing the widest range of approaches methods, and techniques. This, on the one hand, grants unlimited opportunities for research. On the other hand, it puts tangible constraints on the interpretation of research results, and on the possibility of using the findings in other branches of multilingualism.

While the philosophical foundations, goals and methods involved in quantitative, qualitative and complexity research are obviously dissimilar, it would be a mistake to think that some types of research are better than others. Each has its own merits and disadvantages, as well as its limitations and possibilities. Along with employing time-honoured methods of bilingual and multilingual research, both qualitative and quantitative, multilingualism develops methods of its own that explore its highly complex nature. Interdisciplinarity is a conspicuous feature of vibrant multilingualism research.

Further reading

Aronin, Larissa and Ulrike Jessner (2014), 'Methodology in bi- and multilingual studies: from simplification to complexity', *AILA Review*, 27, pp. 56–79.

Burns, Anne (2013), 'Qualitative teacher research', in Carol Chapelle (ed.), *The Encyclopedia of Applied Linguistics*, New York: Wiley-Blackwell.

Chik, A. and S. Melo-Pfeifer (2019), 'Social representations of multilingualism', in G. Barkhuizen (ed.), *Qualitative Research Topics in Language Teacher Education*, London: Routledge, pp. 149–54.

Kramsch, Claire (2014), 'Language and culture', *AILA Review*, 27, pp. 30–55.

Kroll, Judith F. and Eleonora Rossi (2013), 'Bilingualism and multilingualism: quantitative methods', in Carol Chapelle (ed.), *The Encyclopedia of Applied Linguistics*, New York: Wiley-Blackwell.

Porte, Graeme (2010), *Appraising Research in Second Language Learning: A Practical Approach to Critical Analysis of Quantitative Research*, Amsterdam: John Benjamins.

Chapter review

Fill in the table by (1) using material from the chapter, and (2) giving your own examples, considerations and comments.

Concept/keyword	Definition or explanation	Example from the chapter	Your own example	Your considerations and comments
Research				
Triangulation				

Contd

Concept/keyword	Definition or explanation	Example from the chapter	Your own example	Your considerations and comments
Quantitative research				
Qualitative research				
Experiments				
Theoretical thinking/ research				
Study design				
Cross-sectional study				
Longitudinal study				
Complexity				
Matched guise technique				
Language ecology				

Reflective questions

1. What are the particular challenges of research in multilingualism, different from other fields of knowledge?
2. What are the time-honoured methods of research used in multilingualism?
3. What prompts new instrumentation of inquiry in multilingualism research?
4. What can happen if multilinguals are studied as if they are bilinguals?
5. How do complexity science methods enhance research in multilingualism? Give examples.
6. Which research tools of bilingualism can be used in multilingualism research, and which research tools cannot?

Exercises

Exercise 11.1

Choose a study in multilingualism and reflect on the particular methods which were used in this study. Ask yourself and answer questions such as: why were these particular methods chosen by the author to research this particular problem? Could other methods be instrumental in answering the same research questions? How reliable are the methods chosen? If you do not know which study to choose, we suggest the following:

- In neurolinguistics
- In applied linguistics

- In didactics
- In sociology of language.

Exercise 11.2

Kurt Lewin (1890–1947), a renowned scholar in social and applied psychology, wrote 'There is nothing more practical than a good theory' (Lewin 1952: 169). Do you agree? How can you explain this statement in the light of your reading of this chapter?

Exercise 11.3

Benjamin Lee Whorf claimed that the world is different, not for each person but for each language community. The view of Ekkehart Malotki, who also explored the Hopi on the same subject (1983), is different. Which research methodologies are involved there?

12 Models of multilingualism

In the preceding chapter we acquainted ourselves with the methodology of multilingualism and saw that, while theories and models constructed with the view on bilingualism have a contribution to make to multilingualism studies, they alone are not sufficient for a comprehensive explanation of multilingualism. This chapter will deal with theories and models specific to multilingualism.

12.1 What are theories and what are models?

Both theories and models are necessary to reveal fundamental principles and the nature of multilingualism, as both are analytical tools that seek to explain how and why phenomena (that is, things, facts, events and processes, such as language acquisition or language behaviour) happen or exist.

12.1.1 Theories

A theory is usually more developed than a model; a model, if and when verified (rather than shown to be false), can develop into a theory. Theories describe, explain and predict the subject matter of a discipline. For example, the fact that all young children master their mother tongue at an early age, and the common ability of humans to produce speech freely in an infinite number of utterances, have given rise to a number of theories to account for them. These theories come from various perspectives: linguistic, psychological and philosophical, among others.

Consider behaviourist theories in psychology that are based on the axiom that human beings do not act consciously, in that thoughts, feelings, intentions and mental processes do not determine what we do. Behaviourist psychology sees human beings as biological machines that react to stimuli, and whose behaviour is the product of our conditioning and habit formation. Therefore, behaviourist theories place the emphasis on scientific inquiry into observable behaviours, and explain learning as the result of associations that form between Stimulus–Reaction (S-R) (see the works of John Watson, 1878–1958, and the learning theory of Edward Lee Thorndike, 1874–1949) and reinforcement (Burrhus Frederic Skinner, 1904–90). In turn, Chomsky's theory of universal grammar attempts to explain the same fact, the ability of every average human child to master his or her mother tongue, through an innate ability, unique to the human species and shared by all humans (Chomsky 1956).

Various theories describe and explain their subject matter with differing degrees of success; therefore, *descriptive power* and *explanatory power* can vary in different theories. *Predictive power* is also necessary for a theory, and this is the ability to generate predictions that can be easily tested. The more accurate the prediction proves to be, the higher its value. The Periodic Table of Elements by Dmitry Mendeleev (1834–1907) is the foundation for highly valued theory in chemistry and physics because of its strong predictive power. In the last third of the nineteenth century, Mendeleev, then a professor of general chemistry at the University of St. Petersburg, used the trends in his periodic table to predict then undiscovered chemical elements and their properties. The predictions were correct. While, by Mendeleev's time, over 60 elements had been identified, today more than 110 elements are known. The predictive capacity of this theory was recognised even before its meaning could be suitably explained.[1]

The predictive power of a theory is important because the theory can then be used for different applications of the knowledge. In teaching additional languages, those who lean towards universal grammar principles teach and explain grammar to learners together with general principles of language structure. The followers of behaviourism theories emphasise the role of imitation, association, reinforcement and frequent practice in order to form habits and skills that will become automatic. Exercises stress the importance of activity: the precept of 'learning by doing' is observed. The well-known Berlitz language courses, which teach about fifty-two world languages to adults, initially incorporated the ideas of behaviourism in their teaching methods – repetition, imitation, frequency and practice in the form of profuse grammar exercises to reinforce skills. This is a good illustration of how a theory has a practical application.

A multilingualism theory helps us to answer the following questions:

- Why and how is multilingualism qualitatively different from bilingualism?
- Is there one big lexicon or different lexicons for different languages?
- How and why do different languages interact with each other at an individual level?
- What are the additional factors that come into play when a third or subsequent language is being acquired?

Theories also express the axioms and statements that have been proven to be true about the subject matter under consideration. While the complete and unified theory of multilingualism is a matter of the future (not necessarily very far away), there are many statements in the subdomains of multilingualism (such as multilingual education, multilingual individuals, multiple language acquisition and tertiary didactics) that together make up the theory of multilingualism. These theoretical statements not only are descriptive and generally characterise multilingual environments and multilingual individuals, but they also make reasonable predictions possible.

Multilingualism theory includes postulates such as 'The bilingual is not two monolinguals in one person' (after Grosjean 1989), and to the effect that a multilingual is not a total of three or more monolinguals. Multilingualism theory maintains

---

1. <http://www.aip.org/history/curie/periodic.htm> (last accessed 23 August 2021).

that bilingualism and multilingualism are the norm rather than the exception, and trilinguals and multilinguals are treated as fully proficient speakers, setting realistic aims for multilingual learners in accordance with their real linguistic and communicative needs. These and other postulates of multilingualism discussed in previous chapters cumulatively constitute the building blocks of the theory of multilingualism.

12.1.2 Models

In order to imagine how multilingual phenomena and processes occur, a model can be developed, based upon facts and empirical research. Models in science can be physical objects, such as a toy model that may be assembled and even made to work like the object it represents, or mathematical formulas. In bilingualism and multilingualism, at least until now, models have largely been 'conceptual models'. They are generally less formal, less abstract and less 'material' than those in the natural sciences. The humanities and social sciences normally work differently from the natural science research framework, and multilingualism studies often (but not always) rely on subjective and descriptional methodologies. In the rest of this chapter, we will look at an overview of the models specific to multilingualism.

12.2 Models specific to multilingualism

Most of the existing bi- and multilingualism models refer to the process of multiple language acquisition (Green 1986, 1993; De Bot 1992, 2004). The number of specifically multilingual models is still very limited. The best known of them provide frameworks for understanding the nature, processes and phenomena of multilingualism: the Factor Model by Britta Hufeisen (2010, 2018a, 2018b; Hufeisen and Jessner 2019), a Dynamic Model of Multilingualism (DMM) by Philip Herdina and Ulrike Jessner (2002), a Biotic Model of Multilingualism by Aronin and Ó Laoire (Aronin and Ó Laoire 2004), the Role–Function Model by Sarah Williams and Björn Hammarberg (Hammarberg 1998, 2009) and the Multilingual Processing Model suggested by Franz Joseph Meißner (2003).

12.2.1 Factor Model by Hufeisen

This model, by Britta Hufeisen (Hufeisen 2010, 2018a, 2018b), describes stages of language acquisition starting from acquisition of the mother tongue (L1), the first additional language (L2), the second additional language (L3) and further languages (L4 or Ln). Each stage accounts for factors that influence and control the process of language learning. According to this model, learning of the first language requires two groups of factors: Neuropsychological Factors, such as general language acquisition capability and age, and Learner External Factors, such as learning environment, and type and amount of input, as well as L1 learning traditions and cultural heritage. The process of acquiring the second language, in addition to the first two groups of factors, includes three more groups: Affective Factors (motivation, anxiety, attitudes, individual life experience, perceived closeness/distance between languages), Cognitive Factors (language awareness, metalinguistic awareness, individual learning experience, learning strategies) and Linguistic Factors (that is, knowledge of the first language).

The first two groups of factors that play a role in the acquisition of the first language relate to the innate abilities of a speaker, the biological capacities endowed by nature, his/her intelligence and personality traits. These change with age and experience. The Learner External Factors groups encompass a wide range of situations in which a learner finds himself or herself, the family, the parents, and later, nursery and school, quality and type of care and education, the wider environment – the city, country and amount of input for the first language. The heart-breaking experience of the Ukrainian girl Oxana gives us a clue to the importance of Learner External Factors for a child acquiring her first language. Her case, that of a modern feral child, was widely reported in the media as that of the 'Ukrainian dog-girl'.[2] Reportedly, Oxana (born 1983) was abandoned by her parents at the age of two and spent about six years with dogs in a shed behind her house. When she was belatedly noticed by social workers in 1991, she was eight years old and had only minimal elements of human language. Beyond this, her communication consisted in growling and barking like a dog. In other respects, too, she displayed the behaviour and skills of a dog – walking on all fours and crouching in a doglike way, sniffing at her food before she ate it, and having extremely acute senses of hearing, smell and sight. For several formative years, the girl was deprived of a social human environment; in terms of the Factor Model, she did not acquire the social input described as Learner External Factors, although, like any other normal child, she was well endowed with biological abilities. As of 2010, at the age of twenty-six, despite the prognosis of the specialists who did not believe that she would ever be properly rehabilitated into 'normal' society, Oxana was doing amazingly well. She was capable of normal human communication and even of expressing emotions and judgements towards her parents who abandoned her. Oxana's case emphasises the role of society in acquiring the first language, and demonstrates the importance of different groups of factors and their relevance for success in the learning process.

The other groups of factors that feature at the beginning of the acquisition of each additional language are also highly influential. If a learner is not at ease or is emotionally upset, this emotional state can prevent any successful learning and, of course, language acquisition. Cognitive Factors include language awareness, metalinguistic awareness, learner awareness and the learner's ability to deploy and utilise learning strategies. The ability of the learner to learn the language is a critical factor in acquisition.

The group of Linguistic Factors implies the entire language system of one's mother tongue, as well as the cultural aspects that inevitably accompany language – words and grammar patterns, ways of using this language in a variety of situations, the social norms of language use, the cultural repository – for example, legends and fairy tales, proverbs and common abbreviations, along with memory, including reminiscences about childhood or events. In addition, once one language is mastered and the store of experiences and skills accompanying language knowledge

---

2. See <http://www.1tv.ru/documentary/fi=5925> and <http://www.youtube.com/watch?v=93HymGXC_wM> (last accessed 23 August 2021).

is collected, this knowledge and these skills are compared with the second language (L2) a person starts mastering. The first obvious comparison, but not the only one, is that of L1 and L2 as separate systems and their typological relationship (see Chapter 5 for linguistic typologies of languages). Everyone can imagine how difficult the Japanese language is for Europeans, not only because of the difference in vocabulary, pronunciation and grammar, but also because of the difference in Japanese and European writing systems.

The Factor Model is important for understanding multilingualism because it touches the heart of multilingualism theory and ushers in a serious argument for the heated discussions relating to multilingualism: it emphasises the difference between learning an L2 and an L3. Whereas the learner of an L2 is a complete novice in the additional non-native language learning, in the case of learning/acquiring an L3, a learner already has the experience of learning his or her first additional language, the L2.

With learning an L3 (or L4, L5 ... Ln), the Linguistic Factor is 'upgraded', expanding to add the knowledge and skills of L2 in addition to L1, but the principal addition in this figure showing the model is the Foreign Language Specific Factor. This subsumes individual foreign language learning experience, ability to compare features of L2 and L3, ability of learners to transfer lexical and syntactical knowledge from L2 to L3, and vice versa, and to make interlingual connections. Thus the learner of the L2 and the L3 are not the same. Unlike an L2 learner, the L3 learner has a repertoire of experience in learning the L2 that he or she can deliberately evoke and activate. Unlike the L2 novice language learner, the L3 or L4 learner has consciously or unconsciously developed certain strategies and approaches to learning. These Foreign Language Specific Factors are very important in the learning of an L3. The L2, in a way, functions as a bridge to learning the L3.

With each new language learned, as well as with the passage of time, the factors previously involved change or modify; abilities may improve or fade with age or effort, experience may grow and motivation can differ at different periods of life, all of which testifies to the complex and dynamic nature of multilingualism. The Factor Model also stresses the idea that learning further languages – L4, L5 or L12 – is no different in principle from learning an L3, since only one new factor is involved in acquiring additional languages: the Foreign Language Specific Factor. This model visually and logically demonstrates how the learning of the first additional language (L2) is patently different from learning the second and further additional language (L3). In summary, the Factor Model by Hufeisen (2010) conceptualises the third language acquisition process as qualitatively different from that of second language acquisition (SLA), an insight that has direct implications for educational practice.

12.2.2 Dynamic Model by Herdina and Jessner

The Dynamic Model of Multilingualism (DMM) is a highly influential model of multilingualism. This model, proposed by Philip Herdina and Ulrike Jessner (2002), purports to explain individual language learning within the framework of Dynamic Systems Theory (DST). DMM treats the process of an individual's language acquisition as a 'system'. Therefore, the languages of a multilingual are termed psycholin-

Models of multilingualism

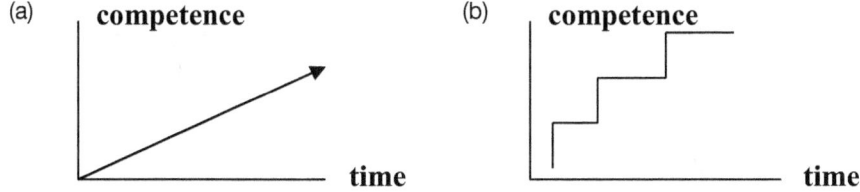

Figure 12.1 (a and b) Previous views of language acquisition development in time (after Herdina and Jessner 2002, reproduced with permission).

guistic *systems* ($LS_1/LS_2/LS_3/LS_4$, etc.) and *open systems*: that is, systems that are open to modifications and changes caused by psychological and social factors.

The process of learning foreign or additional languages from zero to increasing competence is often thought of as an upward straight diagonal line (Fig. 12.1a). More realistic beliefs about language acquisition acknowledge that there are periods during the learning process when the level of mastery does not increase. The gradual rise of language proficiency can be envisaged as a ladder (Fig. 12.1b). Neither assumption, however, can explain the actual process of language learning by a multilingual individual, who, in real life, experiences backward development, intervals of various length, and influences from other languages. Nor can these simplistic views fully explain individual variability, great differences in language mastery levels reached by different individuals under more or less similar conditions. Instead of a straight line representing the imagined ideal advance in learning an additional language, a different dynamic normally occurs in reality. Quick acquisition, phases in the early stages of language learning flatten out in more advanced stages and at any stage language loss of any of an individual's languages, including L1, is very possible for a number of reasons.

Multilingual acquisition is, therefore, understood to be non-linear. This means that acquiring a third language cannot be described as simply acquiring one language linearly after the other, as follows:

$$L1 \longrightarrow L2 \longrightarrow L3$$

Multilingual acquisition (MLA), as represented graphically by Herdina and Jessner, might be more akin to Figure 12.2. We can see that the learning process for each additional language undergoes ups and downs. In keeping with the postulates of the DST approach, language systems of a multilingual (that is, one's mother tongue, and successive languages) are understood to be *dynamic*, which means changing with time and being in constant flux.

The model describes and explains all types of multilingualism and acquisition of all categories of languages: acquisition of first and second languages, foreign language learning, third and successive language acquisition and also language loss. All these processes are interconnected and influence each other.

The DMM model is unique in that it emphasises the importance of the whole and the interdependence of its parts. The emphasis in the DMM is not on dissecting the multiple language acquisition processes into parts, as traditional approaches would, but on the complete system In other words, it views multilingual acquisition

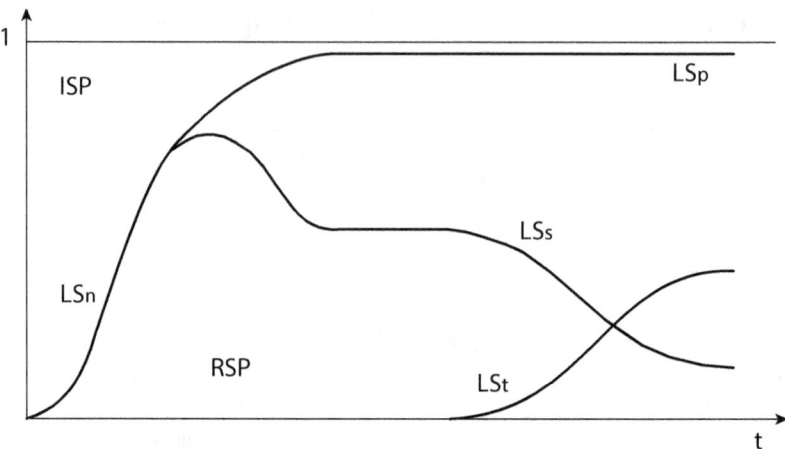

Figure 12.2 Learner multilingualism: overall development (Herdina and Jessner 2002: 124, reproduced with permission). LSn = prior language system(s); LSp = primary language system; LSs = secondary language system; LST = tertiary language system; ISP = ideal native speaker proficiency; RSP = rudimentary speaker proficiency; t = time; l = language level.

in its entirety. While traditional studies investigated multilinguals' mastery or the process of acquisition for each language separately, Herdina and Jessner show that linguistic systems, an individual's languages, interact with one another. In practice, it brings us to the understanding that language performance, language skills and linguistic identity traits should not be assessed separately in multilingual learners.

This 'surplus', beyond the sum of knowledge and skills in each language of a multilingual, is counted by the DMM as an *M-factor* (*Multilingualism Factor*). Jessner defines the M-factor in the following way:

> The M-factor refers to all the effects in multilingual systems that distinguish a multilingual from a monolingual system, that is, all those qualities which develop in a multilingual speaker/learner due to the increase in language contact(s) in a non-additive or cumulative way such as metalinguistic and metacognitive awareness. (Jessner 2008: 26)

The most important notion here is that multilingualism as the natural state of a speaker is not explicable in terms of a single system. In the light of the DMM model, multilinguals have language proficiency that is not simply the sum of their skills in several languages they have mastered or are mastering. Jessner sees multilingual proficiency in the following way:

> [m]ultilingual proficiency (MP) is defined as the dynamic interaction between the various psycholinguistic systems (LS_1, LS_2, LS_3, LS_n), cross-linguistic interaction (CLIL) and the M(ultilingualism)-factor or M-effect as shown in the following formula:

$$LS_1, LS_2, LS_3, LS_n + CLIN + M\text{-factor} = MP \text{ (Jessner 2008: 26)}$$

This model gives a sense of looking at the overall system of languages employed by the multilingual individual in its pattern of convergence, divergence and interaction.

12.2.3 Biotic Model by Aronin and Ó Laoire

This model, proposed by Larissa Aronin and Muiris Ó Laoire (2001, 2004), relates to individual aspects of multilingualism in their entirety, and the notion of *multilinguality* is its central feature (Aronin and Ó Laoire 2001, 2004; Chapter 8 of the present work). Similar to the DMM, the Biotic Model takes a broad, holistic view of the multilingual individual and of multilingualism, and is developed along the lines of the complexity approach. The Biotic Model is different from the other models of multilingualism in that it is largely sociolinguistic in its interest, since it regards the social milieu as an important influence and considers the societal consequences of multilinguality.

The notion of multilinguality refers to an individual, but the Biotic Model is relevant to multilingual societies as well, as it describes and considers social aspects of multilingual existence and multilingual environment (broadly understood) as its focal point of interest (see the notion of multilinguality in Chapter 9). The circumstances and milieu are envisaged as soil in which multilinguals grow. The Biotic Model is also called an *ecological model* of multilingualism because it describes the ecological phenomenon intrinsic to the cycle of nature, thus emphasising the essential dynamics of growth, change, fluctuation, input, absorption and decay, while stressing the complexity of multilingualism.

The three models discussed above are general, considering the language acquisition process and multilinguality as a whole. Each of the next two models focuses on a specific aspects – speech production and comprehension.

12.2.4 Role–Function Model by Williams and Hammarberg

This model, proposed by Sarah Williams and Björn Hammarberg (Hammarberg 1998, 2001), explains the oral production of speech in a tertiary language (L3, L4, L5 ... Ln). The specificity of this model and its relevance to multilingualism theory lie in the fact that it assigns a significant role to other languages in learning an additional language – in particular, to non-native secondary languages. Expanding on the monolingual models of speech production, Williams and Hammarberg developed their model of multilingualism from a longitudinal empirical study. They observed and documented the language learning process of an English-born multilingual, Sarah Williams. Having taken up residence in Sweden, Sarah was learning Swedish. She had lived for six years in Germany before moving to Sweden, and in addition to English and German, her other languages included French and Italian.

Sarah's everyday conversations in Swedish were recorded and analysed. As the next step, the authors determined the influence of Sarah's other languages on her most recent acquisition of Swedish. While learning Swedish, Sarah resorted to her mother tongue in some instances when she wanted to understand a word or tried to explain herself to the interlocutor: that is, not when she was engaged in actual Swedish production, but rather when she was speaking *about* the language and about how the new language was being learned (metalinguistic discourse). But, importantly, she tended to resort to German when searching for a suitable phrase or when lacking a word in Swedish. She also consistently derived rules in Swedish from German. In other words, Sarah used German more often than English, her mother tongue, as a *supplier language* to build her vocabulary and grammar in a new language.

The findings allowed Williams and Hammarberg to come up with the idea that, in learning a new language, other languages, including non-native secondary languages, play a significant role. They termed the language that was dominant in supporting the process of learning an 'instrumental language'. They termed the language that served as a source for building vocabulary and grammar – in Sarah's case, German – for her new language, Swedish, 'a supplier language'.

Which language is assigned the role of 'supplier' and why? The authors of the model put forward four factors, according to which a language is assigned the role of 'a supplier' by the multilingual learner: 'Language proficiency, Linguistic typology; Recency and Foreignness' (L2 status). Any of these factors may prove decisive for a multilingual learner in using a particular one of his or her languages as a *source language*.

12.2.5 Multilingual Processing Model by Meißner

While the focus of the Role–Function Model is on speech production, the Multilingual Processing Model, by Franz-Joseph Meißner (2003), emphasises the receptive processes and skills of a multilingual. Its aim is to explain processing and comprehension in a language not previously learned by multilinguals. Empirical evidence shows that it functions between closely related languages.

The distinctive feature of this model is the premise that, even in the first encounter with a new language, multilingual learners build a *spontaneous hypothetical grammar* for this language. This hypothetical structure of the 'unknown' target language is based on the solid lexical, semantic, syntactical and encyclopaedic knowledge accrued from other languages that a multilingual has already mastered, rather than on knowledge of a target language.

When deciphering and decoding written or oral texts in the target language, learners tend to rely on their previous language knowledge, as well as continuously revising their hypothetical structures to conform to the correct grammar of the target language. Meißner distinguished several stages that learners pass through when processing a new language. Initially, they mainly depend on one of their previous languages, a *bridge* language that facilitates the acquisition of the new lexicon and grammar. As input increases and knowledge of the target language rules grows, a learner puts forward new hypotheses about the new grammar, thus constantly revising and extending it, using the source 'bridge' language to transfer knowledge, skills and strategies to the hypothetic grammar being built. As a result, an interlingual system evolves that provides the learner with a general framework for decoding and understanding a new language. This interlingual grammar system stores all successful transfers from the source language to the target language, furthering progress in the new language.

This algorithm has implications for language teaching and tertiary didactics, and suggests a way to optimise the teaching and learning of additional languages. It is especially valid for adult learners. Ideally, the target language and the bridge language are typologically close (such as Italian and Spanish, or Swedish and Dutch), and the learner is proficient in the bridge language. It is also beneficial to instruct a learner in how to use knowledge of a bridge language better and more efficiently for processing a new language. As the event of intercomprehension gives an insight into the formation of interlanguage, multilingual-processing-based learning and teaching methods can be considered as a language and learning awareness-raising strategy.

12.3 Modelling in multilingualism

The models of multilingualism described above are *conceptual explanatory models*. They are expressed mostly verbally and their characteristic 'brand' figures or diagrams are employed only to illustrate and clarify the verbal explanation. When an analytical explanatory model allows for visual and tangible representation, a replica that is drawn, sketched or produced from various materials, it is called *modelling*.

The analytical model of Dominant Language Constellations (DLCs, referred to in Chapter 10), for instance, is well suited to visual expressions of various kinds and modelling in a variety of forms. While the verbal conceptual model of the DLC approach broadly describes the archetypal, seeking to understand the nature of current multilingual practices, the particular real-life patterns of contemporary language use can be reified and embodied through specific DLC representations for each particular case. In addition to analytical verbal representation, it has a second facet: the capability of being represented visually and tangibly as an interactive model.

Visual and physical models as forms of scientific representation of the world identify and explain patterns that underlie ideas, events and processes. Such models are especially important when, as in case of multilingualism, some phenomena are difficult to observe directly. Although multilingual language practices are seen and heard, their patterns and inner workings are indeed transitory, elusive and hard to capture. Therefore, in addition to analytical models that are, in large part, expressed verbally, modelling representations are used.

The propensity of DLC for being visualised and modelled is variously employed in pedagogy and language teaching with different cohorts of language learners and users, both young and adult.

12.3.1 DLC modelling

DLC Modelling is the process and the result of creating and manipulating external representations of individual or group dominant language constellations in the

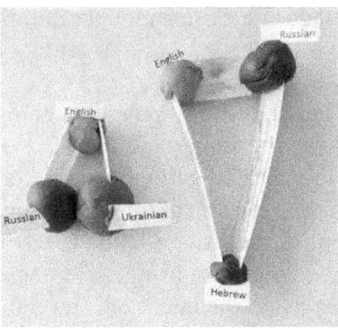

Figure 12.3 Plasticine® DLC models comparing Russian/Ukrainian/English and English/Russian/Hebrew.

form of visual and/or tangible replicas. Perceptible models can be manipulated for the sake of analysis and reflection. DLC modelling is beneficial both for average language users and for those professionally involved with them in multilingual communities. The advantages of modelling lie in enhancing cognition and raising awareness in one's own or others' languages.

Currently, the most popular modelling trend is producing home-made Plasticine®/Play-Doh™ models of individual DLCs. Typically, this is carried out in special class or group sessions, where the students and pupils are offered Plasticine of different colours, along with sticks, so that they can create a tangible embodiment of their unit of languages (such as in Figure 12.3). The simplest models are built on three basic features: (1) which named language – represented by a sphere of a certain colour; (2) perceived proficiency in this language – represented by the size of the sphere; and (3) the linguistic distance between the languages of the language cluster.

For language users and learners, DLC modelling provides not only a cognitive boost, but also advantages around their multilinguality, giving an additional stimulus and input of self-awareness and language awareness to their multilingual identity. During sessions dedicated to creating the physical representation of one's own language identity, apart from engagement and fun, the students reported having associations and thoughts that might not have appeared, if not for the process of making models (see Figure 12.4).

3D Plasticine models of personal DLCs serve as both a cognitive extension and a material symbol of one's own sociolinguistic existence and of the language skills that ensure this existence. For researchers and practitioners, DLC modelling is an external representation of multilingual processes that enables looking at well-known multilingual phenomena from a more comprehensive angle. According to brain scientists, psychologists and data specialists, external representations boost cognition by shortcutting analytical processes, saving internal memory, creating persistent referents and providing structures that can serve as a shareable object of thought (Danaher 2016; Kirsh 2010; Shaw 2014).

If hand-made models are important for awareness and emotional involvement, computer-generated models have a special value in their capacity for being stored as unified data ready for modification and further use by other researchers (Fig. 12.5).

Models of multilingualism 201

 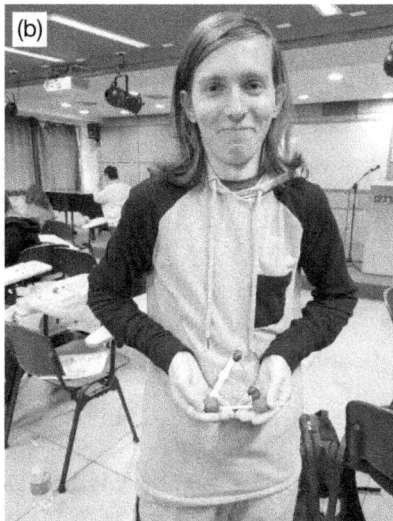

Figure 12.4a and b Creating one's own DLC.

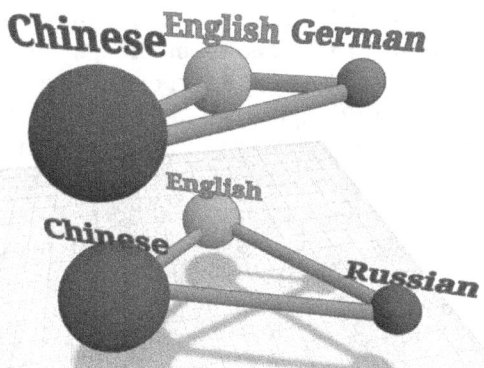

Figure 12.5 Computer-generated 3D Dominant Language Constellations. Illustration by Laurent Moccozet, reproduced with permission.

Computer-assisted DLC modelling with the help of specially designed software allows for tracing the dynamics of individual DLCs in time and space, dealing with smaller and larger cohorts of language users, comparing and categorising DLCs, and identifying their similarities and differing patterns in connection with certain events and in various settings.

Modelling multilingual processes helps us reach integrated and holistic, rather than only partial, understanding of multilingual situations that unfold on the streets and inside schools, universities and organisations. Computer-assisted and, in the near future, online DLC modelling can facilitate the grasping of vast, complicated and ever-fluid bodies of information on multilingualism.

Summary

In this chapter, we distinguished between theories and models, and described some specific multilingual models known in the field.

Three of the five reviewed models are of general scope: the Factor Model, the DMM and the Biotic Model. The Role–Function Model and Multilingual Processing Model delineate their range as language production and language perception and processing.

Complementing and reinforcing each other, the models of multilingualism emphasise the main points of multilingual theory in both similar and different ways. The distinction between bilingualism and multilingualism, bilinguals and tri-linguals or multilinguals, as well as the diversity and complexity of multilingual processes, are at the forefront and are treated as significant characteristic features of multilingual reality in these models. All the models of multilingualism hold that interrelations between the language systems of multilinguals are central and their operations are parallel. All models acknowledge the active role of previously acquired languages in learning a new one.

In keeping with the multilingual holistic approach, all the models recognise, though in different forms, the indispensable emergence of a 'surplus' as an essential property of multilingualism (the whole is always more than the sum of its parts). This is the M-factor in the DMM model, or the cumulative addition of the factor groups in the Factor Model, where the outcome is more than just a sum of the factors. According to Aronin and Ò Laoire, multilinguality is the embodiment of an emergent quality that goes beyond the sum of the physiological, psychological, social, educational and linguistic inputs and influences experienced by an individual and represents the distinctiveness of a multilingual personality. The emergent quality, the surplus, can be felt in a variety of forms. It may also function as a store of knowledge, skills and metalinguistic awareness that allows the learner the benefit of choice in acquisition of a new language. In Williams and Hammarberg's model, we see that multilinguals have a choice in selecting a source language, at least out of two, if the learner is studying a third language, while in the case of bilingualism, only one, the mother tongue, can serve all purposes and roles which might be needed in learning the second language. In Meiβner's model, again, we see that while a learner deciphering a text in a second language has to resort to his or her only previous language as a bridge, a multilingual speaker, in addition to the two language systems already mastered, activates metalinguistic knowledge and has already made comparisons between the two previous languages.

The Dominant Language Constellations approach has two planes. In addition to being an analytical and verbally expressed conceptual model, it can be represented visually and tangibly as an interactive model. Recently, modelling of hand-made representations of DLCs from a variety of materials and computer-assisted DLC modelling have been developed. DLC modelling is the process and the result of creating and manipulating external representations of individual or group DLCs. It is advantageous both for language users and for those who deal professionally with languages in society: teachers, educationalists and policy-makers.

The models of multilingualism, both separately and together, contribute to a coherent view of multilingualism and multiple language acquisition. The more that analytical and interactive representational models specifically tailored to account for the qualitative distinctness of multilingualism are proposed, the better we will be able to deal with complex multilingualism reality.

Further reading

Hammarberg, Björn (1998), 'Bakgrundsspråkens interaktion vid tredjespråksinlärning', in J. Møller, P. Quist, A. Holmen and J. N. Jørgensen (eds), *Nordiske sprog som andetsprog* (Københavnerstudier i tosprogethed 30), Copenhagen: Danmarks Lærerhøjskole, Institut for humanistiske fag.
Hammarberg, Björn (2001), 'Roles of L1 and L2 in L3 production and acquisition', in J. Cenoz, B. Hufeisen and U. Jessner (eds), *Cross-Linguistic Influence in Third Language Acquisition: Psycholinguistic Perspectives*, Clevedon, Bristol: Multilingual Matters, pp. 21–41.
Hammarberg, Björn (2006), 'Activation de L1 et L2 lors de la production orale en L3: étude comparative de deux cas', *Acquisition et Interaction en Langue Étrangère (AILE)*, 24, pp. 45–74.
Hufeisen, Britta (2005), 'Multilingualism: linguistic models and related issues', in B. Hufeisen and R. J. Fouser (eds), *Introductory Readings in L3*, Tübingen: Stauffenburg, pp. 31–45.
Hufeisen, Britta (2010), 'Theoretische Fundierung multiplen Sprachenlernens – Factorenmodell 2.0', in *Jahrbuch Deutsch als Fremdsprache*, 36, pp. 191–8.
Jessner, Ulrike (2008), 'Teaching third languages: findings, trends and challenges', *Language Teaching*, 41(1), pp. 15–56 (on current models of TLA pp. 21–6).
Meißner, F.-J. (2003), EuroComDidact: learning and teaching plurilingual comprehension', in L. Zybatow (ed.), *Sprachkompetenz – Mehrsprachigkeit – Translation. Akten des 35.Linguistischen Kolloquiums*, Innsbruck, 2–22 September 2000. Tübingen: Narr, pp. 33–46.

Chapter review

Fill in the table by (1) using material from the chapter, and (2) giving your own examples, considerations and comments.

Concept/keyword	Definition or explanation	Example from the chapter	Your own example	Your considerations and comments
Theory				
Model				
Factor Model by Britta Hufeisen				

Contd

Concept/keyword	Definition or explanation	Example from the chapter	Your own example	Your considerations and comments
Dynamic Model of Multilingualism (DMM) by Philip Herdina and Ulrike Jessner				
Biotic Model of Multilingualism by Aronin and Ó Laoire				
Role–Function Model by Sarah Williams and Björn Hammarberg				
Multilingual Processing Model by Franz Joseph Meißner				
DLC-modelling				

Reflective questions

1. Why do theories emerge and what can we learn from them?
2. Why does multilingualism need its own models? Why are only bilingual models not sufficient for multilingualism?
3. What aspects of multilingualism are currently explained by theories?
4. What are the additional factors that come into play when a third or subsequent language is being acquired?
5. What evidence for the complexity of multilingualism do you find in this chapter?

Exercises

Exercise 12.1

Draw your own chart of the factors influencing the acquisition of the fifth, sixth or any other additional language of your choice. Specify the particular factors in each group of factors. Discuss the contents of the last group of factors – 'Foreign Language Specific Factors'.

Exercise 12.2

Illustrate the Biotic Model of multilingualism by describing two or three multilinguals known to you and ponder how society, education, life events, attitudes, personal motivations and wishes, and the sociopolitical reality of the time shaped the multilinguality of these particular people. Compare them to see how even small factors change the course of life, thinking or career. Mention other identity characteristics that may be influenced.

Alternatively, compare the multilinguality of any person, or yourself, from the past and now. What are the differences in language use? In your attitudes? In your overall identity? In other words, how different are you now? Which factors (social, psychological, educational or others) were most instrumental to what you are now?

Exercise 12.3

Apply the Role–Function Model to your own multilingual situation.

(a) State from your experience which language usually comes to your mind when you are searching for a word in your target tertiary language?
(b) Discuss which of the factors plays a role in the selection of your supplier language.
(c) State the changes in the influence of languages with time: for example, 'With increasing proficiency in the target (such as Swedish) language, I use the supplier (such as German) language less' or 'I still use my supplier language' or 'My supplier language has changed to [Dutch].'

Exercise 12.4

Find a text in the unknown language on a website, or in a newspaper or book. Define which language is your 'bridge' language. Discuss your experience with your classmates.

Conclusion:
Reflecting on multilingualism

Current multilingualism is unique in many different ways, in terms of the physiological, emotional, cognitive and linguistic impact it has on all of us as individuals – whether monolinguals, bilinguals or multilinguals – and on the whole of humankind. Because it is so tightly woven into daily communication, state practices and aspiring technological and business projects, *whatever we do*, globally or in private, needs contemplation and discussion *in light of multilingualism*.

In considering the various aspects and forms of multilingualism we have discussed in this textbook, several overarching tendencies transpire.

1. The overall picture of multilingualism is striking in the *great complexity and extreme (super-) diversity* that emerge from the *intricate interaction* of *languages,* and in the *people* who reside in and move around various political *and* geographical *environments*. This *constantly transforming reality* results in *manifold forms, kinds and shapes* of linguistic, social and material phenomena (such as language varieties, language policies and materialities), and groupings and subgroupings of people (such as learners, users, populations, multilingual parents and teachers).
2. The resulting emergent phenomena associated with current multilingualism can often be characterised by the adjectives 'fused', 'blended', 'interactive', 'multimodal', 'complex', 'diverse', 'dynamic' and 'plural'. Research operates with 'multilingualis', 'Englishes' and 'multilingualities'. Paradoxically, the plural 's', in terms traditionally used in the singular, expresses both a deep interest in personal identity and, at the same time, concern with the societal.
3. One cannot help but notice *the increasing involvement of the societal dimension*, even in individual manifestations of multilingualism. This is one more special feature of current multilingualism.
4. As for research in multilingualism, it displays *simultaneous tendencies to generalisation and differentiation* and *a shift from dichotomous to holistic* views. Instead of sharp divisions, such as that between native/non-native speakers and teachers, we find holistic understandings and 'continua'. Some *traditional concepts*, such as 'writing' or 'language', *acquire meanings adjusted to a globalised reality*, and *new issues and questions* are occupying the minds of researchers and language users alike.

Multilingualism is currently a thriving area of inquiry that investigates the complex, super-diverse and multimodal reality of humankind using and learning their multiple language varieties in various settings, whether transnational, international or local, individually or in various social groupings.

Conclusion

Chapter review

1. Choose two words from the box, connect them logically, formulate a concrete title/topic and write an essay disclosing the deep interconnection of the two concepts chosen by you, using your theoretical and empirical knowledge.

   > complex   diverse/diversity   blended   continua   multilingualisms   multilingualities   multimodal   dynamic   interaction   emergent   technology   language ownership   multiliteracy   language acquisition   language use   Dominant Language Constellation (DLC)   multilingualism   material culture of multilingualism   third language acquisition (TLA)   translanguaging   multilingual (n)   modelling multilingualities

2. Provide your own examples of the theoretical statements of this précis.
3. Explain how the social dimension is implicated in personal language attitudes.

Bibliography

Abbi, Anvita (2006), *Endangered Languages of the Andaman Islands*, Munich: Lincom Europa.
Abbi, Anvita (2018), 'A sixth language family of India: Great Andamanese, its historical status and salient present-day features', in R. Mesthrie and David Bradley (eds), *The Dynamics of Language: Plenary and Focus Lectures from the 20th International Congress of Linguists, Cape Town, July 2018*, Claremont, Cape Town: UCT Press, pp. 134–52.
Adone, Dany, Anastasia Bauer, Keren Cumberbatch and Elaine L. Maypilama (2012), 'Colour signs in two indigenous sign languages', in Ulrike Zeshan and Connie De Vos (eds), *Sign Languages in Village Communities: Anthropological and Linguistic Insights*, Boston and Berlin: De Gruyter, pp. 53–86.
Aitchison, Jean (2008), *The Articulate Mammal: An Introduction to Psycholinguistics*, 5th edn, New York: Routledge.
Alpatov, Vladimir (2000), *150 Languages and Politics: Socio-linguistic Problems of the USSR and the Post-Soviet Space*, Moscow: Institute Vostokovedeniia. (Алпатов Владимир Михайлович. 2000. 150 языков и политика: 1917–2000. Москва: КРАФТ + ИВ РАН).
Ammon, Ulrich (1995), 'To what extent is German an international language?', in P. Stevenson (ed.), *The German Language and the Real World: Sociolinguistic, Cultural and Pragmatic Perspectives on Contemporary German*, Oxford: Clarendon Press, pp. 25–53.
Anchimbe, Eric, A. (2007), 'Multilingualism, postcolonialism, and linguistic identity: towards a new vision of postcolonial spaces', in Eric A. Anchimbe (ed.), *Linguistic Identity in Postcolonial Multilingual Spaces*, Newcastle: Cambridge Scholars Publishing, pp. 1–18.
Anchimbe, Eric and Stephen A. Mforteh (2011), *Postcolonial Linguistic Voices: Identity Choices and Representations*, Berlin and Boston: Mouton de Gruyter.
Anderson, Stephen (2004), *How Many Languages Are There in the World?*, Washington: Linguistic Society of America.
Andrews, Edna (2014), *Neuroscience and Multilingualism*, Cambridge: Cambridge University Press.
Annamalai, E. (2006), 'India: language situation', in K. Brown (ed.), *Encyclopedia of Language and Linguistics*, Boston: Elsevier, pp. 610–13.
Annamalai, E. (2008), 'Contexts of multilingualism', in Braj B. Kachru, Yamuna Kachru and S. M. Sridhar (eds), *Language in South Asia*, Cambridge: Cambridge University Press, pp. 223–43.
Aronin, Larissa (2006), 'Dominant Language Constellations: an approach to multilingualism studies', in Muiris Ó Laoire (ed.), *Multilingualism in Educational Settings*, Hohengehren: Schneider, pp. 140–59.
Aronin, Larissa (2016), 'Multicompetence and Dominant Language Constellation', in Vivian Cook and Li Wei (eds), *The Cambridge Handbook of Linguistic Multicompetence*, Cambridge: Cambridge University Press, pp. 142–63.

Aronin, Larissa (2018), 'Theoretical underpinnings of the material culture of multilingualism', in Larissa Aronin, Michael Hornsby and Grażyna Kiliańska-Przybyło (eds), *The Material Culture of Multilingualism*, Cham, Switzerland: Springer, pp. 21–45.
Aronin, Larissa, Michael Hornsby and Grażyna Kiliańska-Przybyło (eds), *The Material Culture of Multilingualism*, Cham, Switzerland: Springer.
Aronin, Larissa and Ulrike Jessner (2015), 'Understanding current multilingualism: what can the butterfly tell us?', in Claire Kramsch and Ulrike Jessner (eds), *The Multilingual Challenge*, Berlin and Boston: Mouton de Gruyter, pp. 271–91.
Aronin, Larissa and Muiris Ó Laoire (2001), 'Exploring multilingualism in cultural contexts: Towards a notion of multilinguality', Paper presented at the Third International Conference on Third Language Acquisition and Trilingualism, Leewarden-Liouwert, Netherlands, 13–15 September.
Aronin, Larissa and Muiris Ó Laoire (2004), 'Exploring multilingualism in cultural contexts: towards a notion of multilinguality', in C. Hoffmann and J. Ytsma (eds), *Trilingualism in Family, School and Community*, Clevedon, Bristol: Multilingual Matters, pp. 11–29.
Aronin, Larissa and Muiris Ó Laoire (2013), 'The material culture of multilingualism: moving beyond the linguistic landscape', *International Journal of Multilingualism*, 10(3), pp. 225–35.
Aronin, Larissa, Muiris Ó Laoire and David Singleton (2011), 'The multiple faces of multilingualism: language nominations', *Applied Linguistics Review*, Berlin and Boston: Mouton de Gruyter, 2, pp. 169–90.
Aronin, Larissa and David Singleton (2008), 'Multilingualism as a new linguistic dispensation', *International Journal of Multilingualism*, 5(1), pp. 1–16.
Aronin, Larissa and David Singleton (2010), 'Affordances and the diversity of multilingualism', in Larissa Aronin and David Singleton (eds), *International Journal of the Sociology of Language*, 205, Berlin and Boston: Mouton de Gruyter, pp. 105–29.
Aronin, Larissa and David Singleton (2012), *Multilingualism*, Amsterdam: John Benjamins.
Avery, Hilary and Andrea Gilbert (2006), 'First encounters with Ulster-Scots language, history and culture', in Dónall Ó Riagáin (ed.), *Voces Diversae: Lesser-Used Languages Education in Europe*, Belfast: Clo Ollscoil na Banríona, pp. 64–8.
Baetens Beardsmore, Hugo ([1982] 1986), *Bilingualism: Basic Principles*, 2nd edn. Clevedon, Bristol: Multilingual Matters.
Baker, Anne E. and Kees Hengeveld (eds) (2012), *Linguistics*, Hoboken, NJ: Wiley-Blackwell.
Baker, Colin ([1993, 1996, 2001, 2006, 2011] 2017), *Foundations of Bilingual Education and Bilingualism*, Clevedon, Bristol: Multilingual Matters.
Baker, Colin and S. Prys Jones (eds) (1998), *Encyclopedia of Bilingualism and Bilingual Education*, Clevedon, Bristol: Multilingual Matters.
Bakker, Peter (1997), *A Language of Our Own: The Genesis of Michif, the Mixed Creo-French Language of the Canadian Métis*, Oxford: Oxford University Press.
Banda, Felix (2020), 'Shifting and multi-layered dominant language constellations in dynamic multilingual contexts: African perspectives', in Joseph Lo Bianco and Larissa Aronin (eds), *Dominant Language Constellations: A Perspective on Present-day Multilingualism*, Cham, Switzerland: Springer, pp. 75–93.
Barnard, Alan (2016), *Language in Prehistory*, Cambridge: Cambridge University Press.
Barron-Hauwaert, Suzanne (2003), 'Trilingualism: a study of children growing up with three languages', in T. Tokuhama-Espinosa (ed.), *The Multilingual Mind: Issues Discussed by, for, and about People Living with Many Languages*, Westport, CT: Praeger, pp. 129–50.
Barron-Hauwaert, Suzanne (2004), *Language Strategies for Bilingual Families: The-One-Parent-One-Language Approach*, Clevedon, Bristol: Multilingual Matters.

Bedijs, Kristina and Christiane Maaß (eds) (2017), *Manual of Romance Languages in the Media*, Berlin and Boston: Mouton de Gruyter.

Berkes, Eva and Suzanne Flynn (2012), 'Enhanced L3 . . . Ln acquisition and its implications for language teaching', in D. Gabryś-Barker (ed.), *Cross-linguistic Influences in Multilingual Language Acquisition*, Berlin: Springer, pp. 1–22.

Berlin, Brent and Paul Kay ([1969] 1991), *Basic Color Terms: Their Universality and Evolution*, Berkeley and Los Angeles: University of California Press.

Berthele, Raphael and Gabriele Wittlin (2013), 'Receptive multilingualism in the Swiss army', *International Journal of Multilingualism*, 10(2), pp. 181–95.

Bialystok, Ellen (1991), *Language Processing in Bilingual Children*, Cambridge: Cambridge University Press.

Bialystok, Ellen, Fergus I. M. Craik and Gigi Luk (2012), 'Bilingualism: consequences for mind and brain', *Trends in Cognitive Sciences*, 16(4), pp. 240–50.

Bizri, Fida (2009), 'Sinhala in contact with Arabic: the birth of a new pidgin in the Middle East', in Rajendra Singh (ed.), *Annual Review of South Asian Languages and Linguistics*, Berlin and Boston: Mouton de Gruyter, pp. 135–48.

Bloomfield, Leonard (1933), *Language*, New York: Allen & Unwin.

Bogoras, Waldemar (1922, reprinted 1969), 'Chukchee', in Franz Boas (ed.), *Handbook of American Indian Languages*, 2, Washington: Government Printing Office, pp. 631–903.

Bolton, Kingsley (2020), 'World Englishes: current debates and future directions', in Cecil L. Nelson, Zoya G. Proshina and Daniel R. Davis (eds), *The Handbook of World Englishes*, 2nd edn. Hoboken: John Wiley & Sons, pp. 743–60.

Bolton, Kingsley and Braj B. Kachru (eds), (2006), *World Englishes: Critical Concepts in Linguistics*, 6 vols, London and New York: Routledge.

Bossomaier, Terry and David Green (1998), *Patterns in the Sand: Computers, Complexity, and Everyday Life*, Reading: Perseus Books.

Boyes Braem, Penny and Christian Rathmann (2010), 'Transmission of sign languages in Northern Europe', in Diane Brentari (ed.), *Cambridge Language Surveys: Sign Languages*, Cambridge: Cambridge University Press, pp. 19–45.

Brann, C. M. B. (1981), *Trilingualism in Language Planning for Education in Sub-Saharan Africa*, Paris: UNESCO, ref. ED-81/WS/116.

Bratt Paulston, Christina (2004), Book Review of Rajend Mesthrie (ed.) (2002), 'Language in South Africa', *Language in Society*, 33(4), pp. 632–7.

Braun, Andreas and Tony Cline (2014), *Language Strategies for Trilingual Families: Parents' Perspectives*, Clevedon, Bristol: Multilingual Matters.

Braunmüller, Kurt (2007), 'Receptive multilingualism in Northern Europe in the Middle Ages: a description of a scenario', in J. ten Thije and L. Zeevaert (eds), *Receptive Multilingualism: Linguistic Analyses, Language Policies and Didactic Concepts*, Amsterdam: John Benjamins, pp. 25–47.

Broch, Ingvild and Ernst Hakon Jahr (1984), 'Russenorsk: a new look at the Russo-Norwegian pidgin in Northern Norway', in P. Sture Ureland and Iain Clarkson (eds), *Scandinavian Language Contacts*, Cambridge: Cambridge University Press, pp. 21–5.

Brown, R. W. and E. H. Lenneberg (1954), 'A study in language and cognition', *Journal of Abnormal and Social Psychology*, 49(3), pp. 454–62.

Cameron, Lynne and Alice Deignan (2006), 'The emergence of metaphor in discourse', *Applied Linguistics*, 27, pp. 671–90.

Canadian Official Languages Act (1969). Available at: <http://www.officiallanguages.gc.ca/en/language_rights/act> (last accessed 20 August 2021).

Canagarajah, Suresh (2005), 'Dilemmas in planning English/vernacular relations in post-colonial communities', *Journal of Sociolinguistics*, 9(3), pp. 418–47.

Canagarajah, Suresh (2007), 'Lingua franca English, multilingual communities, and language acquisition', *The Modern Language Journal*, 91, pp. 923–39.
Capra, Fritjof and Pier Luigi Luisi (2014), *The Systems View of Life: A Unifying Vision*, Cambridge: Cambridge University Press.
Cedden, Gülay and Şimşek, Çiğdem Sağın (2012), 'The impact of a third language on executive control processes', *International Journal of Bilingualism*, 16(3), pp. 1–12.
Chertkow, Howard, Victor Whitehead, Natalie Phillips, Christina Wolfson, Julie Atherton and Howard Bergman (2010), 'Multilingualism (but not always bilingualism) delays the onset of Alzheimer disease: evidence from a bilingual community', *Alzheimer Disease & Associated Disorders*, 24(2), pp. 118–25.
Chiswick, Barry R. and Paul W. Miller (2004), 'Language skills and immigrant adjustment: what immigration policy can do!', *IZA Discussion Paper*, No. 1419, SSRN. Available at: <https://ssrn.com/abstract=632341> (last accessed 12 August 2021).
Chiti-Batelli, Andrea (2003), 'Can anything be done about the "glottophagy" of English? A bibliographical survey with a political conclusion', *Language Problems and Language Planning*, 27(2), pp. 137–53.
Chomsky, Noam (1956), 'Three models for the description of language', IRE *Transactions on Information Theory*, 2(3), pp. 113–24. Available at: <http://www.chomsky.info/articles/195609--.pdf> (last accessed 12 August 2021).
Chomsky, Noam (1957), *Syntactic Structures*, The Hague and Paris: Mouton.
Clark, Andy and David Chalmers (1998), 'The extended mind', *Analysis*, 58, pp. 7–19.
Clyne, Michael (1992a), 'Pluricentric languages - introduction', in M. Clyne (ed.), *Pluricentric Languages: Differing Norms in Different Nations*, Berlin and Boston: Mouton de Gruyter, pp. 1–9.
Clyne, Michael (ed.) (1992b), *Pluricentric Languages: Differing Norms in Different Nations*, Berlin and Boston: Mouton de Gruyter.
Clyne, Michael (2003), *Dynamics of Language Contact*, Cambridge: Cambridge University Press.
Colcombe, Stanley and Arthur F. Kramer (2003), 'Fitness effects on the cognitive function of older adults: a meta-analytic study', *Psychological Science*, 14(2), pp. 125–30.
Comrie, Bernard (1989), *Language Universals and Linguistic Typology: Syntax and Morphology*, 2nd edn, Oxford: Blackwell.
Comrie, Bernard, Stephen Matthews and Maria Polinsky (2003), *The Atlas of Languages: The Origin and Development of Languages*, New York: Facts on File Library of Language and Literature Series, a Quarto book.
Cook, Richard, Paul Kay and Terry Regier (2012), 'WCS Data Archives', World Colour Survey. Available at <http://www1.icsi.berkeley.edu/wcs/data.html> (last accessed 20 August 2021).
Cook, Vivian (1992), 'Evidence for multi-competence', *Language Learning*, 42(4), pp. 557–91.
Cook, Vivian (1993), *Linguistics and Second Language Acquisition*, London: Macmillan.
Cook, Vivian (2012), 'Multi-competence', in C. A. Chapelle (ed.), *The Encyclopedia of Applied Linguistics*, Hoboken, NJ: Wiley-Blackwell, pp. 3768–74.
Cook, Vivian (2013), 'ELF: central or atypical form of SLA?', in D. Singleton, J. Fishman, L. Aronin and M. Ó Laoire (eds), *Current Multilingualism: A New Linguistic Dispensation*, Berlin and Boston: Mouton de Gruyter, pp. 27–44.
Cook, Vivian (2016), 'Working definition of multi-competence'. Available at: <http://www.viviancook.uk/Writings/Papers/MCentry.htm> (last accessed 13 August 2021).
Cook Vivian and Li Wei (eds) (2016), *The Cambridge Handbook of Linguistic Multicompetence*, Cambridge: Cambridge University Press.
Cooper, David E. (1973), *Philosophy and the Nature of Language*, London: Longman.

Costa Albert and Mikel Santesteban (2004), 'Lexical access in bilingual speech production: evidence from language switching in highly proficient bilinguals and L2 learners', *Journal of Memory and Language*, 50, pp. 491–511.
Costa, Albert, Mikel Santesteban and Iva Ivanova (2006), 'How do highly proficient bilinguals control their lexicalization process? Inhibitory and language-specific selection mechanisms are both functional', *Journal of Experimental Psychology: Learning, Memory, and Cognition*, 32(5), pp. 1057–74.
Coulmas, Florian (1999), *The Blackwell Encyclopedia of Writing Systems*, Oxford: Blackwell.
Crystal, David (2003), *English as a Global Language*, 2nd edn, Cambridge: Cambridge University Press.
Dada, Shakila, Yvonne Murphy and Kerstin Tönsing (2017), 'Introduction to the special issue on augmentative and alternative communication practices: a descriptive study of the perception of South African speech-language therapists', *AAC*, 33(4), pp. 189–200.
Danaher, John (2016), *How Do We Enhance Cognition Through External Representations? Five Ways*. Philosophical Disquisitions, 13 October. Available at <https://ieet.org/index.php/IEET2/more/Danaher20161013> (last accessed 3 September 2021).
Daniels, Peter and William Bright (eds) (1996), *The World's Writing Systems*, Oxford and New York: Oxford University Press.
Davis, Kathryn (2013), 'Ethnographic approaches to second language acquisition research', in C. A. Chapelle (ed.), *The Encyclopedia of Applied Linguistics*, New York: Wiley Blackwell.
De Angelis, Gessica (2005), 'Multilingualism and non-native lexical transfer: an identification problem', *International Journal of Multilingualism*, 2(1), pp. 1–25.
De Angelis, Gessica and Jean-Marc Dewaele (eds) (2011), *New Trends in Crosslinguistic Influence and Multilingualism Research*, Clevedon, Bristol: Multilingual Matters.
De Bot, Kees (1992), 'A bilingual production model: Levelt's "speaking" model adapted', *Applied Linguistics*, 13(1), pp. 1–24.
De Bot, Kees (2004), 'The multilingual lexicon: modelling selection and control', *International Journal of Multilingualism*, 1(1), pp. 17–32.
De Bot, Kees (2017), 'Complexity Theory and Dynamic Systems Theory: same or different?', in L. Ortega and Z. H. Han (eds), *Complexity Theory and Language Development*, Amsterdam: John Benjamins, pp. 51–8.
De Bot, Kees and Sinfree Makoni (2005), *Language and Aging in Multilingual Contexts*, Clevedon, Bristol: Multilingual Matters.
Delgado, Cesar Ernesto Escobedo (2012), 'Chican Sign Language: a sociolinguistic sketch', in Ulrike Zeshan and Connie De Vos (eds), *Sign Languages in Village Communities: Anthropological and Linguistic Insights*, Boston and Berlin: De Gruyter, pp. 377–80.
Denzin, Norman K. (1978), *The Research Act: A Theoretical Introduction to Sociological Methods*, New York: McGraw-Hill.
Denzin, Norman K. and Yvonna S. Lincoln (eds) (2005), *Handbook of Qualitative Research*, Thousand Oaks, CA: Sage.
Denzin, Norman K., Yvonna S. Lincoln and Linda T. Smith (eds) (2008), *Handbook of Critical and Indigenous Methodologies*. Thousand Oaks, CA: Sage.
De Swaan, Abram (2001), *The Words of the World: The Global Language System*, Cambridge: Polity Press.
Di Carlo, Pierpaolo and Jeff Good (eds) (2020), *African Multilingualisms: Rural Linguistic and Cultural Diversity*, Lanham, MD: Lexington Books.
Dittmar, Norbert and Paul Steckbauer (2013), 'Emerging and conflicting forces of polyphony in the Berlin speech community after the fall of the wall: on the social identity

of adolescents', in D. Singleton, J. Fishman, L. Aronin and M. Ó Laoire (eds), *Current Multilingualism: A New Linguistic Dispensation*, Berlin and Boston: Mouton de Gruyter, pp. 187–229.

Donald, Merlin (1993), 'Précis of Origins of the Modern Mind: three stages in the evolution of culture and cognition', *Behavioral & Brain Sciences*, 16(4), pp. 737–91.

Doyé, Peter (2005), *Intercomprehension: Guide for the Development of Language Education Policies in Europe: From Linguistic Diversity to Plurilingual Education*, Strasbourg: Council of Europe. Available at <https://rm.coe.int/intercomprehension/1680874594> (last accessed 2 September 2021).

Dunbar, Robin ([1996] 2004), *Grooming, Gossip and Evolution of Language*, London: Faber and Faber.

Eberhard, David M., Gary F. Simons and Charles D. Fennig (eds) (2020), *Ethnologue: Languages of the World*, 23rd edn, Dallas: SIL International. Available at: <https://www.ethnologue.com/guides/how-many-languages> (last accessed 12 August 2021).

Ecke, Peter and Christopher J. Hall (2012), 'Tracking tip-of-the-tongue states in a multilingual speaker: evidence of attrition or instability in lexical systems?', *International Journal of Bilingualism*, 17(6), pp. 734–51.

Edelson, Stephen M., 'Autistic savants'. Available at: <https://www.autism.com/understanding_savants> (last accessed 12 April 2019).

Edwards, John (1994), *Multilingualism*, London and New York: Routledge.

Edwards, John (2019), 'Multilingual individuals', in David Singleton and Larissa Aronin (eds), *Twelve Lectures on Multilingualism*, Clevedon, Bristol: Multilingual Matters, pp. 135–61.

Ekpe, M. B. (2007), 'Standard Nigerian English: a stable variety in the emerging evolution of World Englishes', *Journal of the Nigerian English Studies Association*, 3(1), pp. 69–80.

Ellis, Rod (1994), *The Study of Second Language Acquisition*, Oxford: Oxford University Press.

Elmqvist, Niklas and Ji Soo Yi (2012), 'Patterns for visualization evaluation', in *Proceedings of the 2012 BELIV Workshop: Beyond Time and Errors – Novel Evaluation Methods for Visualization*. Article No. 12.

Erard, Michael (2012), *Babel No More: The Search for the World's Most Extraordinary Language Learners*, New York: Free Press.

Ethnologue: Languages of the World (2019), ed. M. Paul Lewis, 22nd edn, Dallas: SIL International. Available at: <http://www.ethnologue.com> (last accessed 23 August 2021).

Ethnologue (2021), 'What are the largest language families?'. Available at: <https://www.ethnologue.com/guides/largest-families> (last accessed 13 May 2020).

European Charter for Regional or Minority Languages (1998), Council of Europe. Available at: <http://conventions.coe.int/Treaty/EN/Treaties/Html/148.htm> (last accessed 12 August 2021).

European Union (2012), *Studies on Translation and Multilingualism. Intercomprehension: Exploring its Usefulness for DGT, the Commission and the EU*, Luxembourg: Publications Office of the European Union.

Fachin, Silvana Schiavi (2006), 'Friulian and other lesser-used languages in education in Friuli Venezia Giulia', in Dónall Ó Riagáin (ed.), *Voces Diversae: Lesser-Used Languages Education in Europe*, Belfast: Clo Ollscoil na Banríona, pp. 52–63.

Fasold, Ralph (1987), *The Sociolinguistics of Society*, Oxford and New York: Blackwell.

Fenlon, Jordan and Erin Wilkinson (2015), 'Sign languages in the world', in Adam C. Schembri and Ceil Lucas (eds), *Sociolinguistics and Deaf Communities*, Cambridge: Cambridge University Press, pp. 5–27.

Ferguson, Charles (1959), 'Diglossia', *Word*, 15, pp. 325–40.

Festman, Julia and Michela Mosca (2016), 'Influence of preparation time on language control: trilingual digit naming', in J. Schwieter (ed.), *The Cognitive Control of Multiple Languages:*

Experimental Studies and New Directions. Bilingual Processing and Acquisition. Amsterdam: John Benjamins, pp. 145–71.
Fishman, Joshua ([1965] 2000), 'Who speaks what language to whom and when?', *La Linguistique*, 2, pp. 67–88.
Fishman, Joshua A. (1967), 'Bilingualism with and without diglossia; diglossia with or without bilingualism', *Journal of Social Issues*, 23, pp. 29–38.
Fishman, Joshua A. ([1972] 1986), 'Domains and the relationship between micro-and macrosociolinguistics', in J. J. Gumperz and D. Hymes (eds), *Directions in Sociolinguistics: The Ethnography of Communication*, New York and Oxford: Basil Blackwell, pp. 435–53.
Fishman, Joshua A. (1997), 'The sociology of language', in N. Coupland, A. Jaworski (eds), *Sociolinguistics*. Modern Linguistics Series, London: Palgrave, pp. 25–30.
Fishman, Joshua A. (1998), 'The new linguistic order', *Foreign Policy*, 113 (Winter), pp. 26–40.
Flick, Uwe (2007), *Triangulation*, Wiesbaden: Verlag für Sozialwissenschaft.
Flores, Nelson and Mark Lewis (2016), 'From truncated to sociopolitical emergence: a critique of super-diversity in sociolinguistics', *International Journal of the Sociology of Language*, 241, pp. 97–124.
François, Alexandre (2012), 'The dynamics of linguistic diversity. Egalitarian multilingualism and power imbalance among northern Vanuatu languages', *International Journal of the Sociology of Language*, (214), pp. 85–110.
Freedman, Morris, Suvarna Alladi, Howard Chertkow, Ellen Bialystok, Fergus I. M. Craik, Natalie A. Phillips, Vasanta Duggirala, Surampudi Bapi Raju and Thomas H. Bak (2014), 'Delaying onset of dementia: are two languages enough?', *Behavioural Neurology*, Article ID 808137. Available at: <https://www.hindawi.com/journals/bn/2014/808137/> (last accessed 12 August 2021).
Gabryś-Barker, Danuta (2005), *Aspects of Multilingual Storage, Processing and Retrieval*, Katowice: Wydawnictwo Uniwersitetu Śląskiego.
Gabryś-Barker, Danuta (2018), 'Introduction', in Danuta Gabryś-Barker (ed.), *Third Age Learners of Foreign Languages*, Clevedon, Bristol: Multilingual Matters, pp. xiii–xxvii.
García, Ofelia and Li Wei (2014), *Translanguaging: Language, Bilingualism, and Education*, London: Palgrave Macmillan.
Gibson, Martha, Britta Hufeisen and Gary Libben (2001), 'Learners of German as an L3 and their production of German prepositional verbs', in Jasone Cenoz, Britta Hufeisen and Ulrike Jessner (eds), *Cross-Linguistic Influence in Third Language Acquisition: Psycholinguistic Perspectives*, Clevedon, Bristol: Multilingual Matters, pp. 138–48.
Goral, Mira and Peggy S. Conner (2013), 'Language disorders in multilingual and multicultural populations', *Annual Review of Applied Linguistics*, 33, pp. 128–61.
Graddol, David (1997), *The Future of English?*, London: British Council.
Graddol, David (2006), *English Next*, London: British Council.
Graddol, David (2010), *English Next India: The Future of English in India*, London: British Council.
Green, David W. (1986), 'Control, activation and resource: a framework and a model for the control of speech in bilinguals', *Brain and Language*, 27, pp. 210–23.
Green, David W. (1993), 'Towards a model of L2 comprehension and production', in R. Schreuder and B. Weltens (eds), *The Bilingual Lexicon*, Amsterdam: John Benjamins, pp. 249–77.
Green, David W. (1998), 'Mental control of the bilingual lexico-semantic system', *Bilingualism: Language and Cognition*, 1, pp. 67–81.
Greenberg, Joseph H. (1956), 'The measurement of linguistic diversity', *Language*, 32(1), pp. 109–15.

Groce, Nora E. (1985), *Everyone Here Spoke Sign Language: Hereditary Deafness on Martha's Vineyard*, Cambridge, MA: Harvard University Press.
Grosjean, François (1982), *Life with Two Languages: An Introduction to Bilingualism*, Cambridge, MA: Harvard University Press.
Grosjean, François (1985), 'The bilingual as a competent but specific speaker–hearer', *Journal of Multilingual and Multicultural Development*, 6, pp. 467–77.
Grosjean, François (1989), 'Neurolinguists, beware! The bilingual is not two monolinguals in one person', *Brain and Language*, 36(1), pp. 3–15.
Grosjean, François (1992), 'Another view of bilingualism', in R. Harris (ed.), *Cognitive Processing in Bilinguals*, Amsterdam: North-Holland, pp. 51–62.
Grosjean, F. (1998), 'Studying bilinguals: methodological and conceptual issues', *Bilingualism: Language and Cognition*, 1(2), pp. 131–49.
Grosjean, François (2001), 'The bilingual's language modes', in J. Nicol (ed.), *One Mind, Two Languages: Bilingual Language Processing*, Oxford: Blackwell, pp. 1–22.
Grosjean, François (2010), *Bilingual Life and Reality*, Cambridge, MA: Harvard University Press.
Gumperz, John (1964), 'Linguistic and social interaction in two communities', *American Anthropologist*, 66(6), pp. 137–53.
Gumperz, John (1968), 'Types of linguistic communities', in J. Fishman (ed.), *Readings in the Sociology of Language*, The Hague: Mouton, pp. 460–72.
Gumperz, John (1971a), 'The speech community', in A. S. Dil (ed.), *Essays by John Gumperz*, Stanford, CA: Stanford University Press, pp. 114–28.
Gumperz, John (1971b), 'Some remarks on regional and social language differences in India', in A. S. Dil (ed.), *Language in Social Groups: Essays by John J. Gumperz*, Stanford, CA: Stanford University Press, pp. 1–11.
Gumperz, John (1982a), *Discourse Strategies*, Cambridge: Cambridge University Press.
Gumperz, John J. (1982b), *Language and Social Identity*, Cambridge: Cambridge University Press.
Halliday, M. A. K. (2020), 'Written language, standard language, global language', in Cecil L. Nelson, Zoya G. Proshina and Daniel R. Davis, *The Handbook of World Englishes*, 2nd edn. Hoboken, NJ: John Wiley & Sons, pp. 333–48.
Hamers, Josiane F. and Michel H. Blanc ([1989] 2000), *Bilinguality and Bilingualism*, Cambridge: Cambridge University Press.
Hammarberg, Björn (1998), 'The learner's word acquisition attempts in conversation', in D. Albrechtsen, B. Henriksen, I. M. Mees and E. Poulsen (eds), *Perspectives on Foreign and Second Language Pedagogy*. Odense: Odense University Press, pp. 177–90. Reprinted in B. Hammarberg (ed.) (2009), *Processes in Third Language Acquisition*, Edinburgh: Edinburgh University Press, pp. 86–100.
Hammarberg, Björn (2001), 'Roles of L1 and L2 in L3 production and acquisition', in J. Cenoz, B. Hufeisen and U. Jessner (eds), *Cross-linguistic Influence in Third Language Acquisition: Psycholinguistic Perspectives*, Clevedon, Bristol: Multilingual Matters, pp. 21–41.
Hammarberg, Björn (ed.) (2009), *Processes in Third Language Acquisition*, Edinburgh: Edinburgh University Press.
Hammarström, Harald, Robert Forkel, Martin Haspelmath and Sebastian Bank (2020), Glottolog 4.2.1, Jena: Max Planck Institute for the Science of Human History. Available at: <http://glottolog.org> (last accessed on 11 June 2020).
Harmon, David and Jonathan Loh (2010), 'The index of linguistic diversity: a new quantitative measure of trends in the status of the world's languages', *Language Documentation & Conservation*, 4, pp. 97–151.
Harmon, David and Jonathan Loh (2018), 'Congruence between species and language

diversity', in Kenneth L. Rehg and Lyle Campbell (eds), *The Oxford Handbook of Endangered Languages*, Oxford: Oxford University Press, pp. 659–82.

Haugen, Einar (1950), 'The analysis of linguistic borrowing', *Language*, 26, pp. 210–331.

Haugen, Einar (1953), *The Norwegian Language in America: A Study in Bilingual Behavior*, Philadelphia: University of Pennsylvania Press.

Haugen, Einar (1972), *The Ecology of Language*, ed. A. S. Dill, Stanford, CA: Stanford University Press.

Haugen, Einar (1987), *Blessings of Babel: Bilingualism and Language Planning*, Berlin and Boston: Mouton de Gruyter.

Hayes, Cathy (1951), *The Ape in Our House*, New York: Harper.

Heeringa, Wilbert (2015), 'Afrikaans and Dutch as closely-related languages: a comparison to West Germanic languages and Dutch dialects', *Stellenbosch Papers in Linguistics Plus*, 47, pp. 1–18.

Herdina, Philip and Ulrike Jessner (2002), *A Dynamic Model of Multilingualism: Perspectives of Change in Psycholinguistics*, Clevedon, Bristol: Multilingual Matters.

Hesson, Sarah, Kate Seltzer and Heather H. Woodley (2014), *Translanguaging in Curriculum and Instruction: A CUNY–NYSIEB Guide for Educators*, New York: CUNY-NYSIEB.

Higby, Eve, Kim Jungna and Loraine K. Obler (2013), 'Multilingualism and the brain', *Annual Review of Applied Linguistics*, 33, pp. 68–101.

Hilgendorf, Suzanne (2020), 'Euro-Englishes', in Cecil L. Nelson, Zoya G. Proshina and Daniel R. Davis (eds), *The Handbook of World Englishes*, 2nd edn, Hoboken, NJ: John Wiley & Sons, pp. 215–31.

Hockett, Charles F. (1960), 'Logical considerations in the study of animal communication', in W. E. Lanyon and W. N. Tavolga (eds), *Animals Sounds and Animal Communication*, Washington: American Institute of Biological Sciences, pp. 392–430.

Hoffmann, Charlotte (2001a), 'The status of trilingualism in bilingualism studies', in J. Cenoz, B. Hufeisen and U. Jessner (eds), *Looking Beyond Second Language Acquisition: Studies in Tri- and Multilingualism*, Tübingen, Stauffenburg, pp. 13–25.

Hoffmann, Charlotte (2001b), 'Towards a description of trilingual competence', *International Journal of Bilingualism*, 5(1), pp. 1–17.

Hornberger, Nancy (1989), 'Bilingual education and language planning in indigenous Latin America', *International Journal of Sociology of Language*, 77, pp. 5–128.

Hornberger, Nancy (2003), 'Afterword: ecology and ideology in multilingual classrooms', in Angela Creese and Peter Martin (eds), *Multilingual Classroom Ecologies*, Clevedon, Bristol: Multilingual Matters, pp. 136–42.

Hornberger, Nancy (2009), 'Multilingual education policy and practice: ten certainties (grounded in indigenous experience)', *Language Teaching*, 42(2), pp. 197–211.

Hornsby, Michael (2018), 'The material cultures of multilingualism in a minoritized setting: the maintenance and transformation of Lemko', in Larissa Aronin, Michael Hornsby and Grażyna Kiliańska-Przybyło (eds), *The Material Culture of Multilingualism*, Cham, Switzerland: Springer, pp. 175–88.

Hosali, Priya (2005), 'Butler English: an account of a highly distinctive variety of English in India', *English Today*, 21, pp. 34–9.

Hufeisen, Britta (2005), 'Multilingualism: linguistic models and related issues', in B. Hufeisen and R. J. Fouser (eds), *Introductory Readings in L3*, Tübingen: Stauffenburg, pp. 31–45.

Hufeisen, Britta (2018a), 'Institutional education and multilingualism: PlurCur® as a prototype of a multilingual whole school policy', *European Journal of Applied Linguistics*, 6(1), pp. 131–70.

Hufeisen, Britta (2018b), 'Models of multilingual competence', in Andreas Bonnet and Peter

Siemund (eds), *Foreign Language Education in Multilingual Classrooms*, Amsterdam: John Benjamins, pp.173–89.

Hufeisen, Britta and Ulrike Jessner (2019), 'The psycholinguistics of multiple language learning and teaching', in D. Singleton and L. Aronin (eds), *Twelve Lectures on Multilingualism*, Cham, Switzerland: Springer, pp. 65–100.

Hufeisen, Britta and Nicole Marx (eds) (2007), *EuroComGerm – Die sieben Siebe: Germanische Sprachen lesen können*, Aachen: Shaker. Available at: <http://docplayer.org/206190070-Eurocomgerm-die-sieben-siebe-germanische-sprachen-lesen-lernen-j.html> (last accessed 1 September 2021).

Humboldt, Wilhelm von (1936), *On Language: The Diversity of Human Language Structure and its Influence on the Mental Development of Mankind*, trans. into English by P. Heath, 1988, Cambridge: Cambridge University Press.

Hymes, Dell H. (1972), 'On communicative competence', in J.B. Pride and J. Holmes (eds), *Sociolinguistics: Selected Readings*, Harmondsworth: Penguin, pp. 269–93.

Hymes, Dell (1974), *Foundations in Sociolinguistics: An Ethnographic Approach*, Philadelphia: University of Pennsylvania Press.

Inglis-Arkell, Esther (2014), 'Yes, sign language has accents', Gizmodo. Available at: <https://gizmodo.com/yes-sign-language-has-accents-1650818475> (last accessed 2 September 2021).

Janesick Valerie J. (1994), 'The dance of qualitative research design: metaphor, methodolatry, and meaning', in N. K. Denzin and Y. S. Lincoln (eds), *Handbook of Qualitative Research*, Thousand Oaks, CA: Sage, pp. 209–19.

Jenkins, Jennifer (2003), *World English: A Resource Book for Students*, London: Routledge.

Jenkins, Jennifer (2009), 'English as a lingua franca: Interpretations and attitudes', *World Englishes*, 28(2):200–7.

Jenkins, Jennifer (2011), 'Accommodating (to) ELF in the international university', *Journal of Pragmatics*, 43(4), pp. 926–36.

Jenkins, J. (2015), 'Repositioning English and multilingualism in English as a lingua franca' *Englishes in Practice*, 2(3), pp. 49–85.

Jenkins, Jennifer (2018), 'The future of English as a lingua franca?', in Jennifer Jenkins, Will Baker and Martin Dewey (eds), *The Routledge Handbook of English as a Lingua Franca*, Routledge, pp. 594–605.

Jenkins, Jennifer, Alessia Cogo and Martin Dewey (2011), 'Review of developments in research into English as a lingua franca', *Language Teaching*, 44(3), pp. 281–315.

Jessner, Ulrike (2006), *Linguistic Awareness in Multilinguals: English as a Third Language*, Edinburgh: Edinburgh University Press.

Jessner, Ulrike (2008), 'Teaching third languages: findings, trends and challenges', *Language Teaching*, 41(1), pp. 15–56.

Josephus (1981), *The Jewish War*, Introduction, notes and appendix by Mary Smallwood, London: Penguin.

Kachru, Braj (ed.) ([1982] 1992), *The Other Tongue: English Across Cultures*, 2nd edn, Urbana: University of Illinois Press.

Kachru, Braj B. (1985), 'Standards, codification and sociolinguistic realism: the English language in the outer circle', in R. Quirk and H. Widdowson (eds), *English in the World: Teaching and Learning the Language and Literatures*, Cambridge: Cambridge University Press, pp. 11–30 (pp. 11–36 with commentaries).

Kachru, Braj (2020), 'World Englishes and culture wars', in Cecil L. Nelson, Zoya G. Proshina and Daniel R. Davis (eds), *The Handbook of World Englishes*, 2nd edn, Hoboken, NJ: John Wiley & Sons, pp. 447–71.

Kachru, Braj B., Yamuna Kachru and Cecil L. Nelson (eds) [(2006] 2009), *The Handbook of World Englishes*, Oxford: Blackwell.

Kachru, Braj B., Yamuna Kachru and Shikaripur N. Sridhar (2008), *Language in South Asia*, Cambridge, UK, and New York: Cambridge University Press.
Kachru, Braj B. and Larry E. Smith (1985), Editorial, *World Englishes*, 4(2), pp. 209–12.
Kalaja, Paula and Silvia Melo-Pfeifer (2019), *Visualising Multilingual Lives: More than Words*, Clevedon, Bristol: Multilingual Matters.
Kamwangamalu, Nkonko M. ([2004] 2016), 'The language planning situation in South Africa', in Richard B. Baldauf and Robert B. Kaplan, *Language Planning and Policy in Africa*, Clevedon, Bristol: Multilingual Matters.
Kannangara, Sarasi (2020), 'The evolution of personal dominant language constellations based on the amount of usage of the languages', in J. L. Lo Bianco and L. Aronin (eds), *Dominant Language Constellations: A Perspective on Present-day Multilingualism*, Cham, Switzerland: Springer, pp.169–86.
Kaplan, Robert B., Baldauf, Richard B. (eds) (1997), *Language Planning from Practice to Theory*. Clevedon, Bristol: Multilingual Matters.
Kavé, Gitit, Nitza Eyal, Aviva Shorek and Jiska Cohen-Mansfield (2008), 'Multilingualism and cognitive state in the oldest old', *Psychology & Aging*, 23(1), pp. 70–8.
Kay, Paul, Brent Berlin, Luisa Maffi and Willam Merrifield (1997), 'Color naming across languages', in C. L. Hardin and L. Maffi (eds), *Color Categories in Thought and Language*, Cambridge: Cambridge University Press, pp. 21–56.
Kay, Paul, Brent Berlin, Luisa Maffi, William Merrifield and Richard Cook (2009), *The World Color Survey*. Stanford, CA: CSLI.
Kay, Paul and Richard S. Cook (2015), 'World Color Survey', in *Encyclopedia of Color Science and Technology*, New York: Springer Science+Business Media.
Kellogg, Winthrop N. and Luella A. Kellogg (1933), *The Ape and the Child: A Comparative Study of the Environmental Influence upon Early Behavior*, New York and London: McGraw-Hill.
Kemp, Charlotte (2007), 'Strategic processing in grammar learning: do multilinguals use more strategies?', *International Journal of Multilingualism*, 4(4), pp. 241–61.
Kemp, Charlotte (2009), 'Defining multilingualism', in L. Aronin and B. Hufeisen, *The Exploration of Multilingualism: Development of Research on L3, Multilingualism and Multiple Language Acquisition*, Amsterdam: John Benjamins, pp. 11–26.
Khubchandani, Lachman Mulchand (1997), *Revisualizing Boundaries: A Plurilingual Ethos*, New Delhi: Sage.
Kiesling, Scott F. (2020), 'English in Australia and New Zealand', in Cecil L. Nelson, Zoya G. Proshina and Daniel R. Davis (eds), *The Handbook of World Englishes*, 2nd edn, Hoboken, NJ: Wiley-Blackwell, pp. 70–86.
Kiran, Swathi and Mira Goral (2012), 'One disorder, multiple languages', *Asha Leader*, 17. Available at: <https://leader.pubs.asha.org/doi/10.1044/leader.FTR4.17072012.22> (last accessed 12 August 2021).
Kirkpatrick, Andy (2007), *World Englishes: Implications for International Communication and English Language Teaching*, Cambridge: Cambridge University Press.
Kirkpatrick, Andy (ed.) (2010a), *The Routledge Handbook of World Englishes*, London and New York: Routledge.
Kirkpatrick, Andy (2010b), *English as a Lingua Franca in ASEAN: A multilingual model*, Hong Kong: Hong Kong University Press.
Kirkpatrick, Andy (2011), 'English as an Asian lingua franca and the multilingual model of ELT', *Language Teaching*, 44(2), pp. 212–24.
Kirkpatrick, Andy (2014), 'English as a medium of instruction in East and Southeast Asian universities', in N. Murray and A. Scarino (eds), *Dynamic Ecologies: A Relational Perspective on Languages Education in the Asia-Pacific Region*, Dordrecht: Springer, pp. 15–29.

Kirkpatrick, Andy and Roland Sussex (eds) (2012), *English as an International Language in Asia: Implications for Language Education*, Dordrecht: Springer.

Kirsh, David (2010), 'Thinking with external representations', *AI and Society*, 25(4), pp. 441–54. Available at <https://philpapers.org/rec/KIRTWE> (last accessed 31 August 2021).

Kondo-Brown, Kimi (2012), 'Teaching Less Commonly Taught Languages' in Carol A. Chapelle (ed.), *The Encyclopedia of Applied Linguistics*, Hoboken, NJ: Wiley Blackwell.

Kornusova, Bosya (2006), 'Developing language teaching strategies: the Kalmyk experience', in Dónall Ó Riagáain (ed.), *Voces Diversae: Lesser-used Languages Education in Europe*, Belfast: Clo Ollscoil na Banríona, pp. 69–77.

Kortlandt, Frederik (2000), 'Initial a- and e- in Old Prussian', *Linguistica Baltica*, 8, pp. 125–7.

Kortlandt, Frederik (2013), 'Balto-Slavic personal pronouns and their accentuation', *Baltistica*, 48(1), pp. 5–11.

Kramsch, Claire (2014), 'Language and culture', *AILA Review*, 27, pp. 30–55.

Kreindler, Isabelle T. (ed.) ([1985] 2015), *Sociolinguistic Perspectives on Soviet National Languages: Their Past, Present and Future*, Contributions to the Sociology of Language [CSL] series, Boston and Berlin: Mouton de Gruyter.

Labov, William (1972), *Sociolinguistic Patterns*, Philadelphia: University of Pennsylvania Press.

Lacey, Alan R. (2001), *A Dictionary of Philosophy*, 3rd edn, London: Routledge.

Ladefoged, Peter (2005), *Vowels and Consonants: An Introduction to the Sounds of Languages*, Malden, MA: Blackwell.

Lane, James (2021), 'The 10 most spoken languages in the world, *Babbel Magazine*, 2 June. Available at: <https://www.babbel.com/en/magazine/the-10-most-spoken-languages-in-the-world> (last accessed 17 May 2020).

Larsen-Freeman, Diane (2013), 'Complexity Theory: a new way to think', *Revista Brasileira de Linguística Aplicada*, 13(2), pp. 369–73.

Larsen-Freeman, Diane (2017), 'Complexity Theory: the lessons continue', in L. Ortega and Z. H. Han (eds), *Complexity Theory and Language Development*, Amsterdam: John Benjamins, pp. 11–50.

Larsen-Freeman, Diane and Lynne Cameron (2008), *Complex systems and Applied Linguistics*, Oxford: Oxford University Press.

Leeson, Lorraine and John I. Saeed (2012), *Irish Sign Language: A Cognitive Linguistic Approach*, Edinburgh: Edinburgh University Press.

Le Goff, Jacques (1991), *Medieval Civilization 400–1500*, Malden, MA: Blackwell.

Leopold, Werner F. (1939–49), *Speech Development of a Bilingual Child: A Linguist's Record*, 4 vols. Evanston, IL: Northwestern University Press.

Levelt, Willem J. M. (1989), *Speaking: From Intention to Articulation*, Cambridge, MA: MIT Press.

Lewin, Kurt (1952), *Field Theory in Social Science*, New York: Harper & Row.

Lim, Lisa (2012), 'Standards of English in South-East Asia', in R. Hickey (ed.), *Standards of English: Codified Varieties around the World* (Studies in English Language). Cambridge: Cambridge University Press, pp. 274–93.

Lo Bianco, Joseph (1987), *National Policy on Languages*, Australian Government Publishing Service.

Lo Bianco, Joseph (2000), 'Multiliteracies and multilingualism', in Bill Cope and Mary Calantzis (eds), *Multiliteracies: Literacy Learning and the Design of Social Futures*, London and New York: Routledge, pp. 92–105.

Lo Bianco, Joseph (2017), 'Accent on the positive: revisiting the "Language as Resource" orientation for bolstering multilingualism in contemporary urban Europe', in H. Peukert and I. Gogolin (eds), *Dynamics of Linguistic Diversity*, Amsterdam: John Benjamins, pp. 31–48.

Lo Bianco, Joseph (2019), 'Uncompromising talk, linguistic grievance, and language policy:

Thailand's Deep South conflict zone', in M. Kelly, H. Footitt and M. Salama-Carr (eds), *Handbook on Languages at War*, London: Palgrave Macmillan.
Lo Bianco, Joseph (2020), 'A meeting of concepts and praxis: multilingualism, language policy and the Dominant Language Constellation', in Joseph Lo Bianco and Larissa Aronin (eds), *Dominant Language Constellations: A New Perspective on Multilingualism*, Cham, Switzerland: Springer, pp. 35–56.
Lo Bianco, Joseph (2021), 'Literacy learning and language education: Dominant Language Constellations and contemporary multilingualism', in L. Aronin, E. Vetter (eds), *Dominant Language Constellations Approach in Education and Language Acquisition. Educational Linguistics*, 51, Cham, Switzerland: Springer.
Lo Bianco, Joseph and Yvette Slaughter (2017), 'Language policy and education in Australia', in Teresa L. McCarty and Stephen May (eds), *Language Policy and Political Issues in Education*, 3rd edn, Cham, Switzerland: Springer, pp. 449–61.
McArthur, Tom (1987), 'The English languages'?, *English Today*, 12, pp. 21–41.
McArthur, Tom (2003), *The Oxford Guide to World Englishes*, Oxford: Oxford University Press.
McCann, William, Horst G. Klein and Tilbert D. Stegmann (2002), *EuroComRom. The Seven Sieves. How to Read all the Romance Languages Right Away*. Aachen: Shaker.
McLoddy, Kadyamusuma, Eve Higbi and Loraine Obler (2019), 'The neurolinguistics of multilingualism', in David Singleton and Larissa Aronin (eds), *Twelve Lectures on Multilingualism*, Clevedon, Bristol: Multilingual Matters, pp. 271–96.
McRae Louise, Robin Freeman and Stefanie Deinet (2014), 'The Living Planet Index', in R. McLellan, L. Iyengar, B. Jeffries and N Oerlemans (eds), *Living Planet Report 2014: Species and Spaces, People and Places*, Gland, Switzerland: WWF.
MacSwan, Jeff (2017), 'A multilingual perspective on translanguaging', *American Educational Research Journal*, 54(1), pp. 167–201.
MacSwan, Jeff (2020), 'Translanguaging, language ontology, and civil rights', *World Englishes*. Wiley Online Library. Available at: <https://terpconnect.umd.edu/~macswan/MacSwan2020-WE.pdf> (last accessed 2 September 2021).
Makoni, Sinfree and Ulrike Meinhof (2003), 'Introducing applied linguistics in Africa', in S. Makoni and U. H. Meinhof (eds), *Africa and Applied Linguistics. AILA Review*, 16, Amsterdam: John Benjamins, pp. 1–12.
Makoni, Sinfree and Alastair Pennycook (2007), 'Disinventing and reconstituting languages', in Sinfree Makoni and Alastair Pennycook (eds), *Disinventing and Reconstituting Languages*, Clevedon, Bristol: Multilingual Matters, pp. 1–41.
Malafouris, Lambros (2009), '"Neuroarchaeology": Exploring the links between neural and cultural plasticity', *Progress in Brain Research*, 178, pp. 251–9.
Malafouris, Lambros (2013), *How Things Shape the Mind: A Theory of Material Engagement*, Cambridge, MA: MIT Press.
Malotki, Ekkehart (1983), 'Hopi time: a linguistic analysis of the temporal concepts in the Hopi language', in Werner Winter (ed.), *Trends in Linguistics. Studies and Monographs*, 20, Berlin, New York and Amsterdam: Mouton.
Marlowe, Frank W. (2010), *The Hadza: Hunter-Gatherers of Tanzania*, Berkeley: University of California Press.
Martin, Peter (2003), 'Interactions and inter-relationships around text: practices and positionings in a multilingual classroom in Brunei', in Angela Creese and Peter Martin (eds), *Multilingual Classroom Ecologies: Inter-relationships, Interactions and Ideologies*, Clevedon, Bristol: Multilingual Matters, pp. 25–41.
Marx, Nicole (2012), 'Reading across the Germanic languages: is equal access just wishful thinking?', *International Journal of Bilingualism*, 16(4), pp. 467–83.
Marx, Nicole and Britta Hufeisen (2003), 'Multilingualism: theory, research methods and

didactics', in G. Bräuer and K. Sanders (eds), *New Visions in Foreign and Second Language Education*, San Diego, CA: LARC Press, pp. 178–203.

Matras, Yaron (2004), 'Romacilikanes – the Romani dialect of Parakalamos', *Romani Studies*, 5, 14(1), pp. 59–109.

Matras, Yaron and Jeanette Sakel (eds) (2007), *Grammatical Borrowing in Cross-linguistic Perspective*, Berlin and Boston: Mouton de Gruyter.

Matras, Yaron and Anton Tenser (eds) (2020), *The Palgrave Handbook of Romani Language and Linguistics*, London: Palgrave Macmillan.

Maurais, Jacques (2003), 'Towards a new linguistic world order', in J. Maurais and M. Morris (eds), *Languages in a Globalizing World*, Cambridge: Cambridge University Press, pp. 13–36.

Meara, Paul (2006), 'Emergent properties of multilingual lexicons', *Applied Linguistics*, 27(4), pp. 620–44.

Meisel, Jürgen M. (2008), 'Child second language acquisition or successive first language acquisition?', in Belma Haznedar and Elena Gavruseva (eds), *Current Trends in Child Second Language Acquisition: A Generative Perspective*, Amsterdam: John Benjamins, pp. 55–80.

Meißner, Franz-Joseph (2003), 'EuroComDidact: learning and teaching plurilingual comprehension', in L. Zybatow (ed.), *Sprachkompetenz–Mehrsprachigkeit –Translation. Akten des 35.Linguistischen Kolloquiums*, Innsbruck, 2–22 September 2000. Tübingen: Narr, pp. 33–46.

Mesthrie, Rajend, Joan Swann, Andrea Deumert and William L. Leap (2009), *Introducing Sociolinguistics*, 2nd edn, Philadelphia: John Benjamins.

Mohanty, Ajit K. (2010), 'Languages, inequality and marginalization: implications of the double divide in Indian multilingualism', *International Journal of the Sociology of Language*, 205, pp. 131–54.

Mosca, Michela (2019), 'Trilinguals' language switching: a strategic and flexible account', *Quarterly Journal of Experimental Psychology*, 72(4), pp. 693–716.

Mufwene, Salikoko (2020), 'Pidgins and creoles', in Cecil L. Nelson, Zoya G. Proshina and Daniel R. Davis (eds), *The Handbook of World Englishes*, 2nd edn, Hoboken, NJ: Wiley-Blackwell, pp. 229–313.

Muñoz, Carmen and David Singleton (2011), 'A critical review of age-related research on L2 ultimate attainment', *Language Teaching*, 44(1), pp. 1–35.

Muñoz, Carmen and David Singleton (2019), 'Age and multilingualism', in D. Singleton and L. Aronin (eds), *Twelve Lectures on Multilingualism*, Clevedon, Bristol: Multilingual Matters, pp. 213–30.

Nelson, Cecil L., Zoya G. Proshina and Daniel R. Davis (eds) (2020), *The Handbook of World Englishes*, 2nd edn, Hoboken, NJ: Wiley-Blackwell.

Neidich, Warren (2014), 'The mind's eye in the age of cognitive capitalism', in C. T. Wolfe (ed.), *Brain Theory: Essays in Critical Neurophilosophy*, Basingstoke: Palgrave Macmillan, pp. 264–86.

Ngalasso, Mwatha Musanji (1990), 'Francophonie africaine, latinité gauloise: destins parallèles?', in Riesz Jànos et Ricard Alain (eds), *Semper aliquid novi: littérature comparée et littératures d'Afrique. Mélanges offerts à Albert Gérard*, Tübingen: Gunter Narr, pp. 21–8.

Ó Ceallaigh, Tadhg J., Muiris Ó Laoire and Máire Uí Chonghaile (2018), 'Comhtháthú ábhar agus teanga san iarbhunscoil lán-Ghaeilge/Ghaeltachta: i dtreo eispéiris forbartha gairmiúla chun dea-chleachtais a nochtadh'. 'Integration of content and language in Irish-medium / Gaeltacht post-primary schools: towards professional development experiences to reveal best practice'. Paper presented at the conference An Tumoideachas: Deiseanna agus Dea-chleachtais, An dara Comhdháil Taighde Uile-Oileánda ar an Tumoideachas. Mary Immaculate College, Limerick, Ireland.

Ó Laoire, Muiris and David Singleton (2009), 'The role of prior language in L3 learning and use: further evidence of psychotypological dimensions', in Larissa Aronin and Britta Hufeisen (eds), *The Exploration of Multilingualism*, Amsterdam: John Benjamins, pp. 79–102.

Official Languages Act, 1963 (as amended, 1967) (Act No. 19 of 1963). Available at: <http://www.languageinindia.com/april2002/officiallanguagesact.html> (last accessed 17 August 2021).

Oštarić, Antonio (2018), 'Commodification of a forsaken script: The Glagolitic script in contemporary Croatian material culture', in Larissa Aronin, Michael Hornsby and Grażyna Kiliańska-Przybyło (eds), *The Material Culture of Multilingualism*, Cham, Switzerland: Springer, pp. 189–208.

Ostler, Nicholas (2003), 'Introduction to language engineering for lesser studied languages –linguistic aspects', in Kemal Oflazer (ed.), *Language Engineering for Lesser-studied Languages*, Amsterdam: IOS Press, pp. 1–20.

Otheguy, Ricardo, Ofelia García and Wallis Reid (2015), 'Clarifying translanguaging and deconstructing named languages: a perspective from linguistics', *Applied Linguistics Review*, 6(3), pp. 281–307.

Otheguy, Ricardo, Ofelia García and Wallis Reid (2019), 'A translanguaging view of the linguistic system of bilinguals', *Applied Linguistics Review*, 10(4), pp. 625–51.

Oxford, Rebecca L. (2018), 'A developmental perspective on third-age learning', in Danuta Gabryś-Barker (ed.), *Third Age Learners of Foreign Languages*, Clevedon, Bristol: Multilingual Matters, pp. 3–18.

Pandey, Geeta (2011), 'An "English goddess" for India's down-trodden', BBC News, 15 February. Available at: <http://www.bbc.co.uk/news/world-south-asia-12355740> (last accessed 16 August 2021).

Pandit, Prabodh Bechardas (1979), 'Perspectives on sociolinguistics in India', in W. C. McCormick and S. A. Wurm (eds), *Language and Society: Anthropological Issues*, The Hague: Mouton.

Paolillo, John C. (2006), *Evaluating Language Statistics: The Ethnologue and Beyond*, Report prepared for UNESCO, Bloomington: Indiana University.

Paradis, Michel (2004), *A Neurolinguistic Theory of Bilingualism*, Amsterdam: John Benjamins.

Pattanayak, D. P. (ed), (1990), *Multilingualism in India*, Clevedon, Bristol: Multilingual Matters.

Pavlov, Ivan (1935), 'The conditioned reflex', *Physiology Journal*, 19(1), pp. 261–75.

Payne, Thomas E. (1997), *Describing Morphosyntax: A Guide for Field Linguists*, Cambridge and New York: Cambridge University Press.

Peal, Elizabeth and Wallace E. Lambert (1962), 'The relation of bilingualism to intelligence', *Psychological Monographs: General and Applied*, 76(27), pp. 1–23.

Pennycook, Alastair (2006), 'Postmodernism in language policy', in T. Ricento (ed.), *An Introduction to Language Policy: Theory and Method*, London: Blackwell, pp. 60–7.

Pennycook, Alastair (2016), 'Mobile times, mobile terms: the trans-super-poly-metro movement', in N. Coupland (ed.), *Sociolinguistics: Theoretical Debates*, Cambridge: Cambridge University Press, pp. 201–16.

Perani, Daniela, Eraldo Paulesu, Nuria S. Galles, Emmanuel Dupoux, Stanislas Dehaene, Valentino Bettinardi, et al. (1998), 'The bilingual brain: proficiency and age of acquisition of the second language', *Brain*, 121 (Pt 10), pp. 1841–52.

Peterson, R. E. (1980), 'Russenorsk: a little known aspect of Russian-Norwegian relations', *Studies in Language*, 4(2), 249–56.

Petroni, Filippo, Maurizio Serva (2008), 'Language distance and tree reconstruction', *Journal of Statistical Mechanics: Theory and Experiment*, August, P08012.

Phipps, Alison (2019), *Decolonising Multilingualism: Struggles to Decreate*, Clevedon, Bristol: Multilingual Matters.

Pinker, Steven (2007), *The Language Instinct*, New York: Harper Perennial Modern Classics.
Pons, Eva and Katharina Jiménez Weese (2021), 'Analysing the EU agreements with Spain and the UK on the use of regional or minority languages: a practical assessment', January, npld.eu. Barcelona: Directorate-General for Language Policy, Department of Culture, Government of Catalonia/NPLD, European Network to Promote Linguistic Diversity.
Porte, Graeme (2010), *Appraising Research in Second Language Learning: A Practical Approach to Critical Analysis of Quantitative Research*, Amsterdam: John Benjamins.
Power, Justin M., Guido W. Grimm and Johann-Mattis List (2020), 'Evolutionary dynamics in the dispersal of sign languages', *Royal Society Open Science*, 7(1), pp. 1–15.
Pütz, Martin (2004), 'Linguistic repertoire/Sprachrepertoire', in U. Ammon, N. Dittmar, K. J. Mattheier and P. Trudgill (eds), *An International Handbook of the Science of Language and Society/Ein internationales Handbuch zur Wissenschaft von Sprache und Gesellschaft*, 2nd edn, Berlin and Boston: Walter de Gruyter, pp. 226–31.
Regier, Terry, Paul Kay, Aubrey Gilbert and Richard Ivry (2010), 'Language and thought: which side are you on, anyway?', in B. Malt and P. Wolff (eds), *Words and the Mind: Perspectives on the Language–Thought Interface*, New York: Oxford University Press, pp. 165–82.
Rimland, Bernard (1978), 'Inside the mind of the autistic savant,' *Psychology Today*, August, pp. 68–80.
Rogers, Henry (2005), *Writing Systems, A Linguistic Approach*, London: Blackwell.
Romaine, Suzanne ([1989] 1995), *Bilingualism*, London: Wiley-Blackwell.
Romaine, Suzanne ([1994] 2000), *Language in Society: An Introduction to Sociolinguistics*, Oxford: Oxford University Press.
Ronjat, Jules (1913), *Le Développment du langage observé chez un enfant bilingue*, Paris: Champion.
Russell, Charles William (1863), *The Life of Cardinal Mezzofanti*, Longman: London. Available at: <https://archive.org/details/lifecardinalmez00russgoog/page/n2/mode/2up> (last accessed 20 August 2021).
Safont-Jordà, Maria Pilar (2012), 'A longitudinal analysis of Catalan, Spanish and English request modifiers in early third language learning', in Danuta Gabryś-Barker (ed.), *Cross-linguistic Influences in Multilingual Language Acquisition*, Berlin: Springer, pp. 99–114.
Safont-Jordà, Maria Pilar (2013), 'Early stages of trilingual pragmatic development: a longitudinal study of requests in Catalan, Spanish and English', *Journal of Pragmatics*, 59, pp. 68–80.
Salzburg Global Seminar (2017), 'Statement for a Multilingual World', Salzburg Global Forum. Available at: <http://www.salzburgglobal.org/topics/article/fellows-co-create-salzburg-statement-for-a-multilingual-world.html> (last accessed 10 January 2020).
Sapir, Edward (1921), *Language*, New York: Harcourt Brace.
Sapir, Edward (1929), 'The status of linguistics as a science', *Language*, 5, pp. 207–14.
Sapir, Edward (1947), *Selected Writings in Language, Culture and Personality*, Berkeley: University of California Press.
Saussure, Ferdinand de ([1916] 1959), *Cours de linguistique générale*, Paris: Payot. English translation: *Course in General Linguistics*, New York: McGraw.
Schembri, Adam C. and Ceil Lucas (eds) (2015), *Sociolinguistics of Deaf Communities*, Cambridge: Cambridge University Press.
Scarmeas, Nikolaos and Yaakov Stern (2003), 'Cognitive reserve and lifestyle', *Journal of Clinical and Experimental Neuropsychology*, 2003(25), pp. 625–33.
Schiffmann, Harold (1996), *Linguistic Culture and Language Policy*, New York: Routledge.
Schjerve-Rindler, Rosita and Eva Vetter (2007), 'Linguistic diversity in Habsburg Austria as a model for modern European language policy', in Jan D. ten Thije and Ludger Zeevaert (eds), *Receptive Multilingualism: Linguistic Analyses, Language Policies and Didactic Concepts*, Amsterdam: John Benjamins, pp. 49–70.

Schuit, Joke (2012), 'Signing in the Arctic: external influences on Inuit Sign Language', in Ulrike Zeshan and Connie De Vos (eds), *Sign Languages in Village Communities: Anthropological and Linguistic Insights*, Boston and Berlin De Gruyter, pp. 181–208.

Seidlhofer, Barbara (2001), 'Closing a conceptual gap: the case for a description of English as a lingua franca', *International Journal of Applied Linguistics*, 11, pp. 133–58.

Seidlhofer, Barbara (2011), *Understanding English as a lingua franca*, Oxford: Oxford University Press.

Seidlhofer, Barbara and H. G. Widdowson (2009), 'Conformity and creativity in ELF and learner English', in Michaela Albl-Mikasa, Sabine Braun and Sylvia Kalina (eds), *Dimensionen der Zweitsprachenforschung / Dimensions of Second Language Research* [Festschrift for Kurt Kohn], Tübingen: Narr, pp. 93–107.

Shaw, Jonathan (2014), 'Why "Big Data" is a big deal', *Harvard Magazine*, March–April, pp. 30–5, 74–5. Available at <https://harvardmagazine.com/2014/03/why-big-data-is-a-big-deal> (last accessed 31 August 2021).

Singleton, David, Larissa Aronin and Lorna Carson (2013a), 'Minority language use in Ireland: the time dimension', in D. Singleton, J. Fishman, L. Aronin and M. Ó Laoire (eds), *Current Multilingualism: A New Linguistic Dispensation*, Berlin and Boston: Mouton de Gruyter, pp. 121–38.

Singleton, David, Joshua Fishman, Larissa Aronin and Muiris Ó Laoire (eds) (2013b), *Current Multilingualism: A New Linguistic Dispensation*, Berlin and Boston: Mouton de Gruyter.

Skutnabb-Kangas, Tove (1981), *Bilingualism or Not: The Education of Minorities*, Clevedon, Bristol: Multilingual Matters.

Skutnabb-Kangas, Tove (2001), 'The globalisation of (educational) language rights', *International Review of Education/Internationale Zeitschrift für Erziehungswissenschaft/Revue internationale l'éducation*, 47(3–4), pp. 201–19.

Skutnabb-Kangas, Tove and Robert Phillipson (eds) (2017), *Language Rights*, vols I–IV, London: Routledge.

Smith, Larry E. and Cecil L. Nelson (2020), 'World Englishes and the issues of intelligibility', in Cecil L. Nelson, Zoya G. Proshina and Daniel R. Davis (eds), *The Handbook of World Englishes*, 2nd edn, Hoboken, NJ: Wiley-Blackwell, pp. 430–46.

Smith, Geoff P. and Jeff Siegel (2013), 'Tok Pisin structure dataset', in Susanne Maria Michaelis, Philippe Maurer, Martin Haspelmath and Magnus Huber (eds), *Atlas of Pidgin and Creole Language Structures Online*, Leipzig: Max Planck Institute for Evolutionary Anthropology. Available at: <http://apics-online.info/contributions/22> (last accessed 13 August 2021).

Snowdon, David A. (1997), 'Aging and Alzheimer's disease: lessons from the Nun Study' *Gerontologist*, 37, pp. 150–6.

Spolsky, Bernard (2009), *Language Management*, Cambridge: Cambridge University Press.

Stivers, Tanya, N. J. Enfield, Penelope Brown, Christina Englert, Makoto Hayashi, Trine Heinemann, Gertie Hoymann, Federico Rossano, Jan Peter de Ruiter, Kyung-Eun Yoon and Stephen C. Levinson (2009), 'Universals and cultural variation in turn-taking in conversation', *PNAS - Proceedings of the National Academy of Sciences of the United States of America*, 30 June, 106(26), pp. 10587–92.

Sutton, John (2010), 'Memory and the extended mind: embodiment, cognition, and culture', in R. Menary (ed.), *The Extended Mind*, Cambridge, MA: MIT Press, pp. 189–225.

ten Thije, Jan (2019), 'Receptive multilingualism', in David Singleton, and Larissa Aronin (eds), *Twelve Lectures on Multilingualism*, Clevedone, Bristol: Multilingual Matters, pp. 329–64).

ten Thije, Jan D. and Ludger Zeevaert (eds) (2007), *Receptive Multilingualism: Linguistic Analyses, Language Policies and Didactic Concepts*, Amsterdam: John Benjamins.

Thomason, Sarah (2010), 'Contact explanations in linguistics', in Raymond Hickey (ed.), *The Handbook of Language Contact*, Oxford: Blackwell, pp. 31–47.
Thomason, Sarah G. (2015), *Endangered Languages: An Introduction*, Cambridge: Cambridge University Press.
Thomason, Sarah Grey ([2001] 2004, 2005), *Language Contact: An Introduction*, Edinburgh; Edinburgh University Press.
Todeva, Elka and Jasone Cenoz (eds) (2009), *The Multiple Realities of Multilingualism: Personal Narratives and Researchers' Perspectives*, Berlin and Boston: Mouton de Gruyter.
Tofts, Darren (2003), 'On mutability', in D. Tofts, A. Johnson and A. Cavallaro (eds), *Prefiguring Cyberculture: An Intellectual History*, Cambridge, MA: MIT Press, pp. 2–5.
'Tok Pisin' (n.d.), Ethnologue. Available at: <http://www.ethnologue.com/show_language.asp?code=tpi> (last accessed 6 August 2011).
'Tok Pisin' (n.d.), mustgo travel. Available at: <https://www.mustgo.com/worldlanguages/tok-pisin/> (last accessed 13 August 2021).
Tolstoy, Leo (n.d.), *War and Peace*, Project Gutenberg. Available at: <https://drive.google.com/file/d/0B7lZ7JU-iHeBOHhEUG9GTGpuRlE/view?resourcekey=0-NGiUKDmiph8jrB-zSuYb0g> (last accessed 3 September 2021).
Tomasello, Michael (1999), *The Cultural Origins of Human Cognition*, Cambridge, MA: Harvard University Press.
Treffert, Darold A. (2009), 'The savant syndrome: an extraordinary condition. A synopsis: past, present, future', *Philosophical Transactions of the Royal Society*, 27 May, 364(1522), pp. 1351–7.
Trudgill, Peter (1999), 'Standard English: what it isn't', in Tony Bex and Richard J. Watts (eds), *Standard English: The Widening Debate*, London: Routledge, pp. 117–28.
Wardhaugh, Ronald (2010), *An Introduction to Sociolinguistics*, Hoboken, NJ: Wiley-Blackwell.
Watt, Jonathan (2010), 'Ancient tribal language becomes extinct as last speaker dies', *The Telegraph*, 10 February. Available at: <https://www.telegraph.co.uk/news/obituaries/7207731/Lives-Remembered.html> (last accessed 18 June 2020).
Wattendorf, Elise, Julia Festman, Birgit Westermann, Ursula Keil, Daniela Zappatore, Rita Franceschini, Georges Luedi, Ernst-Wilhelm Radue, Thomas F. Münte, Günter Rager and Cordula Nitsch (2014), 'Early bilingualism influences early and subsequently later acquired languages in cortical regions representing control functions', *International Journal of Bilingualism*, 18(1), pp. 48–66.
Watts, Thomas (1859), 'On Dr. Russell's Life of Cardinal Mezzofanti', *Transactions of the Philological Society*, 6(1), pp. 227–56.
Wei, Li (2018), 'Translanguaging as a practical theory of language', *Applied Linguistics*, 39(1), pp. 9–30.
Weinreich, Uriel (1953), *Languages in Contact*, The Hague: Mouton.
Whorf, Benjamin Lee (1956ba), *Language, Thought, and Reality: Selected Writings of Benjamin Lee Whorf*, ed. J. B. Carroll, Cambridge, MA: MIT Press.
Whorf, Benjamin Lee (1956b), 'An American Indian model of the universe', in J. B. Carroll (ed.), *Language, Thought and Reality: Selected Writings of Benjamin Lee Whorf*, Cambridge, MA: MIT Press, pp. 57–64.
Wicherkiewicz, Tomasz (2006), 'A decade of Kashubian in education', in Dónall Ó Riagáin, (ed.), *Voces Diversae: Lesser-Used Languages Education in Europe*, Belfast: Clo Ollscoil na Banríona, pp. 103–12.
Wiley, Terrence (2001), 'On defining heritage learners and their speakers', in J. K. Peyton, D. A. Ranard and S. McGinnis (eds), *Heritage Languages in America: Preserving a National Resource*, McHenry, IL: Delta Systems, pp. 109–42.

Wiley, Terrence G. and Guadalupe Valdés (2000), 'Heritage language instruction in the United States' [Special issue], *Bilingual Research Journal*, 24(4).

Winford, Donald (2003), *An Introduction to Contact Linguistics*, Hoboken, NJ: Wiley-Blackwell John Wiley and Sons.

Wolfe, Charles T. (ed.) (2014), *Brain Theory: Essays in Critical Neurophilosophy*, Basingstoke: Palgrave Macmillan.

Wolff, H. Ekkehard (2017), 'Language ideologies and the politics of language in post-colonial Africa', *Stellenbosch Papers in Linguistics Plus*, 51, pp. 1–22.

Wright, Sue (2006), 'French as a lingua franca', *Annual Review of Applied Linguistics*, 26, pp. 35–60.

Yoel, Judith (2009), 'Canada's Maritime Sign Language', unpublished PhD thesis, University of Manitoba, Canada.

Zentella, Ana Celia (1997), *Growing up Bilingual: Puerto Rican Children in New York*, Oxford: Blackwell.

Zentella, Ana Celia (2018), 'LatinUs and linguistics: complaints, conflicts, and contradictions – the anthro-political linguistics solution', in Naomi Shin and Daniel Erker (eds), *Questioning Theoretical Primitives in Linguistic Inquiry: Papers in Honor of Ricardo Otheguy* [Studies in Functional and Structural Linguistics 76], Amsterdam: John Benjamins, pp. 189–207.

Zuckermann, Ghil'ad (2020), *Revivalistics: From the Genesis of Israeli to Language Reclamation in Australia and Beyond*, Oxford: Oxford University Press.

Zuckermann, Ghil'ad, Shiori Shakuto-Neoh and Giovanni Matteo Quer (2014), 'Native tongue title: proposed compensation for the loss of aboriginal languages', *Australian Aboriginal Studies (AAS)*, 1, pp. 55–71.

Languages index

A
Aboriginal languages, 78
African American Vernacular English (AAVE, Ebonics), 19
Afrikaans, 60, 115
Ainu, 78
Akan, 67
Ākhoe Haiǀǀom, 34
Albanian, 98
Alemannic (or Allemannish), 60
Algonquian languages, 97
American Sign Language (ASL), 32, 85
Anêm, 59
Anglo-Romani, 71; *see also* Roma language
Apurinã, 76
Arabic 36, 70, 77, 80–1, 82, 95, 99, 101, 113, 161
Aramaic, 95, 106
Araucano, 111
Aria, 59
Armenian, 76–7
Assyrian, 32
Avar, 79

B
Babylonian, 106
Bahasa Melayu, 95
Balti, 118
Bantu languages, 36, 115
Bari, 37
Bashkir, 59
Basque, 19, 77–8, 109–10
Bavarian, 60
Belizean, 67
Bengali, 80, 81
Berber (Amazigh), 114
Bikol, 59
Bodo, 115
Bolo, 59
Bosnian, 95
Bulgarian, 98, 108, 178
Burmese 76, 77
Butler English, 70

C
Cantonese, 37, 59, 107, 109; *see also* Chinese
Castilian (Spanish), 57, 110
Catalan, 19, 37, 109
Cebuano, 59
Chakesang, 80
Chechen, 79
Cherokee, 36, 76–7, 107
Cheshire dialect, 60
Chinese, 18, 35, 36, 76–7, 80–1, 99, 164; *see also* Mandarin
Chinese Sign Language (CSL), 85–6
Chokwe, 115
Chopi, 115
Church Slavonic, 102
Chuwabu, 115
Circassian, 79
Cockney, 60
Corsican, 80
Cree, 71
Croatian, 58, 98, 108, 170
Czech, 108

D
Dadri, 118
Damara, 115
Danish, 34, 58, 108, 156, 167–9
Deori, 80
Dogri, 118
Dravidian languages, 116
Dusun, 95
Dutch, 60, 62, 108, 115, 168–9
Dutch Sign Language, 85

E
Elamite, 106
English, 18–19, 34, 36, 37, 48–9, 57, 60, 62–6, 70, 76, 77, 80–5, 97, 99, 108, 109, 115–19, 149, 157, 175
Eskimo, 78
Esperanto, 89

Estonian, 77, 108
Etruscan, 78

F
Faroese, 78, 160
Farsi, 95
Filipino, 59
Finnish, 77, 108
Flemish, 101, 147
Frankish (Fränkisch), 60
French, 36, 62, 70–1, 83, 97, 108, 115, 118, 135, 158, 175
French Sign Language (LSF – Langue des Signes Française), 86–7
Frisian, 60, 109
Fulani (FulBe, Fula), 67, 114
Fusha (al-fusha), 101, 158

G
Gaelic, 76, 109
Galician, 109
Georgian, 76, 79
German, 31, 60, 62, 87, 108, 115, 158, 178
German Sign Language, 87
German Sign Language family, 87
Gojri, 118
Goundo, 115
Greek, 36, 83, 97, 98, 108
Guarani, 102, 111
Gujarati, 117
Gullah, 70, 107

H
Hadza, 99
Haitian Creole, 27, 73
Hausa, 67, 76, 82, 83, 114
Hawaiian, 70, 76, 79, 107
Hebrew, 19, 36, 37, 62, 77, 161, 170
Herero, 115
High German, 14
Hiligaynon, 59
Hindi, 18, 80–1, 83, 97, 99, 116, 118
Hindustani, 58, 117
Hiw, 99
Hixkaryana, 76
Hopi, 37, 38, 76, 189
Hungarian, 16, 20, 37, 77
Hungarian Sign Language, 87

I
Iban, 95
Ibo, 37, 67
Icelandic, 78, 168, 169
Ido, 89

Ilokano, 59
Ingush, 79
Interlingua, 89
Irish, 76, 108, 109
Irish Sign Language, 86
Italian, 36, 76, 80, 108, 111, 161, 168

J
Jamaican Creole, 70
Japanese, 35–7, 76, 78, 80, 97
Japanese Sign Language (NS – Nihon Shuwa), 86

K
Kacchi, 117
Kalmyk, 109
Kannada, 81, 104, 116
Kashmiri, 81, 118
Kashubian, 109
Kathiawadil, 117
Kazakh, 30
Khezha, 80
Khmer, 107
Kikongo, 100, 115
Kimbundu, 115
Kimwani, 115
Kinaray-a, 59
Klingon, 89
Konkani, 117
Korean, 34–6, 62, 76, 78
Kormakiti Arabic, 71
Kurdish, 95

L
Ladakhi, 118
Lahauli, 80
Lao, 34, 77, 116
Latin, 32, 36, 75, 77, 83, 97, 140
Latvian, 107, 108
Lehali, 99
Lezgian, 79
Lingala, 114
Lingua Franca, 82
Lithuanian, 107
Lomwe, 115

M
Macedonian, 98, 112
Makhuwa, 115
Makonde, 115
Malagasy, 76
Malay, 79, 80, 81, 82
Malayalam, 37, 81, 116, 118
Malinke, 67
Maltese, 108

Languages index

Mandarin, 18, 79, 82, 99, 107; *see also* Chinese
Mandinka, 67
Manually Coded English (MCE), 149
Māori, 19, 79, 108, 184
Maranao, 59
Marathi, 81, 104, 109, 117, 118
Mbunda, 115
Media Lengua, 71
Michif, 71
Mitteldeutsch (Middle German), 60
Moldavian, 58, 184
Mouk, 59

N
Native American Languages, 78, 97
Navaho, 75
Ndau, 115
Negerhollands, 67
New Guinea Pidgin, 70 (Tok Pisin), 18, 70, 71, 73
Niederdeutsch (Low German/Plattdeutsch), 60
Norwegian, 45, 58, 68–70, 78, 167–9
Novial, 89

O
Occitan, 80
Old Norse, 78
Old Persian, 106
Oshiwambo, 115

P
Pahari, 118
Pangasinan, 59
Pashtu, 95
Penan, 95
Pidgin Madam, 70
Polish, 108, 181
Polish Sign Language, 87
Portuguese, 36, 70, 108, 113, 115
Proto-Indo-European language, 78
Proto-Uralic, 78
Punjabi, 81, 117, 118

Q
Quechua, 71, 111, 182

R
Romani (Roma language), 20, 71
Romanian, 58, 98, 108, 168
Romansh, 95, 111
Ronga, 115
Rukwangali, 115
Russenorsk, 8, 67, 68–70
Russian, 37, 67–70, 75, 77, 80–1, 82, 97, 109, 161
Russian Sign Language (РЖЯ), 85–6

S
Sanskrit, 77, 81, 82, 97, 161, 162
Sena, 115
Serbian, 16, 98, 112
Setswana, 115
Shangaan (Tsonga), 115
sign languages, 84–8
Sign-Supported English (SSE), 149
Silbo Gomero, 101
Silozi, 115
Sinhala, 70
Sino-Tibetan family, 79
Siwi, 37
Slovak, 16, 63, 108
Slovene (Slovenian), 16, 77, 108
Spanish (Castilian), 36, 62, 81, 97, 99, 108, 110, 127, 178
Squamish, 76
Standard British English, 60
Sumerian, 35, 78
Swahili (Kiswahili), 36, 77, 80, 82–3, 114
Swedish, 62, 78, 108, 167–9, 197–8
Swedish Sign Language, 86
Swiss German (Schwyzerdütsch), 61, 105

T
Tabasaran, 59
Tagalog, 37, 59, 107
Tamil, 81, 116
Tatar, 95
Telugu, 116
Thai, 112, 116
Tibetan, 76
Tok Pisin (New Guinea Pidgin), 18, 70–1
Tsonga, 115
Tswa, 115
Turkish, 77
Tzeltal, 34
Tzotsil, 76

U
Ukrainian, 161
Urartian, 32
Urdu, 37, 58, 81, 83, 118
Urhobo, 37

V
Vietnamese, 22, 35, 37, 76–7, 98
Volapük, 89

W
Waray-Waray, 59
Welsh, 19, 76, 109
Wolof, 67, 80, 114
Wu Chinese, 109

X
Xhosa, 32

Y
Yamamadi, 76
Yélî-Dnye, 34
Yiddish, 83, 107, 161

Yorkshire dialect, 60
Yoruba, 67, 77, 114

Z
Zulu, 115
Zuni, 37, 107

Subject Index

A
additional language, 14, 192–5
adult learners, 133, 199
age, 30, 35, 126, 132–5, 143, 150, 192–4
alphabet, 33, 35, 36, 40, 58, 87
anglophone, 115
animal communication, 28–30
applied linguistics, 22, 23
artefact, 22, 169–70
articulation, 141, 142
artificial (constructed) languages, 88–9
attitude
    language attitudes, 14, 21, 158, 170
    scientific attitudes, 42, 179
autochthonous languages, 109
autoethnography, 182

B
behaviourism, 191
bilingual first language acquisition (BFLA), 44
bilingual mixed languages, 67
Biotic Model (Aronin and Ó Laoire), 192
borrowing, 96–8
bridge language, 198–9

C
case study, 182
classifications (of languages), 75–2
code-switching, 165–7
cognates, 63
cognitive reserve, 134–5
colonial languages, 116
    ex-colonial languages, 116
    post-colonial languages, 21, 22
colour terms, 36–7
comparative linguistics, 20
complexity, 126, 183–7
contact linguistics, 96
convergence, 98
creoles, 67, 70

creolisation, 70
cross-linguistic influence, 128–30
cross-linguistic interactions, 126, 128–9
cuneiform, 35, 106
current multilingualism, 18, 32, 49, 206

D
dialect, 57–8, 59–61, 71, 118
dialect continuum, 61
diglossia, 101–2
diversity
    diversity of multilingualism, 20, 114–19, 206
    linguistic diversity, 35–8,
domain, 102–3
Dominant Language Constellation (DLC), 160–3, 199–200
Dynamic Model of Multilingualism (DMM), 194–7

E
ecological approach, 45
ecology of language, 45
emergent (qualities, phenomena), 125–6, 185, 206
ethnic languages, 114

F
factor model (Hufeisen), 192–3
family
    language family, 79, 87, 113, 116, 168
    multilingual family, 144–5
first language (L1), 47, 66, 108, 181, 192–3, 195
first signal system, 28
foreign language, 66, 84, 129, 194
    English as a Foreign Language (EFL), 66, 84
foreignness, 129; *see also* L2 status, 129, 198
francophone, 115

G
genetic classification, 78–9

H
heritage language, 139, 156–7
hieroglyph, 35
historical multilingualism, 16–18
holistic research, 183
home language, 117, 143, 144

I
identity (multilingual), 139–2, 149, 200–1
idiolect, 60
immigrant language, 156
Index of Linguistic Diversity (ILD), 111; *see also Language Diversity Index (LDI)*
indigenous language, 109
individual multilingualism, 14–15, 111, 149

K
Kachru's circles, 63–6

L
language acquisition, 192–6; *see also* SLA, 22, 157, 176; TLA, 22, 157, 176, 186; MLA, 192–6
language competency, 46, 167; *see also* language proficiency; multi-competence
language contact, 67–2, 95–8
language demography, 180–1
language distance (linguistic distance), 62–3, 129
Language Diversity Index (LDI), 110; *see also* Index of Linguistic Diversity (ILD)
language family *see* family
language mode, 126–7
language nomination, 155–9
language policy, 22, 182
language proficiency 15, 44, 47, 128, 129, 130, 132, 133, 134, 163, 175, 195–6, 198, 200
language repertoire (linguistic repertoire), 159–61
language shift, 85, 180–1
language universals, 31–5
language varieties, 19, 27, 57–59, 66–7, 71–2, 81, 82, 98, 155
lesser-used languages, 109
lexicon, 87, 139, 191
lexis, 59, 71, 96–7, 168
lingua franca (plural – *lingua francas* or *lingue franca*), 82–4
 English as a Lingua Franca (ELF), 66, 83
linguistic distance (language distance), 62–3

linguistic diversity *see* diversity
linguistic typology, 75–8, 198
liturgical language, 102
loan words, 97

M
M-factor (Multilingualism Factor), 196
majority language, 108
manual sign codes, 85, 88, 149
matched guise technique, 175
material culture of multilingualism, 49, 169–70
method
 research method/methodology, 62–3, 87, 174–7, 180–3, 186–7
 teaching method, 13, 47, 66, 86, 168, 191
migration, 107
minority language, 85, 108–90
mixed languages, 71–2
modelling in multilingualism, 199–201, 202
models of multilingualism, 192–9, 202–3
monolingual perspective, 43–4, 99
morpheme, 35, 97
morphology, 12, 57, 67, 96, 97, 128
mother tongue, 14, 81, 135, 157
multicompetence, 46–7
multilingual mind, 46–7, 131, 134–5, 140
multilinguality, 138, 141–3, 197
multiple language acquisition (MLA), 192–6
mutual intelligibility, 58–9, 167

N
national language, 81, 108
native speaker, 47, 65–6, 83, 99, 206
neuroplasticity, 135
new linguistic dispensation, 49–1
non-switchers, 131; *see also* switchers
numerals, 27, 36

O
official language, 106–8, 116, 156, 158
one parent – one language OPOL (principle), 44–5, 145

P
performativity, 183
pidgin, 19, 67–70
pluricentric languages, 62, 65, 66
plurilingualism, 14, 117
polyglot, 145–8
post-colonial language, 21–2; *see also* colonial languages
proficiency, 15, 44, 46, 47, 63, 83, 163, 196; *see also* competence, 46, 167
proto-languages, 78
psychotypology, 129

Q
quadrilingualism, 14
qualitative research, 182–3
quantitative research, 179–3

R
recency (of use), 129, 198
recipient language, 97–8
regional language, 81, 118, 157

S
'savants', 148, 150
scheduled languages, 81, 116–18
script, 22, 35–6, 58
second language (L2), 44, 47, 178, 192–5, 202
    English as a Second language (ESL), 66, 157
    Second Language Acquisition (SLA), 22, 157, 176
second signal system, 28
sensitivity to initial conditions, 185
sequential bilingualism, 44
sign language, 84–8
societal multilingualism, 15–16, 23, 111–13
sociolect, 60
sociolinguistics, 20–1, 57
sociology of language, 20–1
source language, 96–7, 98, 199
    speech community (sometimes also 'language community' or 'linguistic community'), 98–101, 112, 117, 149
Sprachbund, 98
standardisation, 48, 61, 71
strategies
    accommodation strategies, 83, 84, 168
    learning strategies, 127, 141, 193
    parental strategies, 44–5, 144
subjectivity, 63, 183
Suffix, 77, 97
switchers, 131
switching costs, 131
syllabary, 33–6
syllable, 34, 36
syntax, 12, 78, 96, 127

T
tertiary didactics, 199
tertiary language, 196, 197
third language acquisition (TLA), 22, 157, 176, 186
titular language, 59
tribal tongue/language, 22, 116, 118
trilingual family, 142, 144–5

V
vernacular, 59, 81, 118
vocabulary, 61–3, 85, 125, 178, 198
vocal apparatus, 27, 32

W
word order typology, 75–6
World Englishes, 63–6
writing system, 35–6

EU representative:
Easy Access System Europe
Mustamäe tee 50, 10621 Tallinn, Estonia
Gpsr.requests@easproject.com

www.ingramcontent.com/pod-product-compliance
Lightning Source LLC
Chambersburg PA
CBHW051807230426
43672CB00012B/2662